Learn Helm

Improve productivity, reduce complexity, and speed up cloud-native adoption with Helm for Kubernetes

Andrew Block

Austin Dewey

Packt>

BIRMINGHAM—MUMBAI

Learn Helm

Commissioning Editor: Vijin Boricha
Acquisition Editor: Rohit Rajkumar
Senior Editor: Rahul Dsouza
Content Development Editor: Alokita Amanna
Technical Editor: Dinesh Pawar
Copy Editor: Safis Editing
Project Coordinator: Neil Dmello
Proofreader: Safis Editing
Indexer: Tejal Daruwale Soni
Production Designer: Joshua Misquitta

First published: June 2020

Production reference: 2081020

Published by Packt Publishing Ltd.
Livery Place
35 Livery Street
Birmingham
B3 2PB, UK.

ISBN 978-1-83921-429-5

www.packt.com

To my mother, whose guidance, work ethic, and attention to detail have made me a better person in almost every facet of my life.

– Andrew Block

To Lindsey, whose love and support I cannot do without.

– Austin Dewey

Packt>

Contributors

About the authors

Andrew Block is a senior principal consultant at Red Hat who guides organizations on adopting container solutions and microservice architectures using automation principles across an array of deployment targets. As the author of *Application Release Strategies with OpenShift*, he preaches the importance of CI/CD methodologies with an emphasis on security to develop and deploy software faster. Andrew also serves as a manager of the Container Community of Practice within Red Hat, which aims to foster awareness around the container ecosystem.

Austin Dewey is a senior consultant at Red Hat, focused on enabling customers in cloud and container technologies. He has helped drive success at many different Fortune 500 companies through his expertise in CI/CD and deployment patterns on Red Hat's Kubernetes-based PaaS, OpenShift Container Platform. Delivering projects centered around DevOps and automation, Austin has guided many different customers to production by building pipelines that ensure fast, stable, and secure deliveries. When Austin is not working with his customers or engaging in the Kubernetes community, he can be found playing guitar and spending time outdoors.

About the reviewer

Matthew Fisher is a software engineer at Microsoft and one of the core maintainers of the Helm project. Born and raised on Vancouver Island, he studied computer systems at the British Columbia Institute of Technology. Outside of work, he has an extensive list of hobbies, which is forever growing. On any given day, he is a musician, a luthier, a woodworker, a blacksmith, a cook, a photographer, and an artist. When he's not practicing with his guitar or rushing to and from the workshop, you'll find him out on another adventure with his wife, Brandy. He goes by the name @bacongobbler on GitHub and Twitter.

To my wife, Brandy: Thank you for your love and support, and for always being there for me. I am so thrilled I get to spend the rest of my life with you.

To my friends: Thank you for the birthdays, the inside jokes, the laughs, the food, and all the board game nights we've shared together since we were kids.

To my fellow Helm maintainers: Each and every one of you made Helm the successful project it is today. Thank you.

Packt is searching for authors like you

If you're interested in becoming an author for Packt, please visit `authors.packtpub.com` and apply today. We have worked with thousands of developers and tech professionals, just like you, to help them share their insight with the global tech community. You can make a general application, apply for a specific hot topic that we are recruiting an author for, or submit your own idea.

Table of Contents

3

Installing your First Helm Chart

Section 2:
Helm Chart Development

4
Understanding Helm Charts

5
Building Your First Helm Chart

6
Testing Helm Charts

Section 3:
Adanced Deployment Patterns

7
Automating Helm Processes Using CI/CD and GitOps

8

Using Helm with the Operator Framework

9

Helm Security Considerations

ASSESSMENTS

Preface

Presently, containerization is said to be the best way to implement DevOps. While Docker introduced containers and changed the DevOps era, Google developed an extensive container orchestration system, Kubernetes, which is now considered the frontrunner in container orchestration. The main goal of this book is to learn about the efficiency of managing applications running on Kubernetes using Helm. This book will start with a short introduction to Helm and how it can benefit the entire container environment. You will then dive into the architectural aspects, along with learning about Helm charts and its use cases. You'll learn how to write Helm charts in order to automate application deployment on Kubernetes. Focused on providing enterprise-ready patterns around Helm and automation, the book covers best practices around application development, delivery, and life cycle management with Helm. By the end of this book, you will know how to leverage Helm to develop an enterprise pattern with a view to application delivery.

Who this book is for

This book targets Kubernetes developers or administrators interested in learning Helm to provide automation around application development on Kubernetes. Basic knowledge of Kubernetes application development would be useful, but prior knowledge of Helm is not required. Basic knowledge of business use cases that automation provides is recommended.

What this book covers

Chapter 1, Understanding Kubernetes and Helm, provides an introduction to Kubernetes and Helm. You will be introduced to the challenges that users face when deploying applications to Kubernetes and how Helm can help simplify deployments and increase productivity.

Chapter 2, Preparing a Kubernetes and Helm Environment, covers the tools required to deploy applications with Helm on a local Kubernetes cluster. In addition, you will also learn about basic Helm configurations that occur post-installation.

Chapter 3, Installing Your First Helm Chart, explains how to deploy an application to Kubernetes by installing a Helm chart and covers the different life cycle phases of an application deployed with Helm.

Chapter 4, Understanding Helm Charts, dives deep into the building blocks of a Helm chart and prepares you with the knowledge required to build your own Helm chart.

Chapter 5, Building Your First Helm Chart, provides an end-to-end walkthrough of building a Helm chart. The chapter begins with the fundamental concepts of building a Helm chart that leverages basic Helm constructs and progresses to modifying the baseline configurations to incorporate more advanced Helm constructs. Finally, you will learn how to deploy a chart to a basic chart repository

Chapter 6, Testing Helm Charts, discusses different methodologies around linting and testing Helm charts.

Chapter 7, Automating Helm Processes Using CI/CD and GitOps, explores an advanced use case in terms of leveraging CI/CD and GitOps models to automate Helm tasks. Namely, developing a process around testing, packaging, and releasing Helm charts. In addition, the management of Helm chart installations across multiple different environments is also introduced.

Chapter 8, Using Helm with the Operator Framework, discusses the fundamental concepts of operators on Kubernetes with a view to building a Helm operator out of an existing Helm chart using the operator-sdk tool provided by the operator framework.

Chapter 9, Helm Security Considerations, dives into some of the security considerations and precautions around using Helm, from the moment the tool is installed to the second it is used to install a Helm chart on a Kubernetes cluster.

To get the most out of this book

While not mandatory, as basic concepts are explained throughout the book, some familiarity with Kubernetes and container technology is recommended.

For the tools used throughout this book, chapters 2-9 will focus on the following key technologies:

Software/hardware covered in the book	OS requirements
Minikube	Windows, macOS X, and Linux (any)
Kubectl	Windows, macOS X, and Linux (any)
Helm	Windows, macOS X, and Linux (any)

The installation of these tools is discussed in detail in *Chapter 2, Preparing a Kubernetes and Helm Environment*. Additional tools that are used throughout the book are chapter-specific, and their installations are described in the chapters in which they are used.

If you are using the digital version of this book, we advise you to type the code yourself or access the code via the GitHub repository (link available in the next section). Doing so will help you avoid any potential errors related to copy/pasting of code.

Download the example code files

You can download the example code files for this book from your account at www.packt.com. If you purchased this book elsewhere, you can visit www.packtpub.com/support and register to have the files emailed directly to you.

You can download the code files by following these steps:

1.   Log in or register at www.packt.com.
2.   Select the Support tab.
3.   Click on Code Downloads.
4.   Enter the name of the book in the Search box and follow the onscreen instructions.

Once the file is downloaded, please make sure that you unzip or extract the folder using the latest version of:

*   WinRAR/7-Zip for Windows
*   Zipeg/iZip/UnRarX for Mac
*   7-Zip/PeaZip for Linux

The code bundle for the book is also hosted on GitHub at https://github.com/PacktPublishing/-Learn-Helm. In case there's an update to the code, it will be updated on the existing GitHub repository.

We also have other code bundles from our rich catalog of books and videos available at https://github.com/PacktPublishing/. Check them out!

Code in action

Code in action videos for this book can be viewed at https://bit.ly/2AEAGvm.

Download the color images

We also provide a PDF file that has color images of the screenshots/diagrams used in this book. You can download it here: http://www.packtpub.com/sites/default/files/downloads/9781839214295_ColorImages.pdf.

Conventions used

There are a number of text conventions used throughout this book.

Code in text: Indicates code words in text, database table names, folder names, filenames, file extensions, pathnames, dummy URLs, user input, and Twitter handles. Here is an example: "Mount the downloaded WebStorm-10*.dmg disk image file as another disk in your system."

A block of code is set as follows:

```
html, body, #map {
  height: 100%;
  margin: 0;
  padding: 0
}
```

When we wish to draw your attention to a particular part of a code block, the relevant lines or items are set in bold:

```
[default]
exten => s,1,Dial(Zap/1|30)
exten => s,2,Voicemail(u100)
exten => s,102,Voicemail(b100)
exten => i,1,Voicemail(s0)
```

Any command-line input or output is written as follows:

```
$ mkdir css
$ cd css
```

Bold: Indicates a new term, an important word, or words that you see on screen. For example, words in menus or dialog boxes appear in the text like this. Here is an example: "Select **System info** from the **Administration** panel."

Tips or important notes
Appear like this.

Get in touch

Feedback from our readers is always welcome.

General feedback: If you have questions about any aspect of this book, mention the book title in the subject of your message and email us at `customercare@packtpub.com`.

Errata: Although we have taken every care to ensure the accuracy of our content, mistakes do happen. If you have found a mistake in this book, we would be grateful if you would report this to us. Please visit `www.packtpub.com/support/errata`, selecting your book, clicking on the Errata Submission Form link, and entering the details.

Piracy: If you come across any illegal copies of our works in any form on the internet, we would be grateful if you would provide us with the location address or website name. Please contact us at `copyright@packt.com` with a link to the material.

If you are interested in becoming an author: If there is a topic that you have expertise in, and you are interested in either writing or contributing to a book, please visit `authors.packtpub.com`.

Reviews

Please leave a review. Once you have read and used this book, why not leave a review on the site that you purchased it from? Potential readers can then see and use your unbiased opinion to make purchase decisions, we at Packt can understand what you think about our products, and our authors can see your feedback on their book. Thank you!

For more information about Packt, please visit `packt.com`.

Section 1: Introduction and Setup

This section will present the problem statement that Helm addresses, as well as the solution that it provides, by walking you through real-world examples.

This section comprises the following chapters:

1
Understanding Kubernetes and Helm

Thank you for choosing this book, Learn Helm. If you are interested in this book, you are probably aware of the challenges that modern applications bring. Teams face tremendous pressure to ensure that applications are lightweight and scalable. Applications must also be highly available and able to withstand varying loads. Historically, applications have most commonly been deployed as monoliths, or large, single-tiered applications served on a single system. As time has progressed, the industry has shifted toward a microservice approach, or toward small, multi-tiered applications served on multiple systems. Often deployed using container technology, the industry has started leveraging tools such as Kubernetes to orchestrate and scale their containerized microservices.

Kubernetes, however, comes with its own set of challenges. While it is an effective container orchestration tool, it presents a steep learning curve that can be difficult for teams to overcome. One tool that helps simplify the challenges of running workloads on Kubernetes is Helm. Helm allows users to more simply deploy and manage the life cycle of Kubernetes applications. It abstracts many of the complexities behind configuring Kubernetes applications and allows teams to be more productive on the platform.

In this book, you will explore each of the benefits offered by Helm and discover how Helm makes application deployments much simpler on Kubernetes. You will first assume the role of an end user, consuming Helm charts written by the community and learning the best practices behind leveraging Helm as a package manager. As this book progresses, you will assume the role of a Helm chart developer and learn how to package Kubernetes applications in ways that are easily consumable and efficient. Toward the end of this book, you'll learn about advanced patterns around application management and security with Helm.

Let's begin by first understanding microservices, containers, Kubernetes, and the challenges that these bring with regards to application deployment. Then, we will discuss the key features and benefits of Helm. In this chapter, we will cover the following main topics:

- Monoliths, microservices, and containers
- An overview of Kubernetes
- How Kubernetes applications are deployed
- Challenges in configuring Kubernetes resources
- Benefits that Helm provides to simplify life application deployments on Kubernetes

From monoliths to modern microservices

Software applications are a foundational component of most modern technology. Whether they take the form of a word processor, web browser, or media player, they enable user interaction to complete one or more tasks. Applications have a long and storied history, from the days of ENIAC—the first general-purpose computer—to taking man to the moon in the Apollo space missions, to the rise of the World Wide Web, social media, and online retail.

These applications can operate on a wide range of platforms and system. We said in most cases they run on virtual or physical resources, but aren't these technically the only options? Depending on their purpose and resource requirements, entire machines may be dedicated to serving the compute and/or storage needs of an application. Fortunately, thanks in part to the realization of Moore's law, the power and performance of microprocessors initially increased with each passing year, along with the overall cost associated with the physical resources. This trend has subsided in recent years, but the advent of this trend and its persistence for the first 30 years of the existence of processors was instrumental to the advances in technology.

Software developers took full advantage of this opportunity and bundled more features and components in their applications. As a result, a single application could consist of several smaller components, each of which, on their own, could be written as their own individual services. Initially, bundling components together yielded several benefits, including a simplified deployment process. However, as industry trends began to change and businesses focused more on the ability to deliver features more rapidly, the design of a single deployable application brought with it a number of challenges. Whenever a change was required, the entire application and all of its underlying components needed to be validated once again to ensure the change had no adverse features. This process potentially required coordination from multiple teams, which slowed the overall delivery of the feature.

Delivering features more rapidly, especially across traditional divisions within organizations, was also something that organizations wanted. This concept of rapid delivery is fundamental to a practice called DevOps, whose rise in popularity occurred around the year 2010. DevOps encouraged more iterative changes to applications over time, instead of extensive planning prior to development. In order to be sustainable in this new model, architectures evolved from being a single large application to instead favoring several smaller applications that can be delivered faster. Because of this change in thinking, the more traditional application design was labeled as **monolithic**. This new approach of breaking components down into separate applications coined the name for these components as **microservices**. The traits that were inherent in microservice applications brought with them several desirable features, including the ability to develop and deploy services concurrently from one another as well as to scale (increase the number of instances) them independently.

The change in software architecture from monolithic to microservices also resulted in re-evaluating how applications are packaged and deployed at runtime. Traditionally, entire machines were dedicated to either one or two applications. Now, as microservices resulted in the overall reduction of resources required for a single application, dedicating an entire machine to one or two microservices was no longer viable.

Fortunately, a technology called **containers** was introduced and gained popularity for filling in the gaps for many missing features needed to create a microservices runtime environment. Red Hat defines a container as 'a set of one or more processes that are isolated from the rest of the system and includes all of the files necessary to run' (`https://www.redhat.com/en/topics/containers/whats-a-linux-container`). Containerized technology has a long history in computing, dating back to the 1970s. Many of the foundational container technologies, including **chroot** (the ability to change the root directory of a process and any of its children to a new location on the filesystem) and **jails**, are still in use today.

The combination of a simple and portable packaging model, along with the ability to create many isolated sandboxes on each physical or virtual machine, led to the rapid adoption of containers in the microservices space. This rise in container popularity in the mid-2010s can also be attributed to Docker, which brought containers to the masses through simplified packaging and a runtime that could be utilized on Linux, macOS, and Windows. The ability to distribute container images with ease led to the increase in popularity of container technologies. This was because first-time users did not need to know how to create images but instead could make use of existing images that were created by others.

Containers and microservices became a match made in heaven. Applications had a packaging and distribution mechanism, along with the ability to share the same compute footprint while taking advantage of being isolated from one another. However, as more and more containerized microservices were deployed, the overall management became a concern. How do you ensure the health of each running container? What do you do if a container fails? What happens if your 0my underlying machine does not have the compute capacity required? Enter Kubernetes, which helped answer this need for container orchestration.

In the next section, we will discuss how Kubernetes works and provides value to an enterprise.

What is Kubernetes?

Kubernetes, often abbreviated as **k8s** (pronounced as **kaytes**), is an open source container orchestration platform. Originating from Google's proprietary orchestration tool, Borg, the project was open sourced in 2015 and was renamed Kubernetes. Following the v1.0 release on July 21, 2015, Google and the Linux Foundation partnered to form the **Cloud Native Computing Foundation** (**CNCF**), which acts as the current maintainer of the Kubernetes project.

The word Kubernetes is a Greek word meaning 'helmsman' or 'pilot'. A helmsman is the person who is in charge of steering a ship and works closely with the ship's officer to ensure a safe and steady course, along with the overall safety of the crew. Kubernetes has similar responsibilities with regards to containers and microservices. Kubernetes is in charge of the orchestration and scheduling of containers. It is in charge of 'steering' those containers to proper worker nodes that can handle their workloads. Kubernetes will also help ensure the safety of those microservices by providing high availability and health checks.

Let's review some of the ways Kubernetes helps simplify the management of containerized workloads.

Container Orchestration

The most prominent feature of Kubernetes is container orchestration. This is a fairly loaded term, so we'll break it down into different pieces.

Container orchestration is about placing containers on certain machines from a pool of compute resources based on their requirements. The simplest use case for container orchestration is for deploying containers on machines that can handle their resource requirements. In the following diagram, there is an application that requests 2 Gi of memory (Kubernetes resource requests typically use their 'power of two' values, which in this case is roughly equivalent to 2 GB) and one CPU core. This means that the container will be allocated 2 Gi of memory and 1 CPU core from the underlying machine that it is scheduled on. It is up to Kubernetes to track which machines, which in this case are called nodes, have the required resources available and to place an incoming container on that machine. If a node does not have enough resources to satisfy the request, the container will not be scheduled on that node. If all of the nodes in a cluster do not have enough resources to run the workload, the container will not be deployed. Once a node has enough resources free, the container will be deployed on the node with sufficient resources:

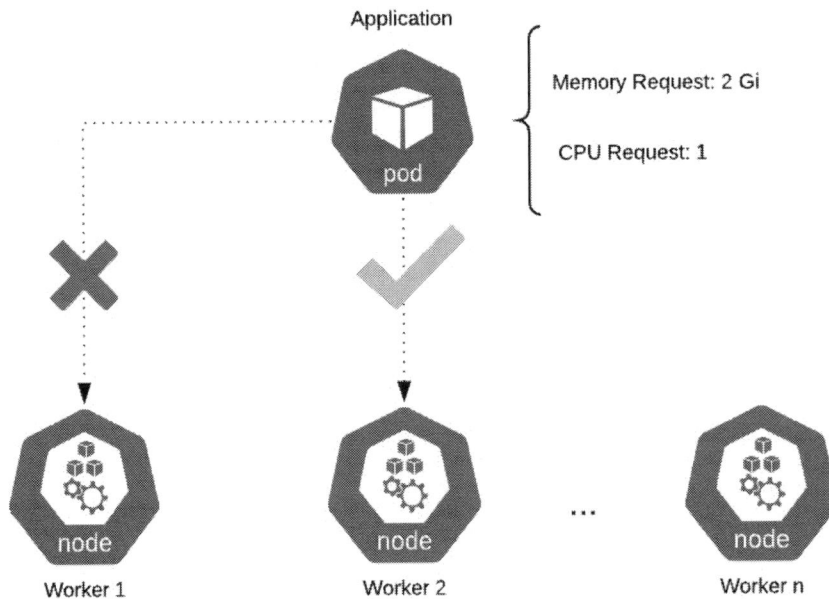

Figure 1.1 - Kubernetes orchestration and scheduling

Container orchestration relieves you of putting in the effort to track the available resources on machines at all times. Kubernetes and other monitoring tools provide insight into these metrics. So, a day-to-day developer does not need to worry about available resources. A developer can simply declare the amount of resources they expect a container to use and Kubernetes will take care of the rest on the backend.

High availability

Another benefit of Kubernetes is that it provides features that help take care of redundancy and high availability. High availability is a characteristic that prevents application downtime. It's performed by a load balancer, which splits incoming traffic across multiple instances of an application. The premise of high availability is that if one instance of an application goes down, other instances are still available to accept incoming traffic. In this regard, downtime is avoided and the end user, whether a human or another microservice, remains completely unaware that there was a failed instance of the application. Kubernetes provides a networking mechanism, called a Service, that allows applications to be load balanced. We will talk about Services in greater detail later on in the *Deploying a Kubernetes application* section of this chapter.

Scalability

Given the lightweight nature of containers and microservices, developers can use Kubernetes to rapidly scale their workloads, both horizontally and vertically.

Horizontal scaling is the act of deploying more container instances. If a team running their workloads on Kubernetes were expecting increased load, they could simply tell Kubernetes to deploy more instances of their application. Since Kubernetes is a container orchestrator, developers would not need to worry about the physical infrastructure that those applications would be deployed on. It would simply locate a node within the cluster with the available resources and deploy the additional instances there. Each extra instance would be added to a load-balancing pool, which would allow the application to continue to be highly available.

Vertical scaling is the act of allocating additional memory and CPU to an application. Developers can modify the resource requirements of their applications while they are running. This will prompt Kubernetes to redeploy the running instances and reschedule them on nodes that can support the new resource requirements. Depending on how this is configured, Kubernetes can redeploy each instance in a way that prevents downtime while the new instances are being deployed.

Active community

The Kubernetes community is an incredibly active open source community. As a result, Kubernetes frequently receives patches and new features. The community has also made many contributions to documentation, both to the official Kubernetes documentation as well as to professional or hobbyist blog websites. In addition to documentation, the community is highly involved in planning and attending meetups and conferences around the world, which helps increase education and innovation of the platform.

Another benefit of Kubernetes's large community is the number of different tools built to augment the abilities that are provided. Helm is one of those tools. As we'll see later in this chapter and throughout this book, Helm—a tool built by members of the Kubernetes community—vastly improves a developer's experience by simplifying application deployments and life cycle management.

With an understanding of the benefits Kubernetes brings to managing containerized workloads, let's now discuss how an application can be deployed in Kubernetes.

Deploying a Kubernetes application

Deploying an application on Kubernetes is fundamentally similar to deploying an application outside of Kubernetes. All applications, whether containerized or not, must have configuration details around topics that include the following:

- Networking
- Persistent storage and file mounts
- Availability and redundancy
- Application configuration
- Security

Configuring these details on Kubernetes is done by interacting with the Kubernetes **application programming interface (API)**.

The Kubernetes API serves as a set of endpoints that can be interacted with to view, modify, or delete different Kubernetes resources, many of which are used to configure different details of an application.

Let's discuss some of the basic API endpoints users can interact with to deploy and configure an application on Kubernetes.

Deployment

The first Kubernetes resource we will explore is called a Deployment. Deployments determine the basic details required to deploy an application on Kubernetes. One of these basic details consists of the container image that Kubernetes should deploy. Container images can be built on local workstations using tools such as `docker`, and `jib` but images can also be built right on Kubernetes using `kaniko`. Because Kubernetes does not expose a native API endpoint for building container images, we will not go into detail about how a container image is built prior to configuring a Deployment resource.

In addition to specifying the container image, Deployments also specify the number of replicas, or instances, of an application to deploy. When a Deployment is created, it spawns an intermediate resource, called a ReplicaSet. The ReplicaSet deploys as many instances of the application as determined by the `replicas` field on the Deployment. The application is deployed inside a container, which itself is deployed inside a construct called a Pod. A Pod is the smallest unit in Kubernetes and encapsulates at least one container.

Deployments can additionally define an application's resource limits, health checks, and volume mounts. When a Deployment is created, Kubernetes creates the following architecture:

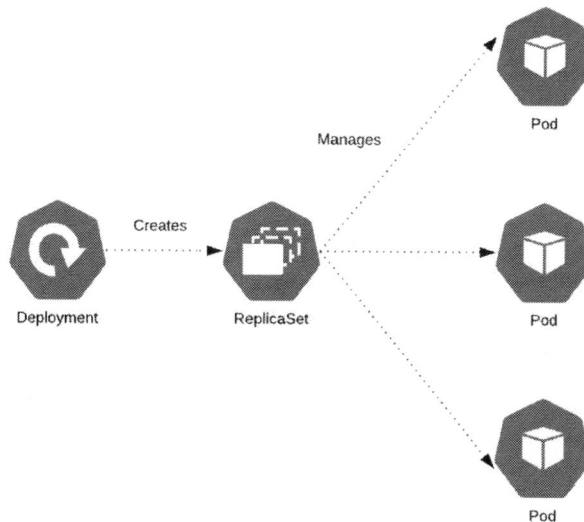

Figure 1.2 - A Deployment creates a set of Pods

Another basic API endpoint in Kubernetes is used to create Service resources, which we will discuss next.

Services

While Deployments are used to deploy an application to Kubernetes, they do not configure the networking components that allow an application to be communicated with Kubernetes exposes a separate API endpoint used to define the networking layer, called a Service. Services allow users and other applications to talk to each other by allocating a static IP address to a Service endpoint. The Service endpoint can then be configured to route traffic to one or more application instances. This kind of configuration provides load balancing and high availability.

An example architecture using a Service is described in the following diagram. Notice that the Service sits in between the client and the Pods to provide load balancing and high availability:

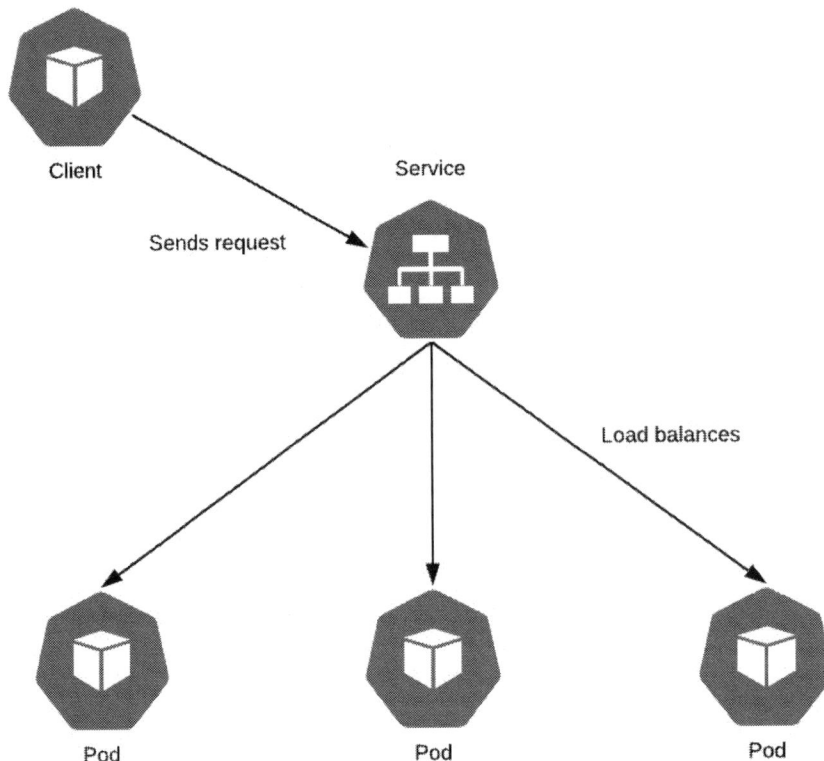

Figure 1.3 - A Service load balancing an incoming request

As a final example, we will discuss the `PersistentVolumeClaim` API endpoint.

PersistentVolumeClaim

Microservice-style applications embrace being self-sufficient by maintaining their state in an ephemeral manner. However, there are numerous use cases where data must live beyond the life span of a single container. Kubernetes addresses this issue by providing a subsystem for abstracting the underlying details of how storage is provided and how it is consumed. To allocate persistent storage for their application, users can create a `PersistentVolumeClaim` endpoint, which specifies the type and amount of storage that is desired. Kubernetes administrators are responsible for either statically allocating storage, expressed as `PersistentVolume`, or dynamically provisioning storage using `StorageClass`, which allocates `PersistentVolume` in response to a `PersistentVolumeClaim` endpoint. `PersistentVolume` captures all of the necessary storage details, including the type (such as network file system [NFS], internet small computer systems interface [iSCSI], or from a cloud provider), along with the size of the storage. From a user's perspective, regardless of which method of the `PersistentVolume` allocation method or storage backend that is used within the cluster, they do not need to manage the underlying details of managing storage. The ability to leverage persistent storage within Kubernetes increases the number of potential applications that can be deployed on the platform.

An example of persistent storage being provisioned is depicted in the following diagram. The diagram assumes that an administrator has configured dynamic provisioning via `StorageClass`:

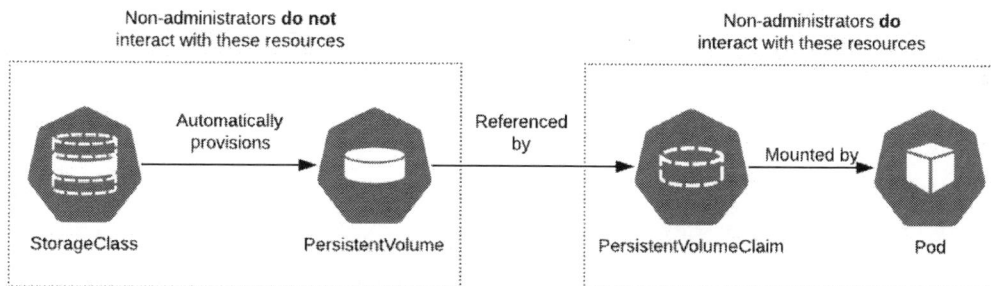

Figure 1.4 - A Pod mounting PersistentVolume created by PersistentVolumeClaim

There are many more resources in Kubernetes, but by now, you have probably got the picture. The question now is how are these resources actually created?

We will explore this question further in the next section.

Approaches in resource management

In order to deploy an application on Kubernetes, we need to interact with the Kubernetes API to create resources. `kubectl` is the tool we use to talk to the Kubernetes API. `kubectl` is a **command-line interface (CLI)** tool used to abstract the complexity of the Kubernetes API from end users, allowing them to more efficiently work on the platform.

Let's discuss how `kubectl` can be used to manage Kubernetes resources.

Imperative and declarative configuration

The `kubectl` tool provides a series of subcommands to create and modify resources in an imperative fashion. The following is a small list of these commands:

- `create`
- `describe`
- `edit`
- `delete`

The `kubectl` commands follow a common format:

```
kubectl <verb> <noun> <arguments>
```

The verb refers to one of the `kubectl` subcommands and the noun refers to a particular Kubernetes resource. For example, the following command can be run to create a Deployment:

```
kubectl create deployment my-deployment --image=busybox
```

This would instruct `kubectl` to talk to the Deployment API and create a new Deployment called `my-deployment`, using the `busybox` image from Docker Hub.

You could use `kubectl` to get more information on the Deployment that was created by using the `describe` subcommand:

```
kubectl describe deployment my-deployment
```

This command would retrieve information about the Deployment and format the result in a readable format that allows developers to inspect the live `my-deployment` Deployment on Kubernetes.

If a change to the Deployment was desired, a developer could use the `edit` subcommand to modify it in place:

```
kubectl edit deployment my-deployment
```

This command would open a text editor, allowing you to modify the Deployment.

When it comes to deleting the resource, the user can run the `delete` subcommand:

```
kubectl delete deployment my-deployment
```

This would instruct the API to delete the Deployment called `my-deployment`.

Kubernetes resources, once created, exist in the cluster as JSON resource files, which can be exported as YAML files for greater human readability. An example resource in YAML format can be seen here:

```
apiVersion: apps/v1
kind: Deployment
metadata:
  name: busybox
spec:
  replicas: 1
  selector:
    matchLabels:
      app: busybox
  template:
    metadata:
      labels:
        app: busybox
    spec:
      containers:
        - name: main
          image: busybox
          args:
            - sleep
            - infinity
```

The preceding YAML format presents a very basic use case. It deploys the `busybox` image from Docker Hub and runs the `sleep` command indefinitely to keep the Pod running.

While it may be easier to create resources imperatively using the `kubectl` subcommands we have just described, Kubernetes allows you to directly manage the YAML resources in a declarative fashion to gain more control over resource creation. The `kubectl` subcommands do not always let you configure all the possible resource options, but creating the YAML files directly allows you to more flexibly create resources and fill in the gaps that the `kubectl` subcommands may contain.

When creating resources declaratively, users first write out the resource they want to create in YAML format. Next, they use the `kubectl` tool to apply the resource against the Kubernetes API. While in imperative configuration developers use `kubectl` subcommands to manage resources, declarative configuration relies primarily on only one subcommand—`apply`.

Declarative configuration often takes the following form:

```
kubectl apply -f my-deployment.yaml
```

This command gives Kubernetes a YAML resource that contains a resource specification, although the JSON format can be used as well. Kubernetes infers the action to perform on resources (create or modify) based on whether or not they exist.

An application may be configured declaratively by following these steps:

1. First, the user can create a file called `deployment.yaml` and provide a YAML-formatted specification for the deployment. We will use the same example as before:

```
apiVersion: apps/v1
kind: Deployment
metadata:
  name: busybox
spec:
  replicas: 1
  selector:
    matchLabels:
      app: busybox
  template:
    metadata:
      labels:
```

```
        app: busybox
  spec:
    containers:
      - name: main
        image: busybox
        args:
          - sleep
          - infinity
```

2. The Deployment can then be created with the following command:

```
kubectl apply -f deployment.yaml
```

Upon running this command, Kubernetes will attempt to create the Deployment in the way you specified.

3. If you wanted to make a change to the Deployment, say by changing the number of replicas to 2, you would first modify the deployment.yaml file:

```
apiVersion: apps/v1
kind: Deployment
metadata:
  name: busybox
spec:
  replicas: 2
  selector:
    matchLabels:
      app: busybox
  template:
    metadata:
      labels:
        app: busybox
    spec:
      containers:
        - name: main
          image: busybox
          args:
            - sleep
```

```
        - infinity
```

4. You would then apply the change with `kubectl apply`:

    ```
    kubectl apply -f deployment.yaml
    ```

    After running that command, Kubernetes would apply the provided Deployment declaration over the previously applied `deployment`. At this point, the application would scale up from a `replica` value of 1 to 2.

5. When it comes to deleting an application, the Kubernetes documentation actually recommends doing so in an imperative manner; that is, using the `delete` subcommand instead of `apply`:

    ```
    kubectl delete -f deployment.yaml
    ```

6. The `delete` subcommand can be made more declarative by passing in the `-f` flag and a filename. This gives `kubectl` the name of the resource to delete that is declared in a specific file and it allows the developers to continue managing resources with declarative YAML files.

With an understanding of how Kubernetes resources are created, let's now discuss some of the challenges involved in resource configuration.

Resource configuration challenges

In the previous section, we covered how Kubernetes has two different configuration methods—imperative and declarative. One question to consider is what challenges do users need to be aware of when creating Kubernetes resources with imperative and declarative methodologies?

Let's discuss some of the most common challenges.

The many types of Kubernetes resources

First of all, there are many, *many* different resources in Kubernetes. Here's a short list of resources a developer should be aware of:

- Deployment
- StatefulSet
- Service

- Ingress
- ConfigMap
- Secret
- StorageClass
- PersistentVolumeClaim
- ServiceAccount
- Role
- RoleBinding
- Namespace

Out of the box, deploying an application on Kubernetes is not as simple as pushing a big red button marked `Deploy`. Developers need to be able to determine which resources are required to deploy their application and they need to understand those resources at a deep enough level to be able to configure them appropriately. This requires a lot of knowledge of and training on the platform. While understanding and creating resources may already sound like a large hurdle, this is actually just the beginning of many different operational challenges.

Keeping the live and local states in sync

A method of configuring Kubernetes resources that we would encourage is to maintain their configuration in source control for teams to edit and share, which also allows the source control repository to become the source of truth. The configuration defined in source control (referred to as the 'local state') is then created by applying them to the Kubernetes environment and the resources become 'live' or enter what can be called the 'live state.' This sounds simple enough, but what happens when developers need to make changes to their resources? The proper answer would be to modify the local files and apply the changes to synchronize the local state to the live state in an effort to update the source of truth. However, this isn't what usually ends up happening. It is often simpler, in the short term, to modify the live resource in place with `kubectl patch` or `kubectl edit` and completely skip over modifying the local files. This results in a state inconsistency between local and live states and is an act that makes scaling on Kubernetes difficult.

Application life cycles are hard to manage

Life cycle management is a loaded term, but in this context, we'll refer to it as the concept of installing, upgrading, and rolling back applications. In the Kubernetes world, an installation would create resources to deploy and configure an application. The initial installation would create what we refer to here as `version 1` of an application.

An upgrade, then, can be thought of as an edit or modification to one or many of those Kubernetes resources. Each `batch` of edits can be thought of as a single upgrade. A developer could modify a single Service resource, which would bump the version number to `version 2`. The developer could then modify a Deployment, a ConfigMap, and a Service, bumping the version count to `version 3`.

As newer versions of an application continue to be rolled out onto Kubernetes, it becomes more difficult to keep track of the changes that have occurred. Kubernetes, in most cases, does not have an inherent way of keeping a history of changes. While this makes upgrades harder to keep track of, it also makes restoring a prior version of an application much more difficult. Say a developer previously made an incorrect edit on a particular resource. How would a team know where to roll back to? The `n-1` case is particularly easy to work out, as that is the most recent version. What happens, however, if the latest stable release was five versions ago? Teams often end up scrambling to resolve issues because they cannot quickly identify the latest stable configuration that worked previously.

Resource files are static

This is a challenge that primarily affects the declarative configuration style of applying YAML resources. Part of the difficulty in following a declarative approach is that Kubernetes resource files are not natively designed to be parameterized. Resource files are largely designed to be written out in full before being applied and the contents remain the source of truth until the file is modified. When dealing with Kubernetes, this can be a frustrating reality. Some API resources can be lengthy, containing many different customizable fields, and it can be quite cumbersome to write and configure YAML resources in full.

Static files lend themselves to becoming boilerplate. Boilerplate represents text or code that remains largely consistent in different but similar contexts. This becomes an issue if developers manage multiple different applications, where they could potentially manage multiple different Deployment resources, multiple different Services, and so on. In comparing the different applications' resource files, you may find large numbers of similar YAML configuration between them.

The following figure depicts an example of two resources with significant boilerplate configuration between them. The blue text denotes lines that are boilerplate, while the red text denotes lines that are unique:

```
apiVersion: v1                          apiVersion: v1
kind: Deployment                        kind: Deployment
metadata:                               metadata:
  name: my-k8s-app                        name: your-k8s-app
spec:                                   spec:
  replicas: 1                             replicas: 1
  selector:                               selector:
    matchLabels:                            matchLabels:
      app: my-k8s-app                         app: your-k8s-app
  strategy:                               strategy:
    rollingUpdate:                          rollingUpdate:
      maxSurge: 25%                           maxSurge: 25%
      maxUnavailable: 25%                     maxUnavailable: 25%
  template:                               template:
    metadata:                               metadata:
      labels:                                 labels:
        app: my-k8s-app                         app: your-k8s-app
    spec:                                   spec:
      containers:                             containers:
      - image: my-k8s-app:v1                  - image: your-k8s-app:v3
        imagePullPolicy: IfNotPresent           imagePullPolicy: IfNotPresent
        name: app                               name: app
```

Figure 1.5 - An example of two resources with boilerplate

Notice, in this example, that each file is almost exactly the same. When managing files that are as similar as this, boilerplate becomes a major headache for teams managing their applications in a declarative fashion.

Helm to the rescue!

Over time, the Kubernetes community discovered that creating and maintaining Kubernetes resources to deploy applications is difficult. This prompted the development of a simple yet powerful tool that would allow teams to overcome the challenges posed by deploying applications on Kubernetes. The tool that was created is called Helm. Helm is an open source tool used for packaging and deploying applications on Kubernetes. It is often referred to as the **Kubernetes Package Manager** because of its similarities to any other package manager you would find on your favorite OS. Helm is widely used throughout the Kubernetes community and is a CNCF graduated project.

Given Helm's similarities to traditional package managers, let's begin exploring Helm by first reviewing how a package manager works.

Understanding package managers

Package managers are used to simplify the process of installing, upgrading, reverting, and removing a system's applications. These applications are defined in units, called **packages**, which contain metadata around target software and its dependencies.

The process behind package managers is simple. First, the user passes the name of a software package as an argument. The package manager then performs a lookup against a package repository to see whether that package exists. If it is found, the package manager installs the application defined by the package and its dependencies to the specified locations on the system.

Package managers make managing software very easy. As an example, let's imagine you wanted to install htop, a Linux system monitor, to a Fedora machine. Installing this would be as simple as typing a single command:

```
dnf install htop --assumeyes
```

This instructs dnf, the Fedora package manager since 2015, to find htop in the Fedora package repository and install it. dnf also takes care of installing the htop package's dependencies, so you would not have to worry about installing its requirements beforehand. After dnf finds the htop package from the upstream repository, it asks you whether you're sure you want to proceed. The --assumeyes flag automatically answers yes to this question and any other prompts that dnf may potentially ask.

Over time, newer versions of htop may appear in the upstream repository. dnf and other package managers allow users to efficiently upgrade to new versions of the software. The subcommand that allows users to upgrade using dnf is upgrade:

```
dnf upgrade htop --assumeyes
```

This instructs dnf to upgrade htop to its latest version. It also upgrades its dependencies to the versions specified in the package's metadata.

While moving forward is often better, package managers also allow users to move backward and revert an application back to a prior version if necessary. dnf does this with the downgrade subcommand:

```
dnf downgrade htop --assumeyes
```

This is a powerful process because the package manager allows users to quickly roll back if a critical bug or vulnerability is reported.

If you want to remove an application completely, a package manager can take care of that as well. `dnf` provides the `remove` subcommand for this purpose:

```
dnf remove htop --assumeyes
```

In this section, we reviewed how the `dnf` package manager on Fedora can be used to manage a software package. Helm, as the Kubernetes package manager, is similar to `dnf`, both in its purpose and functionality. While `dnf` is used to manage applications on Fedora, Helm is used to manage applications on Kubernetes. We will explore this in greater detail next.

The Kubernetes package manager

Given that Helm was designed to provide an experience similar to that of package managers, experienced users of `dnf` or similar tools will immediately understand Helm's basic concepts. Things become more complicated, however, when talking about the specific implementation details. `dnf` operates on RPM packages that provide executables, dependency information, and metadata. Helm, on the other hand, works with **charts**. A Helm chart can be thought of as a Kubernetes package. Charts contain the declarative Kubernetes resource files required to deploy an application. Similar to an RPM, it can also declare one or more dependencies that the application needs in order to run.

Helm relies on repositories to provide widespread access to charts. Chart developers create declarative YAML files, package them into charts, and publish them to chart repositories. End users then use Helm to search for existing charts to deploy onto Kubernetes, similar to how end users of `dnf` will search for RPM packages to deploy to Fedora.

Let's go through a basic example. Helm could be used to deploy `Redis`, an in-memory cache, to Kubernetes by using a chart published to an upstream repository. This could be performed using Helm's `install` command:

```
helm install redis bitnami/redis --namespace=redis
```

This would install the `redis` chart from the bitnami chart repository to a Kubernetes namespace called `redis`. This installation would be referred to as the initial **revision**, or the initial deployment of a Helm chart.

If a new version of the `redis` chart becomes available, users can upgrade to a new version using the `upgrade` command:

```
helm upgrade redis bitnami/redis --namespace=redis
```

This would upgrade `Redis` to meet the specification defined by the newer
`redis-ha` chart.

With operating systems, users should be concerned about rollbacks if a bug or
vulnerability is found. The same concern exists with applications on Kubernetes, and
Helm provides the rollback command to handle this use case:

```
helm rollback redis 1 --namespace=redis
```

This command would roll `Redis` back to its first revision.

Finally, Helm provides the ability to remove `Redis` altogether with the
`uninstall` command:

```
helm uninstall redis --namespace=redis
```

Compare `dnf`, Helm's subcommands, and the functions they serve in the following table.
Notice that `dnf` and Helm offer similar commands that provide a similar user experience:

The dnf subcommands	The Helm subcommands	Purpose
install	install	Install an application and its dependencies.
upgrade	upgrade	Upgrade an application to a newer version. Upgrade dependencies as specified by the target package.
downgrade	rollback	Revert an application to a previous version. Revert dependencies as specified by the target package.
remove	uninstall	Delete an application. Each tool has a different philosophy around handling dependencies.

With an understanding of how Helm functions as a package manager, let's discuss in
greater detail the benefits that Helm brings to Kubernetes. The benefits of Helm

Earlier in this chapter, we reviewed how Kubernetes applications are created by managing
Kubernetes resources, and we discussed some of the challenges involved. Here are few
ways that Helm can overcome these challenges.

The abstracted complexity of Kubernetes resources

Let's assume that a developer has been given the task of deploying a MySQL database onto Kubernetes. The developer would need to create the resources required to configure its containers, network, and storage. The amount of Kubernetes knowledge required to configure such an application from scratch is high and is a big hurdle for new and even intermediate Kubernetes users to clear.

With Helm, a developer tasked with deploying a MySQL database could simply search for MySQL charts in upstream chart repositories. These charts would have already been written by chart developers in the community and would already contain the declarative configuration required to deploy a MySQL database. In this regard, developers with this kind of task would act as simple end users that use Helm in a similar way to any other package manager.

The ongoing history of revisions

Helm has a concept called release history. When a Helm chart is installed for the first time, Helm adds that initial revision to the history. The history is further modified as revisions increase via upgrades, keeping various snapshots of how the application was configured at varying revisions.

The following diagram depicts an ongoing history of revisions. The squares in blue illustrate resources that have been modified from their previous versions:

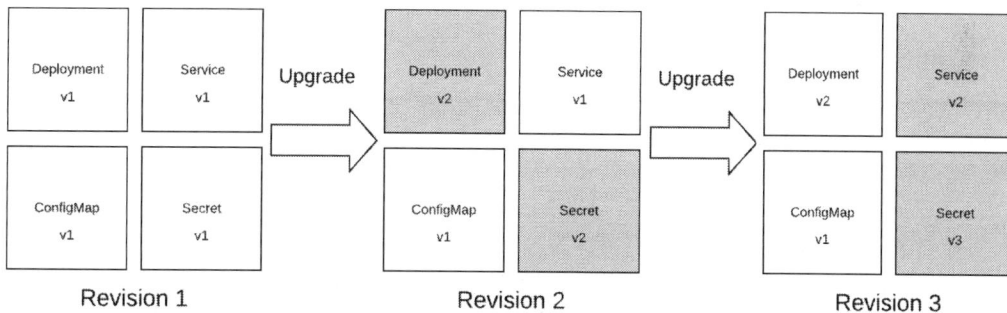

Figure 1.6 - An example of a revision history

The process of tracking each revision provides opportunities for rollback. Rollbacks in Helm are very simple. Users simply point Helm to a previous revision and Helm reverts the live state to that of the selected revision. With Helm, gone are the days of the n-1 backup. Helm allows users to roll back their applications as far back as they desire, even back to the very first installation.

Dynamically configured declarative resources

One of the biggest hassles with creating resources declaratively is that Kubernetes resources are static and cannot be parameterized. As you may recall from earlier, this results in resources becoming boilerplate across applications and similar configurations, making it more difficult for teams to configure their applications as code. Helm alleviates these issues by introducing **values** and **templates**.

Values are simply what Helm calls parameters for charts. Templates are dynamically generated files based on a given set of values. These two constructs provide chart developers the ability to write Kubernetes resources that are automatically generated based on values that end users provide. By doing so, applications managed by Helm become more flexible, less boilerplate, and easier to maintain.

Values and templates allow users to do things such as the following:

- Parameterize common fields, such as the image name in a Deployment and the ports in a Service
- Generate long pieces of YAML configuration based on user input, such as volume mounts in a Deployment or the data in a ConfigMap
- Include or exclude resources based on user input

The ability to dynamically generate declarative resource files makes it simpler to create YAML-based resources while still ensuring that applications are created in an easily reproducible fashion.

Consistency between the local and live states

Package managers prevent users from having to manage an application and its dependencies manually. All management can be done through the package manager itself. The same idea holds true with Helm. Because a Helm chart contains a flexible configuration of Kubernetes resources, users shouldn't have to make modifications directly to live Kubernetes resources. Users that want to modify their applications can do so by providing new values to a Helm chart or by upgrading their application to a more recent version of the associated chart. This allows the local state (represented by the Helm chart configuration) and the live state to remain consistent across modifications, giving users the ability to provide a source of truth for their Kubernetes resource configurations.

Intelligent Deployments

Helm simplifies application deployments by determining the order that Kubernetes resources need to be created. Helm analyzes each of a chart's resources and orders them based on their types. This pre-deterministic order exists to ensure that resources that commonly have resources dependent on them are created first. For example, Secrets and ConfigMaps should be created before Deployments, since a Deployment would likely consume those resources as volumes. Helm performs this ordering without any interaction from the user, so this complexity is abstracted and prevents users from needing to worry about the order that these resources are applied.

Automated life cycle hooks

Similar to other package managers, Helm provides the ability to define life cycle hooks. Life cycle hooks are actions that take place automatically at different stages of an application's life cycle. They can be used to do things such as the following:

- Perform a data backup on an upgrade.
- Restore data on a rollback.
- Validate a Kubernetes environment prior to installation.

Life cycle hooks are valuable because they abstract complexities around tasks that may not be Kubernetes-specific. For example, a Kubernetes user may not be familiar with the best practices behind backing up a database or may not know when such a task should be performed. Life cycle hooks allow experts to write automation that performs those best practices when recommended so that users can continue to be productive without needing to worry about those details.

Summary

In this chapter, we began by exploring the change in architectural trends of adopting microservice-based architectures to decompose applications into several smaller applications instead of deploying one large monolith. The creation of applications that are more lightweight and easier to manage has led to utilizing containers as a packaging and runtime format to produce releases more frequently. By adopting containers, additional operational challenges were introduced and solved by using Kubernetes as a container orchestration platform to manage the container life cycle.

Our discussion turned to the various ways that Kubernetes applications can be configured, including Deployments, Services, and PersistentVolumeClaims. These resources can be expressed using two distinct styles of application configuration: imperative and declarative. Each of these configuration styles contributes to a set of challenges involved in deploying Kubernetes applications, including the amount of knowledge required to understand how Kubernetes resources work and the challenge of managing application life cycles.

To better manage each of the assets that comprise an application, Helm was introduced as the package manager for Kubernetes. Through its rich feature set, the full life cycle of applications from install, upgrade, rollback, and removal can be managed with ease.

In the next chapter, we'll walk through the process of configuring a Helm environment. We will also install the tooling required for consuming the Helm ecosystem and following along with the examples provided in this book.

Further reading

For more information about the Kubernetes resources that make up an application, please see the *Understanding Kubernetes Objects* page from the Kubernetes documentation at `https://kubernetes.io/docs/concepts/overview/working-with-objects/kubernetes-objects/`.

To reinforce some of the benefits of Helm discussed in this chapter, please refer to the *Using Helm* page of the Helm documentation at `https://helm.sh/docs/intro/using_helm/`. (This page also dives into some basic usage around Helm, which will be discussed throughout this book in greater detail.)

Questions

1. What is the difference between a monolithic and a microservices application?

2. What is Kubernetes? What problems was it designed to solve?

3. What are some of the `kubectl` commands commonly used when deploying applications to Kubernetes?

4. What challenges are often involved in deploying applications to Kubernetes?

5. How does Helm function as a package manager for Kubernetes? How does it address the challenges posed by Kubernetes?

6. Imagine you want to roll back an application deployed on Kubernetes. What Helm command allows you to perform this action? How does Helm keep track of your changes to make this rollback possible?

7. What are the four primary Helm commands that allow Helm to function as a package manager?

2
Preparing a Kubernetes and Helm Environment

Helm is a tool that provides a variety of benefits that help users deploy and manage Kubernetes applications more easily. Before users can start experiencing these benefits, however, they must satisfy several prerequisites. First, a user must have access to a Kubernetes cluster. Next, a user should have the command-line tools for both Kubernetes and Helm. Finally, a user should be aware of Helm's basic configuration options in order to be productive with as little friction as possible.

In this chapter, we will outline the tools and concepts that are required in order to begin working with Helm. The following topics will be covered in this chapter:

- Preparing a local Kubernetes environment with Minikube
- Setting up `kubectl`
- Setting up Helm
- Configuring Helm

Technical requirements

In this chapter, you will install the following technologies to your local workstation:

- Minikube
- VirtualBox
- Helm

These tools can be installed with a package manager or by downloading them directly from a download link. We will provide instructions for using the `Chocolatey` package manager on Windows, the `Homebrew` package manager on macOS, the `apt-get` package manager for Debian-based Linux distributions, and the `dnf` package manager for RPM-based Linux distributions.

Preparing a local Kubernetes environment with Minikube

Helm won't be able to deploy applications without access to a Kubernetes cluster. For this reason, let's discuss one option that users can follow to run their own cluster on their machine—Minikube.

Minikube is a community-driven tool that allows users to easily deploy a small, single-node Kubernetes cluster to their local machine. A cluster created with Minikube is created inside a **virtual machine (VM)**, so it can be created and later discarded in a way that is isolated from the host operating system that the VM is running on. Minikube presents an excellent way to experiment with Kubernetes and it can also be used to learn how to use Helm alongside the examples provided throughout this book.

In the next few sections, we'll cover how Minikube can be installed and configured so that you have a Kubernetes cluster available while learning how to use Helm. For more comprehensive instructions, please refer to the *Getting Started* page from the official Minikube website at `https://minikube.sigs.k8s.io/docs/start/`.

Installing Minikube

Minikube, like the other tools that will be installed within this chapter, has binaries compiled for the Windows, macOS, and Linux operating systems. The easiest way to install the latest version of Minikube on Windows and macOS is via a package manager, such as `Chocolatey` for Windows and `Homebrew` for macOS.

Linux users will find it easier to install the latest `minikube` binary by downloading it from Minikube's GitHub releases page, though this method can also be used on Windows and macOS as well.

The following steps describe how you can install Minikube based on your machine and installation preference. Please note that Minikube version v1.5.2 was used during the writing and development of the examples used throughout this book.

To install it via a package manager (on Windows and macOS), do the following:

- Use the following command for Windows:

```
> choco install minikube
```

- Use the following command for macOS:

```
$ brew install minikube
```

The following steps show you how to install it via a download link (on Windows, macOS, and Linux).

The `Minikube` binary can be downloaded directly from its releases page on GitHub at `https://github.com/kubernetes/minikube/releases/`:

1. At the bottom of the releases page, there is a section called *Assets*, which consists of the Minikube binaries available for the various supported platforms:

▼ Assets 15	
📦 docker-machine-driver-hyperkit	10.8 MB
📦 docker-machine-driver-hyperkit.sha256	65 Bytes
📦 docker-machine-driver-kvm2	13.9 MB
📦 docker-machine-driver-kvm2.sha256	65 Bytes
📦 minikube-1.5.2.rpm	12.2 MB
📦 minikube-darwin-amd64	47.1 MB
📦 minikube-darwin-amd64.sha256	65 Bytes
📦 minikube-installer.exe	20.6 MB
📦 minikube-linux-amd64	46.3 MB
📦 minikube-linux-amd64.sha256	65 Bytes
📦 minikube-windows-amd64.exe	47.6 MB
📦 minikube-windows-amd64.exe.sha256	65 Bytes
📦 minikube_1.5.2.deb	15.2 MB
📄 Source code (zip)	
📄 Source code (tar.gz)	

Figure 2.1: The minikube binaries from the GitHub releases page

2. Under the **Assets** section, the binary that corresponds to the target platform should be downloaded. Once downloaded, you should rename the binary to `minikube`. If you are downloading the Linux binary, for example, you would run the following command:

```
$ mv minikube-linux-amd64 minikube
```

3. In order to execute `minikube`, Linux and macOS users may need to add the executable bit by running the `chmod` command:

```
$ chmod u+x
```

4. `minikube` should then be moved to a location managed by the PATH variable so that it can be executed from any location in your command line. The locations that the PATH variable contains vary depending on your operating system. For macOS and Linux users, these locations can be determined by running the following command in the Terminal:

```
$ echo $PATH
```

5. Windows users can determine the PATH variable's locations by running the following command in Command Prompt or PowerShell:

```
> $env:PATH
```

6. You can then move the `minikube` binary to a new location by using the `mv` command. The following example moves `minikube` to a common PATH location on Linux:

```
$ mv minikube /usr/local/bin/
```

7. You can verify your Minikube installation by running `minikube version` and ensuring that the displayed version corresponds with the version that was downloaded:

```
$ minikube version
minikube version: v1.5.2
commit: 792dbf92a1de583fcee76f8791cff12e0c9440ad-dirty
```

Although you have downloaded Minikube, you will also need a hypervisor to be able to run your local Kubernetes cluster. This can be done by installing VirtualBox, which we will describe in the next section.

Installing VirtualBox

Minikube depends on the existence of hypervisors in order to install a single-node Kubernetes cluster on a VM. For this book, we have chosen to discuss VirtualBox as the hypervisor option, since it is the most flexible and is available on the Windows, macOS, and Linux operating systems. Additional hypervisor options for each operating system can be found in the official Minikube documentation at `https://minikube.sigs.k8s.io/docs/start/`.

Like Minikube, VirtualBox is easily installed via Chocolatey or Homebrew, but can also be easily installed using `apt-get` for Debian-based Linux and `dnf` for RPM/RHEL-based Linux:

- Use the following code to install VirtualBox on Windows:

  ```
  > choco install virtualbox
  ```

- Use the following code to install VirtualBox on macOS:

  ```
  $ brew cask install virtualbox
  ```

- Use the following code to install VirtualBox on Debian-based Linux:

  ```
  $ apt-get install virtualbox
  ```

- Use the following code to install VirtualBox on RHEL-based Linux:

  ```
  $ dnf install VirtualBox
  ```

Alternative methods of installing VirtualBox can be found at its official download page at `https://www.virtualbox.org/wiki/Downloads`.

With VirtualBox installed, Minikube must be configured to leverage VirtualBox as its default hypervisor. This configuration will be made in the next section.

Configuring VirtualBox as the designated hypervisor

VirtualBox can be made the default hypervisor by setting the `vm-driver` option of `minikube` to `virtualbox`:

```
$ minikube config set vm-driver virtualbox
```

Note that this command may produce the following warning:

```
These changes will take effect upon a minikube delete and then
a minikube start
```

This message can be safely ignored if there are no active Minikube clusters on the workstation. This command states that any existing Kubernetes clusters will not make use of VirtualBox as the hypervisor until the cluster is deleted and then recreated.

The change to VirtualBox can be confirmed by assessing the value of the `vm-driver` configuration option:

```
$ minikube config get vm-driver
```

If all is well, the output will be as follows:

```
Virtualbox
```

In addition to configuring the default hypervisor, you can also configure the resources that are allocated to a Minikube cluster, discussed in the next section.

Configuring Minikube resource allocation

By default, Minikube will allocate two CPUs and 2 GB of RAM to its VM. These resources are sufficient for each of the examples in this book except for those in Chapter 7, which are more resource intensive. If your machine has the available resources, you should increase the default memory allocation to 4 GB (the CPU allocation can remain the same).

Run the following command to increase the default memory allocation of new Minikube VMs to 4 GB (4000 MB).

```
$ minikube config set memory 4000
```

This change can be verified by running the `minikube config get memory` command, similar to the way the `vm-driver` change was verified previously.

Let's continue exploring Minikube by discussing its basic usage.

Exploring the basic usage

Throughout this book, it will be handy to understand the key commands used in a typical Minikube operation. They will also be essential to understand during the execution of the examples provided throughout the course of this book. Fortunately, Minikube is an easy tool to get started with.

Minikube has three key subcommands:

- `start`
- `stop`
- `delete`

The `start` subcommand is used to create a single-node Kubernetes cluster. It will create a VM and bootstrap the cluster within it. The command will terminate once the cluster is ready:

```
$ minikube start
  minikube v1.5.2 on Fedora 30
    Creating virtualbox VM (CPUs=2, Memory=4000MB, Disk=20000MB)
  ...
    Preparing Kubernetes v1.16.2 on Docker '18.09.9' ...
    Pulling images ...
    Launching Kubernetes ...
  Waiting for: apiserver
    Done! kubectl is now configured to use 'minikube'
```

The `stop` subcommand is used to shut down the cluster and the VM. The state of the cluster and VM are saved to the disk, allowing users to run the `start` subcommand again to quickly begin working, rather than having to build a new VM from scratch. You should try to get into the habit of running `minikube stop` when you have finished working with a cluster that you would like to return to later:

```
$ minikube stop
  Stopping 'minikube' in virtualbox ...
  'minikube' stopped.
```

The delete subcommand is used to delete a cluster and the VM. This command erases the state of the cluster and VM, freeing up the space on the disk that was previously allocated. The next time minikube start is executed, a fresh cluster and VM will be created. You should run the delete subcommand when you would like to remove all of the allocated resources and work on a fresh Kubernetes cluster on your next invocation of minikube start:

```
$ minikube delete
  Deleting 'minikube' in virtualbox ...
  The 'minikube' cluster has been deleted.
  Successfully deleted profile 'minikube'
```

There are more Minikube subcommands available, but these are the main ones that you should be aware of.

With Minikube installed and configured on a local machine, you can now install kubectl, the Kubernetes command-line tool, and satisfy the remaining prerequisites for working with Helm.

Setting up Kubectl

As mentioned in *Chapter 1, Understanding Kubernetes and Helm*, Kubernetes is a system that exposes different API endpoints. These API endpoints are used to perform various actions on a cluster, such as creating, viewing, or deleting resources. To provide simpler user experience, developers need a way of interacting with Kubernetes without having to manage the underlying API layer.

While you will predominantly use the Helm command-line tool throughout the course of this book to install and manage applications, kubectl is an essential tool for common tasks.

Read on to learn how to install kubectl on a local workstation. Note that the kubectl version used at the time of writing is v1.16.2.

Installing Kubectl

Kubectl can be installed using Minikube or it can be obtained via a package manager or through direct download. We will first describe how to obtain kubectl using Minikube.

Installing Kubectl via Minikube

The installation of kubectl is straightforward with Minikube. Minikube provides a subcommand called kubectl, which will download the Kubectl binary. Begin by running minikube kubectl:

```
$ minikube kubectl version
  Downloading kubectl v1.16.2
```

This command will install kubectl to the $HOME/.kube/cache/v1.16.2 directory. Note that the version of Kubectl included in the path will depend on the version of Minikube that you are using. To access kubectl, you can use the following syntax:

```
      minikube kubectl -- <subcommand> <flags>
```

Here's an example command:

```
$ minikube kubectl -- version -client
Client Version: version.Info{Major:'1',
Minor:'16', GitVersion:'v1.16.2',
GitCommit:'c97fe5036ef3df2967d086711e6c0c405941e14b',
GitTreeState:'clean', BuildDate:'2019-10-15T19:18:23Z',
GoVersion:'go1.12.10', Compiler:'gc', Platform:'linux/amd64'}
```

While invoking kubectl with minikube kubectl will suffice, the syntax is more unwieldy than that of invoking kubectl directly. This can be overcome by copying the kubectl executable from the local Minikube cache into a location managed by the PATH variable. Performing this action is similar on each operating system, but the following is an example of how it can be achieved on a Linux machine:

```
$ sudo cp ~/.kube/cache/v1.16.2/kubectl /usr/local/bin/
```

Once complete, kubectl can be invoked as a standalone binary, as illustrated:

```
$ kubectl version -client
Client Version: version.Info{Major:'1',
Minor:'16', GitVersion:'v1.16.2',
GitCommit:'c97fe5036ef3df2967d086711e6c0c405941e14b',
GitTreeState:'clean', BuildDate:'2019-10-15T19:18:23Z',
GoVersion:'go1.12.10', Compiler:'gc', Platform:'linux/amd64'}
```

Installing Kubectl without Minikube

Kubectl can also be installed without Minikube. The Kubernetes upstream documentation provides several different mechanisms to do so for a variety of target operating systems at `https://kubernetes.io/docs/tasks/tools/install-kubectl/`.

Using a package manager

One way that `kubectl` can be installed without Minikube is with native package management. The following list demonstrates how this can be done on different operating systems:

- Use the following command to install `kubectl` on Windows:

```
> choco install kubernetes-cli
```

- Use the following command to install `kubectl` on macOS:

```
$ brew install kubernetes-cli
```

- Use the following command to install `kubectl` on Debian-based Linux:

```
$ sudo apt-get update && sudo apt-get install -y
apt-transport-https gnupg2
```
```
$ curl -s https://packages.cloud.google.com/apt/doc/
apt-key.gpg | sudo apt-key add -
```
```
$ echo 'deb https://apt.kubernetes.io/ kubernetes-xenial
main' | sudo tee -a /etc/apt/sources.list.d/kubernetes.
list
```
```
$ sudo apt-get update
```
```
$ sudo apt-get install -y kubectl
```

- Use the following command to install `kubectl` RPM-based Linux:

```
$ cat <<EOF > /etc/yum.repos.d/kubernetes.repo
[kubernetes]
name=Kubernetes
baseurl=https://packages.cloud.google.com/yum/repos/
kubernetes-el7-x86_64
enabled=1
gpgcheck=1
repo_gpgcheck=1
```

```
gpgkey=https://packages.cloud.google.com/yum/doc/
yum-key.gpg https://packages.cloud.google.com/yum/doc/
rpm-package-key.gpg
EOF
$ yum install -y kubectl
```

We will discuss the final Kubectl installation method next.

Downloading directly from a link

Kubectl can also be downloaded directly from a download link. The download link will contain the version of Kubectl that will be downloaded. You can determine the latest version of Kubectl by going to `https://storage.googleapis.com/kubernetes-release/release/stable.txt` in your browser.

The following example instructions display how version v1.16.2 can be downloaded, which is the version of Kubectl that is used throughout this book:

- Download Kubectl for Windows from `https://storage.googleapis.com/kubernetes-release/release/v1.16.2/bin/windows/amd64/kubectl.exe`.

- Download Kubectl for macOS from `https://storage.googleapis.com/kubernetes-release/release/v1.16.2/bin/darwin/amd64/kubectl`.

- Download Kubectl for Linux from `https://storage.googleapis.com/kubernetes-release/release/v1.16.2/bin/linux/amd64/kubectl`.

The Kubectl binary can then be moved to somewhere managed by the PATH variable. On the macOS and Linux operating systems, be sure to grant the executable permission:

```
$ chmod u+x kubectl
```

The Kubectl installation can be verified by running the following command.

```
$ kubectl version -client
Client Version: version.Info{Major:'1',
Minor:'16', GitVersion:'v1.16.2',
GitCommit:'c97fe5036ef3df2967d086711e6c0c405941e14b',
GitTreeState:'clean', BuildDate:'2019-10-15T19:18:23Z',
GoVersion:'go1.12.10', Compiler:'gc', Platform:'linux/amd64'}
```

Now that we've covered how to set up `kubectl`, we're ready to get into the key technology of this book—Helm.

Setting up Helm

Once Minikube and `kubectl` are installed, the next logical tool to configure is Helm. Note that the version of Helm used when writing this book was `v3.0.0`, but you are encouraged to use the latest version available of the Helm v3 release to receive the latest vulnerability and bug fixes.

Installing Helm

Helm packages exist for Chocolatey and Homebrew to allow easy installation on Windows or macOS. On these systems, the following commands can be run to install Helm with a package manager:

- Install Helm on Windows using the following command:

```
> choco install kubernetes-helm
```

- Install Helm on macOS using the following command:

```
$ brew install helm
```

Linux users, or users who would rather install Helm from a direct downloadable link, can download an archive from Helm's GitHub releases page by following these steps:

1. Find the section called **Installation** on Helm's GitHub releases page at `https://github.com/helm/helm/releases`:

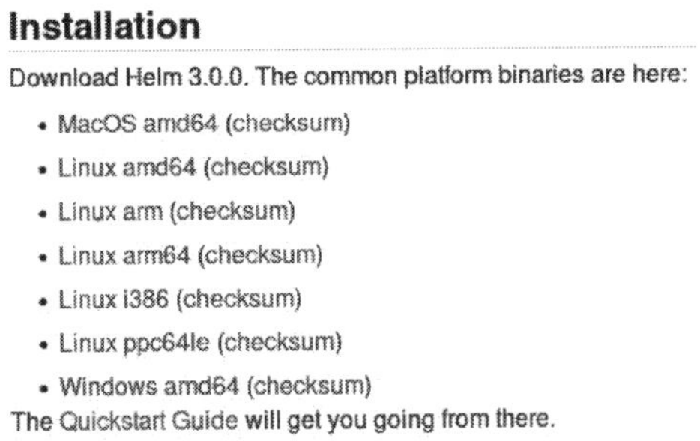

   Installation

   Download Helm 3.0.0. The common platform binaries are here:

   - MacOS amd64 (checksum)
   - Linux amd64 (checksum)
   - Linux arm (checksum)
   - Linux arm64 (checksum)
   - Linux i386 (checksum)
   - Linux ppc64le (checksum)
   - Windows amd64 (checksum)

   The Quickstart Guide will get you going from there.

   Figure 2.2: The Installation section on the Helm GitHub releases page

2. Download the archive file associated with the operating system you are using for the desired version.

3. Once downloaded, the file will need to be unarchived. One way that this can be achieved is by using the `Expand-Archive` cmdlet function on PowerShell or by using the `tar` utility on Bash:

- For Windows/PowerShell, use the following example :

```
> Expand-Archive -Path helm-v3.0.0-windows-amd64.zip
  -DestinationPath $DEST
```

- For Linux and Mac, use the following example :

```
$ tar -zxvf helm-v3.0.0-linux.amd64.tgz
```

Be sure to specify the version that corresponds to the version downloaded. The `helm` binary can be found in the unarchived folder. It should be moved to a location managed by the `PATH` variable.

The following example shows you how to move the `helm` binary to the `/usr/local/bin` folder on a Linux system:

```
$ mv ~/Downloads/linux-amd64/helm /usr/local/bin
```

Regardless of the way that Helm was installed, verification can be performed by running the `helm version` command. If the resulting output is similar to that of the following output, then Helm has been successfully installed:

```
$ helm version
version.BuildInfo{Version:'v3.0.0',
 GitCommit:'e29ce2a54e96cd02ccfce88bee4f58bb6e2a28b6',
 GitTreeState:'clean', GoVersion:'go1.13.4'}
```

With Helm installed on your machine, proceed to the next section to learn about the basic Helm configuration topics.

Configuring Helm

Helm is a tool with sensible defaults that allow users to be productive without needing to perform a large number of tasks post-installation. With that being said, there are several different options users can change or enable to modify Helm's behavior. We will cover these options in the following sections, beginning with the configuration of upstream repositories.

Adding upstream repositories

One way that users can begin to modify their Helm installation is by adding upstream chart repositories. In *Chapter 1, Understanding Kubernetes and Helm*, we described how chart repositories contain Helm charts, which are used to package Kubernetes resource files. Helm, being the Kubernetes package manager, can connect to various chart repositories to install Kubernetes applications.

Helm provides the `repo` subcommand to allow users to manage configured chart repositories. This subcommand contains additional subcommands that can be used to perform actions against specified repositories.

Here are the five `repo` subcommands:

- `add`: To add a chart repository
- `list`: To list chart repositories
- `remove`: To remove a chart repository
- `update`: To update information on available charts locally from chart repositories
- `index`: To generate an index file given a directory containing packaged charts

Using the preceding list as a guide, adding a chart repository can be accomplished using the `repo add` subcommand, as shown:

```
$ helm repo add $REPO_NAME $REPO_URL
```

Adding chart repositories is required in order to install the charts managed within them. Chart installation will be discussed in detail throughout this book.

You can confirm whether a repository has been successfully added by leveraging the `repo list` subcommand:

```
$ helm repo list
NAME              URL
bitnami           https://charts.bitnami.com/bitnami
```

Repositories that have been added to the Helm client will appear in this output. The preceding example shows that the `bitnami` repository was added, so it appears in the list of repositories known by the Helm client. If additional repositories are added, they will also appear in this output.

Over time, updates to charts will be published and released to these repositories. Repository metadata is cached locally. As a result, Helm is not automatically aware when a chart is updated. You can instruct Helm to check for updates from each added repository by running the `repo update` subcommand. Once this command is executed, you will be able to install the latest charts from each repository:

```
$ helm repo update
Hang tight while we grab the latest from your chart
repositories...
...Successfully got an update from the 'bitnami' chart
repository
Update Complete. Happy Helming!
```

You may also need to remove repositories that have been added previously. This can be accomplished by using the `repo remove` subcommand:

```
$ helm repo remove bitnami
'bitnami' has been removed from your repositories
```

The last remaining `repo` subcommand form is `index`. This subcommand is used by repository and chart maintainers to publish new or updated charts. This task will be covered more extensively in *Chapter 5*, *Building your First Helm Chart*.

Next, we will discuss Helm plugin configurations.

Adding plugins

Plugins are add-on capabilities that can be used to provide additional features to Helm. Most users will not need to worry about plugins and plugin management with Helm. Helm is a powerful tool on its own and is complete with the features it promises out of the box. With that being said, the Helm community maintains a variety of different plugins that can be used to enhance Helm's capabilities. A list of these plugins can be found at `https://helm.sh/docs/community/related/`.

Helm provides a `plugin` subcommand for managing plugins, which contain further subcommands, described in the following table:

Plugin subcommand	Description	Usage
`install`	Installs one or more Helm plugins	`helm plugin install $URL`
`list`	List installed Helm plugins	`helm plugin list`
`uninstall`	Uninstalls one or more Helm plugins	`helm plugin uninstall $PLUGIN`
`update`	Updates one or more Helm plugins	`helm plugin update $PLUGIN`

Plugins can provide a variety of different productivity enhancements.

The following are several examples of the upstream plugins:

- `helm diff`: Performs a diff between a deployed release and a proposed Helm upgrade
- `helm secrets`: Used to help conceal secrets from Helm charts
- `helm monitor`: Used to monitor a release and perform a rollback if certain events occur
- `helm unittest`: Used to perform unit testing on a Helm chart

We will continue discussing Helm configuration options by reviewing the different environment variables that can be set to change various aspects of Helm's behavior.

Environment variables

Helm relies on the existence of externalized variables to configure low-level options. The Helm documentation lists six primary environment variables used to configure Helm:

- **XDG_CACHE_HOME**: Sets an alternative location for storing cached files
- **XDG_CONFIG_HOME**: Sets an alternative location for storing Helm configuration
- **XDG_DATA_HOME**: Sets an alternative location for storing Helm data
- **HELM_DRIVER**: Sets the backend storage driver
- **HELM_NO_PLUGINS**: Disables plugins
- **KUBECONFIG**: Sets an alternative Kubernetes configuration file

Helm adheres to The **XDG Base Directory Specification**, which is designed to provide a standardized way of defining where different files are located on an operating system's filesystem. Based on the XDG specification, Helm automatically creates three different default directories on each operating system as required:

Operating system	Cache path	Configuration path	Data path
Windows	`%TEMP%\helm`	`%APPDATA%\helm`	`%APPDATA%\helm`
macOS	`$HOME/Library/Caches/helm`	`$HOME/Library/Preferences/helm`	`$HOME/Library/helm`
Linux	`$HOME/.cache/helm`	`$HOME/.config/helm`	`$HOME/.local/share/helm`

Helm uses the **cache path** for charts that are downloaded from upstream chart repositories. Installed charts are cached to the local machine to enable faster installation of the chart the next time it is referenced. To update the cache, a user can run the `helm repo update` command, which will refresh the repository metadata with the most recent information available, as well as save the chart to the local cache.

The **configuration path** is used to save repository information that was added by running the `helm repo add` command. When a chart that has not been cached is installed, Helm uses the configuration path to look up the URL of the chart repository. Helm uses that URL to understand where the chart resides for it to be downloaded.

The **data path** is used to store plugins. When a plugin is installed using the `helm plugin install` command, the plugin data is stored in this location.

Regarding the remaining environment variables we previously detailed, `HELM_DRIVER` is used to determine how the release state is stored in Kubernetes. The default value is `secret`, which is also the recommended value. `Secret` will Base64-encode the state in a Kubernetes **Secret**. Other options are `configmap`, which will store state in a plaintext Kubernetes ConfigMap and `memory`, which will store the state in the local process's memory. The use of local memory is intended for testing purposes and is not suitable for general purpose or production environments.

The `HELM_NO_PLUGINS` environment variable is used to disable plugins. If unset, the default value that keeps plugins enabled is `0`. To disable plugins, the variable should be set to `1`.

The `KUBECONFIG` environment variable is used to set the file used for authentication to the Kubernetes cluster. If unset, the default value will be `~/.kube/config`. In most cases, users will not need to modify this value.

Another component of Helm that can be configured is tab completion, discussed next.

Tab completion

Bash and Z shell users can enable tab completion to simplify Helm usage. Tab completion allows Helm commands to be auto-completed when the *Tab* key is pressed, allowing users to perform tasks faster and helping prevent input mistakes.

This is similar to how most modern terminal emulators behave by default. When the *Tab* key is pressed, terminals try to guess what the next argument needs to be by observing the state of the command and the environment. For example, the `cd /usr/local/b` input can be tab-completed to `cd /usr/local/bin` in a Bash shell. Similarly, an input such as `helm upgrade hello-` can be tab-completed to read `helm upgrade hello-world`.

Tab completion can be enabled by running the following command:

```
$ source <(helm completion $SHELL)
```

The `$SHELL` variable must be either `bash` or `zsh`. Note that auto-completion will only exist in terminal windows that run the preceding command, so other windows will need to run this command as well to experience the auto-completion feature.

Authentication

Helm needs to be able to authenticate with a Kubernetes cluster in order to deploy and manage applications. It authenticates by referencing a `kubeconfig` file, which specifies different Kubernetes clusters and how to authenticate against them.

Those of you who are using Minikube when following this book will not need to configure authentication, as Minikube automatically configures a `kubeconfig` file each time a new cluster is created. Those of you who aren't running Minikube, however, will likely need to create a `kubeconfig` file or have one provided, depending on the Kubernetes distribution you are using.

A `kubeconfig` file can be created by leveraging three different `kubectl` commands:

- The first command is `set-cluster`:

```
kubectl config set-cluster
```

The `set-cluster` command will define a `cluster` entry in the `kubeconfig` file. It determines the Kubernetes cluster's hostname or IP address, along with its certificate authority.

- The next command is `set-credentials`:

```
kubectl config set-credentials
```

The `set-credentials` command will define the name of a user along with its authentication method and details. This command can configure a username and password pair, client certificate, bearer token, or authentication provider to allow users and administrators the ability to specify varying different methods of authentication.

- Then, we have the `set-context` command:

```
kubectl config set-context
```

The `set-context` command is used to associate a credential to a cluster. Once an association between a credential and a cluster is established, the user will be able to authenticate to the specified cluster using the credential's authentication method.

The `kubectl config view` command can be used to view the `kubeconfig` file. Notice how the `clusters`, `contexts`, and `user` stanzas of `kubeconfig` correspond to the previously described commands, as shown:

```
$ kubectl config view
apiVersion: v1
clusters:
- cluster:
    certificate-authority: /home/helm-user/.minikube/ca.crt
    server: https://192.168.99.102:8443
  name: minikube
contexts:
- context:
    cluster: minikube
    user: minikube
  name: minikube
current-context: minikube
kind: Config
```

```
preferences: {}
users:
- name: minikube
  user:
    client-certificate: /home/helm-user/.minikube/client.crt
    client-key: /home/helm-user/.minikube/client.key
```

Once a valid kubeconfig file is present, Kubectl and Helm will be able to interact with a Kubernetes cluster.

In the next section, we will discuss how authorization is handled against a Kubernetes cluster.

Authorization/RBAC

While authentication is a means of confirming identity, authorization defines the actions that an authenticated user is allowed to perform. Kubernetes uses **role-based access control** (**RBAC**) to perform authorization on Kubernetes. RBAC is a system of designing roles and privileges that can be assigned to a given user or group of users. The actions a user is permitted to perform on Kubernetes depends on the roles that the user has been assigned.

Kubernetes provides many different roles on the platform. Three common roles are listed here:

- `cluster-admin`: Allows a user to perform any action against any resource throughout the cluster
- `edit`: Allows a user to read and write to most resources within a namespace or a logical grouping of Kubernetes resources
- `view`: Prevents a user from modifying existing resources, and only allows users to read resources within a namespace

Since Helm authenticates to Kubernetes using the credentials defined in the kubeconfig file, Helm is given the same level of access as the users defined in the file. If edit access is enabled, Helm can be assumed to have sufficient permission to install applications, in most cases. For only view access, Helm will not be able to install applications, as this level of access is read-only.

Users that run Minikube are given `cluster-admin` by default after cluster creation. While this would not be best practice in a production environment, it is acceptable for learning and experimenting. Those of you running Minikube will not have to worry about configuring authorization in order to follow along with both the concepts and examples provided in this book. Those of you using other Kubernetes clusters that aren't Minikube will need to make sure they are given at least the edit role to be able to deploy most applications with Helm. This can be done by asking an administrator to run the following command:

```
$ kubectl create clusterrolebinding $USER-edit
 --clusterrole=edit --user=$USER
```

Best practices around RBAC will be discussed in *Chapter 9, Helm Security Considerations* when we discuss, in greater detail, the concepts related to security, including how to appropriately apply roles to prevent mistakes or malicious intent in   the cluster.

Summary

There are a variety of different components you will need to have available in order to start using Helm. In this chapter, you learned how to install Minikube to provide a local Kubernetes cluster that can be used throughout this book. You also learned how to install Kubectl, which is the official tool for interacting with the Kubernetes API. Finally, you learned how to install the Helm client and explored the various ways that Helm can be configured, which includes adding repositories and plugins, modifying environment variables, enabling tab completion, and configuring authentication and authorization against a Kubernetes cluster.

Now that you have the prerequisite tooling installed, you can begin to learn how to deploy your first application with Helm. In the next chapter, you will install a Helm chart from an upstream chart repository, as well as learn about life cycle management and application configuration. After finishing the chapter, you will have an understanding of how Helm acts as the package manager for Kubernetes.

Further reading

Check out the following links to learn more about the installation options available for Minikube, Kubectl, and Helm:

- Minikube: `https://kubernetes.io/docs/tasks/tools/install-minikube/`

- Kubectl: `https://kubernetes.io/docs/tasks/tools/install-kubectl/`

- Helm: `https://helm.sh/docs/intro/install/`

We covered various different ways of configuring Helm post-installation. Check out the following links to learn more about the following topics:

- Repository management: `https://helm.sh/docs/intro/quickstart/#initialize-a-helm-chart-repository`

- Plugin management: `https://helm.sh/docs/topics/plugins/`

- Environment variables and the `helm help` output: `https://helm.sh/docs/helm/helm/`

- Tab completion: `https://helm.sh/docs/helm/helm_completion/`

- Authentication and authorization via the `kubeconfig` file: `https://kubernetes.io/docs/tasks/access-application-cluster/configure-access-multiple-clusters/`

Questions

1. Can you list the various methods you can use to install the Helm client?

2. How does Helm authenticate to a Kubernetes cluster?

3. What mechanism is in place to provide authorization to the Helm client? How can an administrator manage these privileges?

4. What is the purpose of the `helm repo add` command?

5. What are the three XDG environment variables used by Helm? What purpose do they serve?

6. Why is Minikube a good choice for learning how to use Kubernetes and Helm? What does Minikube automatically configure for users to allow them to get started more rapidly?

3
Installing your First Helm Chart

Earlier in this book, we referred to Helm as the "Kubernetes package manager" and compared it to an operating system's package manager. A package manager allows users to quickly and easily install applications of varying complexities and manages any dependencies that an application might have. Helm works in a similar fashion.

Users simply determine the application they want to deploy on Kubernetes and Helm does the rest of the work for them. A Helm chart—a packaging of Kubernetes resources—contains the logic and components required to install an application, allowing users to perform installations without needing to know the specific resources required. Users can also pass in parameters, called values, to a Helm chart to configure different aspects of the application without needing to know the specific details about the Kubernetes resources that are being configured. You will explore these features in this chapter by leveraging Helm as a package manager to deploy a WordPress instance onto Kubernetes.

We will cover the following main topics in this chapter:

- Finding a WordPress chart on Helm Hub
- Creating the Kubernetes environment
- Additional installation notes

- Installing a WordPress chart
- Accessing a WordPress application
- Upgrading a WordPress release
- Rolling back a WordPress release
- Uninstalling a WordPress release

Technical requirements

This chapter will use the following software technologies:

- `minikube`
- `kubectl`
- `helm`

We will assume that these components have already been installed on your system. For additional information on each of these tools, including installation and configuration, please refer to *Chapter 2, Preparing a Kubernetes and Helm Environment.*

Understanding the WordPress application

In this chapter, you will use Helm to deploy **WordPress** on Kubernetes. WordPress is an open source **Content Management System (CMS)** used to create websites and blogs. Two different variants are available—`WordPress.com` and `WordPress.org`. `WordPress.com` is a **Software-As-A-Service (SaaS)** version of the CMS, meaning the WordPress application and its components are already hosted and managed by WordPress. In this case, users do not need to worry about installing their own WordPress instance as they can simply access instances that are already available. `WordPress.org`, on the other hand, is the self-hosted option. It requires users to deploy their own WordPress instances and requires expertise to maintain.

Since `WordPress.com` is easier to start with, it may sound like the more desirable option. This SaaS version of WordPress, however, has many disadvantages over the self-hosted `WordPress.org`:

- It does not provide as many features as `WordPress.org`.
- It does not give users full control over their website.

- It requires users to pay for premium features.
- It does not provide the ability to modify the backend code of a website.

The self-hosted `WordPress.org` variation, on the other hand, gives users complete control over their website and WordPress instances. It provides the full WordPress feature set, from installing plugins to modifying backend code.

A self-hosted WordPress instance requires users to deploy a few different components. First, WordPress needs a database to save the website and administrative data. `WordPress.org` states that the database must be either **MySQL** or **MariaDB**, which serves as both the website's location and the administrative portal. In Kubernetes, deploying these components means creating a variety of different resources:

- `secrets` for database and admin console authentication
- A `ConfigMap` for externalized database configuration
- `services` for networking
- A `PersistentVolumeClaim` for database storage
- A `StatefulSet` for deploying the database in a stateful fashion
- A `Deployment` for deploying the frontend

Creating these Kubernetes resources requires both WordPress and Kubernetes expertise. It requires WordPress expertise because the user needs to know the physical components that are required as well as how to configure them. Kubernetes expertise is required because users need to know how to express the WordPress requirements as Kubernetes resources. Given the complexity and number of resources that are required, deploying WordPress on Kubernetes can be a daunting task.

The challenge presented by this task is a perfect use case for Helm. Rather than focus on creating and configuring each of the Kubernetes resources we have described, users can leverage Helm as a package manager to deploy and configure WordPress on Kubernetes without expertise. To begin, we'll explore a platform called **Helm Hub** to first find a WordPress Helm chart. After that, we'll deploy WordPress to your Kubernetes cluster using Helm and explore basic Helm features along the way.

Finding a WordPress chart

Helm Charts can be made available for consumption by being published to a chart repository. A chart repository is a location where packaged charts can be stored and shared. A repository is simply hosted as an HTTP server and can take the form of various implementations, including GitHub pages, an Amazon S3 bucket, or a simple web server such as Apache HTTPD.

To be able to use existing charts that are stored in a repository, Helm needs to first be configured to a repository that it can use. This is accomplished by adding repositories using `helm repo add`. One challenge involved with adding repositories is that there are numerous different chart repositories available for consumption; it may be difficult to locate the particular repository that fits your use case. To make it easier to find chart repositories, the Helm community created a platform called Helm Hub.

Helm Hub is a centralized location for upstream chart repositories. Powered by a community project called **Monocular**, Helm Hub is designed to aggregate all known public chart repositories and provide a search functionality. In this chapter, we will use the Helm Hub platform to search for WordPress Helm charts. Once an appropriate chart is found, we will add the repository that this chart belongs so that it can be installed, afterward.

To begin, interaction with Helm Hub can be accomplished either from the command line or from a web browser. When using the command line to search for Helm charts, the results that are returned provide a URL to Helm Hub, which can be used to find additional information on the chart and instructions on how to add its chart repository.

Let's follow this workflow to add a chart repository containing a WordPress chart.

Searching for WordPress charts from the command line

In general, Helm contains two different search commands to assist us in finding Helm charts:

- To search for charts in Helm Hub or an instance of Monocular, use the following command:

```
helm search hub
```

- To search repositories for a keyword in Charts, use the following command:

```
helm search repo
```

If repositories have not been added previously, users should run the `helm search hub` command to locate Helm charts available across all public chart repositories. After repositories are added, users can run `helm search repo` to search across these repositories.

Let's search Helm Hub for any existing WordPress charts. Each chart in Helm Hub has a set of keywords that can be searched against. Execute the following command to locate charts containing the `wordpress` keyword:

```
$ helm search hub wordpress
```

Upon running this command, an output similar to the following should be displayed:

```
URL                                            CHART VERSION   APP VERSION   DESCRIPTION
https://hub.helm.sh/charts/bitnami/wordpress   8.1.0           5.3.2         Web publishing
https://hub.helm.sh/charts/presslabs/wordpress-...   v0.6.3    v0.6.3        Presslabs Word
https://hub.helm.sh/charts/presslabs/wordpress-...   v0.7.4    v0.7.4        A Helm chart
```

Figure 3.1 – The output from running `helm search hub wordpress`

Each line of the output returned by this command is a chart from Helm Hub. The output will display the URL to each chart's Helm Hub page. It will also display the chart version, which is the latest version of the Helm chart, and the app version, which is the version of the application that the chart is defaulted to deploy. This command will also print a description of each chart, which will often state the application that the chart deploys.

As you may have noticed, some of the values returned are truncated. This is due to the fact that the default output of `helm search hub` is a table, causing the results to be returned in a table format. By default, columns wider than 50 characters are truncated. This truncation can be avoided by specifying the `--max-col-width=0` flag.

Try running the following command by including the `--max-col-width` flag to view the untruncated results in table format:

```
$ helm search hub wordpress  --max-col-width=0
```

The result, in table format, will display each field in full, including the URLs and descriptions.

The URLs are as follows:

- `https://hub.helm.sh/charts/bitnami/wordpress`
- `https://hub.helm.sh/charts/presslabs/wordpress-site`
- `https://hub.helm.sh/charts/presslabs/wordpress-operator`

The descriptions are as follows:

- Web publishing platform for building blogs and websites.
- A Helm chart for deploying a WordPress site on Presslabs Stack
- Presslabs WordPress Operator Helm Chart

Alternatively, users can pass the --output flag and specify either a yaml or json output, which will print the search results in full.

Try running the previous command again with the --output yaml flag:

```
$ helm search hub wordpress --output yaml
```

The result will be in YAML format, similar to the output shown here:

```
- app_version: 5.3.2
  description: Web publishing platform for building blogs and websites.
  url: https://hub.helm.sh/charts/bitnami/wordpress
  version: 8.1.0
- app_version: v0.6.3
  description: Presslabs WordPress Operator Helm Chart
  url: https://hub.helm.sh/charts/presslabs/wordpress-operator
  version: v0.6.3
- app_version: v0.7.4
  description: A Helm chart for deploying a WordPress site on Presslabs Stack
  url: https://hub.helm.sh/charts/presslabs/wordpress-site
  version: v0.7.4
```

Figure 3.2 – The output for helm search hub wordpress--output yaml

For this example, we will choose to install the first chart that was returned in the preceding sample output. To learn more about this chart and how it is installed, we can go to https://hub.helm.sh/charts/bitnami/wordpress, which will help us view the chart from Helm Hub.

The resulting content will be explored in the next section.

Viewing the WordPress chart in a browser

Using helm search hub is the fastest way of searching for charts on Helm Hub. However, it does not provide all of the details needed for the installation. Namely, users need to know a chart's repository URL in order to add its repository and install the chart. A chart's Helm Hub page can provide this URL, along with other installation details.

Once you have pasted the WordPress chart's URL into a browser window, a page similar to the following should be displayed:

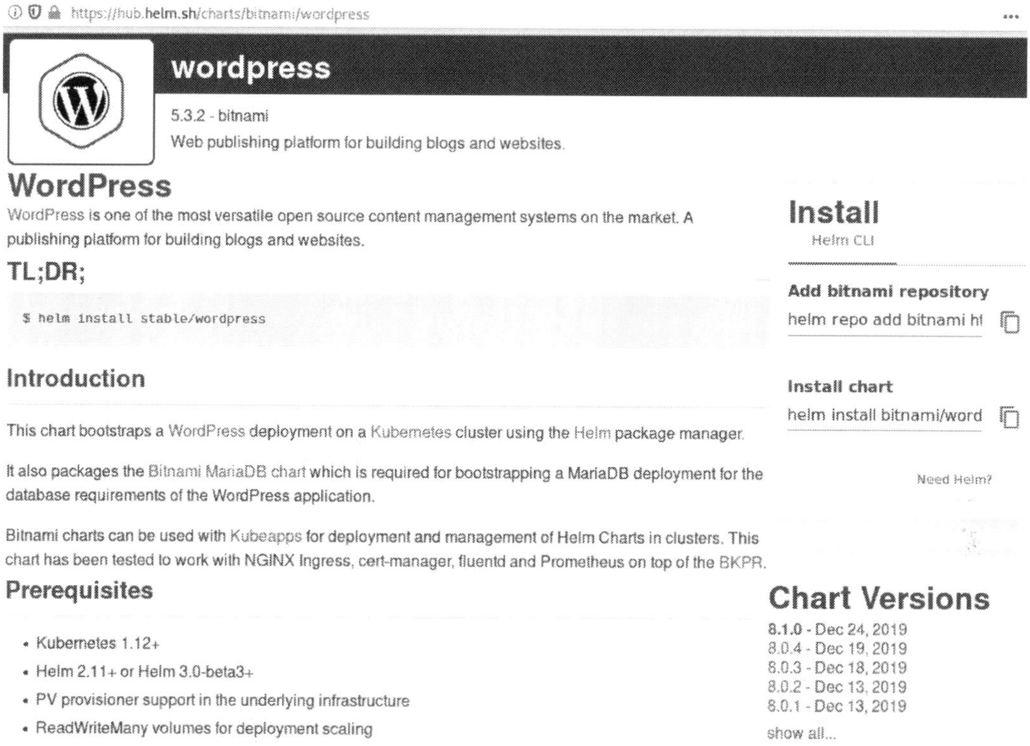

Figure 3.3 – A WordPress Helm chart from Helm Hub

The WordPress chart's page from Helm Hub provides many details, including the maintainer of the chart (**Bitnami**, which is a company that provides software packages that are deployable to different environments) and a brief introduction on the chart (stating that this chart will deploy a WordPress instance to Kubernetes along with a Bitnami MariaDB chart as a dependency). The web page also provides installation details, including the chart's supported values, used to configure the installation, along with Bitnami's chart repository URL. These installation details give users the ability to add this repository and install the WordPress chart.

On the right-hand side of the page, you should see a section labeled **Add bitnami repository**. This section contains the command that can be used to add the Bitnami chart repository. Let's look at how to use it:

1. Run the following command in your command line:

```
$ helm repo add bitnami https://charts.bitnami.com/
bitnami
```

2. Verify that the chart has been added by running `helm repo list`:

```
$ helm repo list
NAME          URL
bitnami       https://charts.bitnami.com/bitnami
```

We can do a little more now that we have added the repository.

3. Run the following command to view charts from locally configured repositories that contain the `bitnami` keyword:

```
$ helm search repo bitnami --output yaml
```

A shortened list of the results returned is shown in the following output:

```
- app_version: 1.10.6
  description: Apache Airflow is a platform to programmatically author, schedule and
    monitor workflows.
  name: bitnami/airflow
  version: 4.0.16
- app_version: 2.4.41
  description: Chart for Apache HTTP Server
  name: bitnami/apache
  version: 7.3.0
- app_version: 0.0.8
  description: Chart with custom templates used in Bitnami charts.
  name: bitnami/bitnami-common
  version: 0.0.8
- app_version: 3.11.5
  description: Apache Cassandra is a free and open-source distributed database management
    system designed to handle large amounts of data across many commodity servers,
    providing high availability with no single point of failure. Cassandra offers
    robust support for clusters spanning multiple datacenters, with asynchronous masterless
    replication allowing low latency operations for all clients.
  name: bitnami/cassandra
  version: 4.1.11
```

Figure 3.4 – The output for `helm search repo bitnami --output yaml`

Similar to the `helm search hub` command, the `helm search repo` command takes a keyword as an argument. Using `bitnami` as a keyword will return all the charts under the `bitnami` repository, as well as charts outside of that repository that may also contain the `bitnami` keyword.

To ensure that you now have access to the WordPress chart, run the following `helm search repo` command with the `wordpress` argument:

```
$ helm search repo wordpress
```

The output will display the WordPress chart that you found on Helm Hub and observed in your browser:

```
NAME                      CHART VERSION     APP VERSION       DESCRIPTION
bitnami/wordpress         8.1.0             5.3.2             Web publishing
```

Figure 3.5 – The output for `helm search repo wordpress`

The value in the NAME field before the slash (/) indicates the name of the repository containing the Helm chart that was returned. The latest version of the WordPress chart from the bitnami repository, as of the time of writing, is version 8.1.0. This is the version that will be used for the installation. Previous versions can be observed by passing the --versions flag to the search command:

```
$ helm search repo wordpress --versions
```

You should then see a new line for each version of the available WordPress charts:

```
NAME                      CHART VERSION     APP VERSION       DESCRIPTION
bitnami/wordpress         8.1.0             5.3.2             Web publishing
bitnami/wordpress         8.0.4             5.3.2             Web publishing
bitnami/wordpress         8.0.3             5.3.1             Web publishing
bitnami/wordpress         8.0.2             5.3.1             Web publishing
```

Figure 3.6 – The version lists for WordPress charts on the bitnami repository

Now that a WordPress chart has been identified and the chart's repository has been added, we will explore how you can use the command line to find out more about the chart to prepare for installation in the next section.

Showing the WordPress chart information from the command line

You can find a lot of important details about a Helm chart on its Helm Hub page. Once a chart's repository is added locally, this information (and more) can also be viewed from the command line with the four `helm show` subcommands described in the following list:

- This command shows the chart's metadata (or chart definition):

```
helm show chart
```

- This command shows the chart's README file:

```
helm show readme
```

- This command shows the chart's values:

```
helm show values
```

- This command shows the chart's definition, README files, and values:

```
helm show all
```

Let's use these commands with the Bitnami WordPress chart. In each of these commands, the chart should be referenced as `bitnami/wordpress`. Note that we will be passing the `--version` flag to retrieve information about version `8.1.0` of this chart. If this flag is omitted, information from the latest version of the chart will be returned.

Run the `helm show chart` command to retrieve the metadata for the chart:

```
$ helm show chart bitnami/wordpress --version 8.1.0
```

The result of this command will be the **chart definition** of the WordPress chart. A chart definition describes information such as the chart's version, its dependencies, keywords, and maintainers:

```
apiVersion: v1
appVersion: 5.3.2
dependencies:
- condition: mariadb.enabled
  name: mariadb
  repository: https://kubernetes-charts.storage.googleapis.com/
  tags:
  - wordpress-database
  version: 7.x.x
description: Web publishing platform for building blogs and websites.
home: http://www.wordpress.com/
icon: https://bitnami.com/assets/stacks/wordpress/img/wordpress-stack-220x234.png
keywords:
- wordpress
- cms
- blog
- http
- web
- application
- php
maintainers:
- email: containers@bitnami.com
  name: Bitnami
name: wordpress
sources:
- https://github.com/bitnami/bitnami-docker-wordpress
version: 8.1.0
```

Figure 3.7 – The WordPress chart definition

Run the `helm show readme` command to view the chart's README file from the command line:

```
$ helm show readme bitnami/wordpress --version 8.1.0
```

The results of this command may look familiar, as a chart's README file is also displayed on its Helm Hub page. Leveraging this option from the command line provides a quick way to view the README file without having to open a browser:

```
# WordPress

[WordPress](https://wordpress.org/) is one of the most versatile open source content management
systems on the market. A publishing platform for building blogs and websites.

## TL;DR;

```console
$ helm install stable/wordpress
```

Introduction

This chart bootstraps a [WordPress](https://github.com/bitnami/bitnami-docker-wordpress) deploym
ent on a [Kubernetes](http://kubernetes.io) cluster using the [Helm](https://helm.sh) package ma
nager.
```

Figure 3.8 – The WordPress chart's README file shown in the command line

We use `helm show values` to inspect a chart's values. Values serve as parameters that users can provide in order to customize a chart installation. We will run this command later on in this chapter in the *Creating a values file for configuration* section when we install the chart.

Finally, `helm show all` aggregates all of the information from the previous three commands together. Use this command if you want to inspect all of a chart's details at once.

Now that we have found and inspected a WordPress chart, let's set up a Kubernetes environment that we can later install this chart to.

Creating a Kubernetes environment

To create a Kubernetes environment in this chapter, we will use Minikube. We learned how to install Minikube in *Chapter 2, Preparing a Kubernetes and Helm Environment*.

Let's follow these steps to set up Kubernetes:

1. Start your Kubernetes cluster by running the following command:

```
$ minikube start
```

2. After a short amount of time, you should see a line in the output that resembles the following:

```
Done! kubectl is now configured to use 'minikube'
```

3. Once the Minikube cluster is up and running, create a dedicated namespace for this chapter's exercise. Run the following command to create a namespace called chapter3:

```
$ kubectl create namespace chapter3
```

Now that the cluster setup is complete, let's begin the process of installing the WordPress chart to your Kubernetes cluster.

Installing the WordPress chart

Installing a Helm chart is a simple process that can begin with the inspection of a chart's values. In the next section, we will inspect the values that are available on the WordPress chart and describe how to create a file that allows customizing the installation. Finally, we will install the chart and access the WordPress application.

Creating a values file for configuration

You can override the values defined in charts by providing a YAML-formatted values file. In order to properly create a values file, you need to inspect the supported values that the chart provides. This can be done by running the helm show values command, as explained earlier.

Run the following command to inspect the WordPress chart's values:

```
$ helm show values bitnami/wordpress --version 8.1.0
```

The result of this command should be a long list of possible values that you can set, many of which already have default values set:

```
## Global Docker image parameters
## Please, note that this will override the image parameters, including depend
## Current available global Docker image parameters: imageRegistry and imagePu
##
# global:
#   imageRegistry: myRegistryName
#   imagePullSecrets:
#     - myRegistryKeySecretName
#   storageClass: myStorageClass

## Bitnami WordPress image version
## ref: https://hub.docker.com/r/bitnami/wordpress/tags/
##
image:
  registry: docker.io
  repository: bitnami/wordpress
  tag: 5.3.2-debian-9-r0
  ## Specify a imagePullPolicy
  ## Defaults to 'Always' if image tag is 'latest', else set to 'IfNotPresent'
  ## ref: http://kubernetes.io/docs/user-guide/images/#pre-pulling-images
  ##
  pullPolicy: IfNotPresent
  ## Optionally specify an array of imagePullSecrets.
  ## Secrets must be manually created in the namespace.
  ## ref: https://kubernetes.io/docs/tasks/configure-pod-container/pull-image-
  ##
  # pullSecrets:
  #   - myRegistryKeySecretName
```

Figure 3.9 – A list of values generated by running `helm show values`

The preceding output shows the beginning of the WordPress chart's values. Many of these properties already have defaults set, meaning these values will represent how the chart is configured if they are not overridden. For example, if the `image` value is not overridden in a `values` file, the image used by the WordPress chart will use the `bitnami/wordpress` container image from the `docker.io` registry against the `5.3.2-debian-9-r0` tag.

Lines in the chart's values that begin with a hash sign (#) are comments. Comments can be used to explain a value or a block of values, or they can be used to comment values in order to unset them. An example of unsetting values by commenting them is shown in the `global` YAML stanza at the top of the preceding output. Each of these values will be unset by default unless set explicitly by the user.

If we explore the `helm show values` output further, we can find values that pertain to configuring the WordPress blog's metadata:

```
## User of the application
## ref: https://github.com/bitnami/bitnami-docker-wordpress#environment-variables
##
wordpressUsername: user

## Application password
## Defaults to a random 10-character alphanumeric string if not set
## ref: https://github.com/bitnami/bitnami-docker-wordpress#environment-variables
##
# wordpressPassword:

## Admin email
## ref: https://github.com/bitnami/bitnami-docker-wordpress#environment-variables
##
wordpressEmail: user@example.com

## First name
## ref: https://github.com/bitnami/bitnami-docker-wordpress#environment-variables
##
wordpressFirstName: FirstName

## Last name
## ref: https://github.com/bitnami/bitnami-docker-wordpress#environment-variables
##
wordpressLastName: LastName

## Blog name
## ref: https://github.com/bitnami/bitnami-docker-wordpress#environment-variables
##
wordpressBlogName: User's Blog!
```

Figure 3.10 – The values returned by running the `helm show values` command

These values appear to be important for configuring a WordPress blog. Let's override them by creating a `values` file. Create a new file on your machine called `wordpress-values.yaml`. In that file, enter the following content:

```
wordpressUsername: helm-user
wordpressPassword: my-pass
wordpressEmail: helm-user@example.com
wordpressFirstName: Helm_is
wordpressLastName: Fun
wordpressBlogName: Learn Helm!
```

Feel free to get more creative with these values if you'd like. Continuing down the list of values from `helm show values`, there is one more important value that should be added to the `values` file before starting the installation, as shown:

```
## Kubernetes configuration
## For minikube, set this to NodePort, elsewhere use LoadBalancer or ClusterIP
##
service:
  type: LoadBalancer
```

Figure 3.11 – The LoadBalancer value returned after running `helm show values`

As described in the comments, this value states that if we are working with Minikube, we'll need to change the default `LoadBalancer` type to `NodePort`. A `LoadBalancer` service type in Kubernetes is used to provision a load balancer from a public cloud provider. While this value can be supported by leveraging the `minikube tunnel` command, setting this value to `NodePort` will instead allow you to directly access the WordPress application against a local port, instead of having to make use of the `minikube tunnel` command.

Add this value to your `wordpress-values.yaml` file:

```
service:
  type: NodePort
```

Once this value is added to your `values` file, your complete `values` file should look as follows:

```
wordpressUsername: helm-user
wordpressPassword: my-pass
wordpressEmail: helm-user@example.com
wordpressFirstName: Helm_is
wordpressLastName: Fun
wordpressBlogName: Learn Helm!
service:
  type: NodePort
```

Now that the `values` file is complete, let's run the installation.

Running the installation

We use `helm install` to install a Helm chart. The standard syntax is as follows:

```
helm install [NAME] [CHART] [flags]
```

The NAME parameter is the name you would like to give your Helm release. A **release** captures the Kubernetes resources that were installed with a chart and tracks an application's life cycle. We will explore how releases work throughout this chapter.

The CHART parameter is the name of the Helm chart that is installed. Charts from a repository can be installed by following the <repo name>/<chart name> form.

The flags option in helm install allows you to further customize the installation. flags allow users to define and override values, specify the namespace to work against, and more. The list of flags can be viewed by running helm install --help. We can pass --help to other commands as well to view their usage and supported options.

Now, with a proper understanding of the helm install usage, run the following command:

```
$ helm install wordpress bitnami/wordpress --values=wordpress-
values.yaml --namespace chapter3 --version 8.1.0
```

This command will install a new release called wordpress using the bitnami/ wordpress Helm chart. It will use the values defined in the wordpress-values. yaml file to customize the installation, and the chart will be installed in the chapter3 namespace. It will also deploy the 8.1.0 version, as defined by the --version flag. Helm will install the latest version of the Helm chart without this flag.

If the chart installation is successful, you should see the following output:

```
NAME: wordpress
LAST DEPLOYED: Sun Dec 22 08:01:04 2019
NAMESPACE: chapter3
STATUS: deployed
REVISION: 1
NOTES:
1. Get the WordPress URL:

   export NODE_PORT=$(kubectl get --namespace chapter3 -o jsonpath="{.spec.ports[0].no
dePort}" services wordpress)
   export NODE_IP=$(kubectl get nodes --namespace chapter3 -o jsonpath="{.items[0].sta
tus.addresses[0].address}")
   echo "WordPress URL: http://$NODE_IP:$NODE_PORT/"
   echo "WordPress Admin URL: http://$NODE_IP:$NODE_PORT/admin"

2. Login with the following credentials to see your blog

   echo Username: helm-user
   echo Password: $(kubectl get secret --namespace chapter3 wordpress -o jsonpath="{.d
ata.wordpress-password}" | base64 --decode)
```

Figure 3.12 – The output of a successful WordPress chart installation

This output displays information about the installation, including the name of the release, the time it was deployed, the namespace it was installed to, the status of the deployment (which is `deployed`), and the revision number (which is set to `1` since this was the initial installation of the release).

The output also displays a list of notes related to the installation. Notes are used to provide users with additional information about their installation. In the case of the WordPress chart, these notes provide information about how to access and authenticate the WordPress application. While these notes appear directly after installation, they can be retrieved at any time with the `helm get notes` command, as explained in the next section.

With your first Helm installation complete, let's inspect the release to observe the resources and configurations that were applied.

Inspecting your release

One of the easiest ways to inspect a release and verify its installation is to list all the Helm releases in a given namespace. For this, Helm provides the `list` subcommand.

Run the following command to view the list of releases in the `chapter3` namespace:

```
$ helm list --namespace chapter3
```

You should see only one release in this namespace, as shown:

```
NAME          NAMESPACE      REVISION      UPDATED
wordpress     chapter3       1             2019-12-22 08:01:04.179076712 -0500 EST
```

Figure 3.13 – The output from the `helm list` command that lists the Helm releases

The `list` subcommand provides the following information:

- The release name
- The release namespace
- The latest revision number of the release
- A timestamp of the latest revision
- The release status
- The chart name
- The application version

Note that the status, chart name, and application version are truncated from the preceding output.

While the `list` subcommand is useful for providing high-level release information, there are additional items that users might want to know about a particular release. Helm provides the `get` subcommand to provide more information about a release. The following list describes the commands that can be used to provide a set of detailed release information:

- To get all the hooks for a named release, run the following command:

```
helm get hooks
```

- To get the manifest for a named release, run the following command:

```
helm get manifest
```

- To get the notes for a named release, run the following command:

```
helm get notes
```

- To get the values for a named release, run the following command:

```
helm get values
```

- To get all the information about a named release, run the following command:

```
helm get all
```

The first command from the preceding list, `helm get hooks`, is used to display the hooks for a given release. Hooks will be explored in more detail in *Chapter 5, Building Your First Helm Chart* and *Chapter 6, Testing Helm Charts*, when you learn about building and testing Helm charts. For now, hooks can be thought of as the actions that Helm performs during certain phases of an application's life cycle.

Run the following command to view the hooks that are included in this release:

```
$ helm get hooks wordpress --namespace chapter3
```

In the output, you will find two Kubernetes Pod manifests with the following annotation:

```
'helm.sh/hook': test-success
```

This annotation denotes a hook that is run during the execution of the `test` subcommand, which we will explore in greater detail in *Chapter 6, Testing Helm Charts*.

These test hooks provide a mechanism for chart developers to confirm that a chart is functioning as designed and can be safely ignored by end users.

Since both of the hooks included in this chart are for testing purposes, let's move on to the next command from the preceding list to continue with the release inspection.

The `helm get manifest` command can be used to get a list of the Kubernetes resources that were created as part of the installation. Run this command as shown in the following example:

```
$ helm get manifest wordpress --namespace chapter3
```

After you run this command, you'll see the following Kubernetes manifests:

- Two `secrets` manifests.
- Two `ConfigMaps` manifests (the first is used to configure the WordPress application, while the second is used for testing, which is performed by chart developers and so can be ignored).
- One `PersistentVolumeClaim` manifest.
- Two `services` manifests.
- One `Deployment` manifest.
- One `StatefulSet` manifest.

From this output, you can observe where your values had an effect when configuring the Kubernetes resources. One example to note is within the WordPress service whose `type` has been set to `NodePort`:

```
# Source: wordpress/templates/svc.yaml
apiVersion: v1
kind: Service
metadata:
  name: wordpress
  labels:
    app: "wordpress"
    chart: "wordpress-8.1.0"
    release: "wordpress"
    heritage: "Helm"
  annotations:
spec:
  type: NodePort
  externalTrafficPolicy: "Cluster"
  ports:
    - name: http
      port: 80
      targetPort: http
    - name: https
      port: 443
      targetPort: https
  selector:
    app: "wordpress"
```

Figure 3.14 – Setting `type` to `NodePort`

You can also observe the other values that we set for the WordPress user. These values are defined as environment variables in the WordPress deployment, as shown:

```
- name: WORDPRESS_USERNAME
  value: "helm-user"
- name: WORDPRESS_PASSWORD
  valueFrom:
    secretKeyRef:
      name: wordpress
      key: wordpress-password
- name: WORDPRESS_EMAIL
  value: "helm-user@example.com"
- name: WORDPRESS_FIRST_NAME
  value: "Helm_is"
- name: WORDPRESS_LAST_NAME
  value: "Fun"
```

Figure 3.15 – Values set as environment variables

Most of the default values provided by the chart were left untouched. Those defaults have been applied to the Kubernetes resources and can be observed through the `helm get manifest` command. If these values had been changed, the Kubernetes resources would be configured differently.

Let's move on to the next `get` command. The `helm get notes` command is used to display the notes from a Helm release. As you may recall, the release notes were displayed when the WordPress chart was installed. These notes provide important information about accessing the application and they can be displayed again by running the following command:

```
$ helm get notes wordpress --namespace chapter3
```

The `helm get values` command is useful for recalling the values that were used for a given release. Run the following command to view the values that were provided in the `wordpress` release:

```
$ helm get values wordpress --namespace chapter3
```

The results of this command should look familiar as they should match the values specified in the `wordpress-values.yaml` file:

```
USER-SUPPLIED VALUES:
service:
  type: NodePort
wordpressBlogName: Learn Helm!
wordpressEmail: helm-user@example.com
wordpressFirstName: Helm_is
wordpressLastName: Fun
wordpressPassword: my-pass
wordpressUsername: helm-user
```

Figure 3.16 –User-supplied values in the wordpress release

While recalling the user-supplied values is useful, it may be necessary in some cases to return all of the values used by a release, including the defaults. This can be accomplished by passing in an additional --all flag, as shown:

```
$ helm get values wordpress --all --namespace chapter3
```

For this chart, the output will be lengthy. The first few values are shown in the following output:

```
COMPUTED VALUES:
affinity: {}
allowEmptyPassword: true
allowOverrideNone: false
customHTAccessCM: null
externalDatabase:
  database: bitnami_wordpress
  host: localhost
  password: ""
  port: 3306
  user: bn_wordpress
extraEnv: []
extraVolumeMounts: []
extraVolumes: []
healthcheckHttps: false
image:
  pullPolicy: IfNotPresent
  registry: docker.io
  repository: bitnami/wordpress
  tag: 5.3.2-debian-9-r0
```

Figure 3.17 – A subset of all the values for the wordpress release

Finally, Helm provides a helm get all command, which can be used to aggregate all of the information from the various helm get commands:

```
$ helm get all wordpress --namespace chapter3
```

Aside from the commands provided by Helm, the `kubectl` CLI can also be used to inspect an installation more closely. For example, instead of getting all of the Kubernetes resources created by the installation, `kubectl` can be used to narrow the scope down to just one type of resource, such as a deployment. To ensure that the resources returned belong to the Helm release, a label defined on the deployment can be provided to the `kubectl` command that denotes the name of the release. Helm charts often add an `app` label to their Kubernetes resources. Use the `kubectl` CLI to retrieve the deployments that contain this label by running the following command:

```
$ kubectl get all -l app=wordpress --namespace chapter3
```

You'll find that the following deployment exists in the `chapter3` namespace:

```
NAME        READY   UP-TO-DATE   AVAILABLE   AGE
wordpress   1/1     1            1           6m22s
```

Figure 3.18 – The wordpress deployment in the `chapter3` namespace

Additional installation notes

Soon, we will explore the WordPress application that we just installed. First, there are several areas of consideration that should be mentioned before leaving behind the topic of installation.

The -n flag

The `-n` flag can be used instead of the `--namespace` flag to reduce the typing effort when entering commands. This holds true for the `upgrade` and `rollback` commands, which we will describe later in this chapter. From here on, we will use the `-n` flag when we denote the namespace that Helm should interact with.

The HELM_NAMESPACE environment variable

You can also set an environment variable to denote the namespace that Helm should interact with.

Let's look at how we can set this environment variable on various operating systems:

- You can set the variable on macOS and Linux as follows:

```
$ export HELM_NAMESPACE=chapter3
```

- Windows users can set this environment variable by running this command in PowerShell:

```
> $env:HELM_NAMESPACE = 'chapter3'
```

This variable's value can be verified by running the `helm env` command:

```
$ helm env
```

You should see the `HELM_NAMESPACE` variable in the resulting output. By default, the variable is set to `default`.

In this book, we will not rely on the `HELM_NAMESPACE` variable but will instead pass in the `-n` flag alongside each command so that it is clearer which namespace we intend to work with. Providing the `-n` flag is also the best way that the namespace for Helm can be specified, as it ensures that we are targetting the namespace that we expect.

Choosing between --set and --values

For the `install`, `upgrade`, and `rollback` commands, you can choose one of two ways to pass values to your chart:

- To pass a value in from the command line, use the following command:

```
--set
```

- To specify values in a YAML file or URL, use the following command:

```
--values
```

In this book, we will treat the `--values` flag as the preferred method of configuring chart values. The reason for this is that it is easier to configure multiple values in this fashion. Maintaining a `values` file will also allow us to save these assets in a **Source Code Management** (**SCM**) system, such as `git`, which allows installations to be more easily reproducible. Take note that sensitive values, such as passwords, should never be stored in a source-control repository. We will cover the topic of security in *Chapter 9, Helm Security Considerations*. For the time being, it is important to remember not to push `secrets` into a source control repository. When secrets need to be provided in a chart, the recommended approach is to use the `--set` flag explicitly.

The `--set` flag is used to pass values directly from the command line. This is an acceptable method for values that are simple, as well as for when there are few values that need to be configured. Once again, using the `--set` flag is not the preferred approach as it limits the ability to make the installation more reproducible. It is also much more difficult to configure complex values in this fashion, such as values in the form of lists or complex maps. There are other related flags, such as `--set-file` and `--set-string`; the `--set-file` flag is used to pass along a file that has configured values in a `key1=val1` and `key2=val2` format, while the `--set-string` flag is used to set all the values provided in a `key1=val1` and `key2=val2` format as strings.

With this explanation out of the way, let's explore the WordPress application that we just installed.

Accessing the WordPress application

The WordPress chart's release notes provide four commands that you can run to access your WordPress application. Run the four commands listed here:

- For macOS or Linux, run the following:

```
$ export NODE_PORT=$(kubectl get --namespace chapter3 -o
jsonpath="{.spec.ports[0].nodePort}" services wordpress)
$ export NODE_IP=$(kubectl get nodes --namespace chapter3
-o jsonpath="{.items[0].status.addresses[0].address}")
$ echo "WordPress URL: http://$NODE_IP:$NODE_PORT/"
$ echo "WordPress Admin URL: http://$NODE_IP:$NODE_PORT/
admin"
```

- For Windows PowerShell, run the following:

```
> $NODE_PORT = kubectl get --namespace chapter3 -o
jsonpath="{.spec.ports[0].nodePort}" services wordpress |
Out-String
> $NODE_IP = kubectl get nodes --namespace chapter3 -o
jsonpath="{.items[0].status.addresses[0].address}" |
Out-String
> echo "WordPress URL: http://$NODE_IP:$NODE_PORT/"
> echo "WordPress Admin URL: http://$NODE_IP:$NODE_PORT/
admin"
```

After defining the two environment variables based on a series of `kubectl` queries, the resulting `echo` commands will reveal the URLs to access WordPress. The first URL is to view the home page and is where visitors would access your site. The second URL is to reach the admin console, which is used by website administrators to configure and manage the site content.

Paste the first URL into a browser and you should be presented with a page that appears similar to the content displayed here:

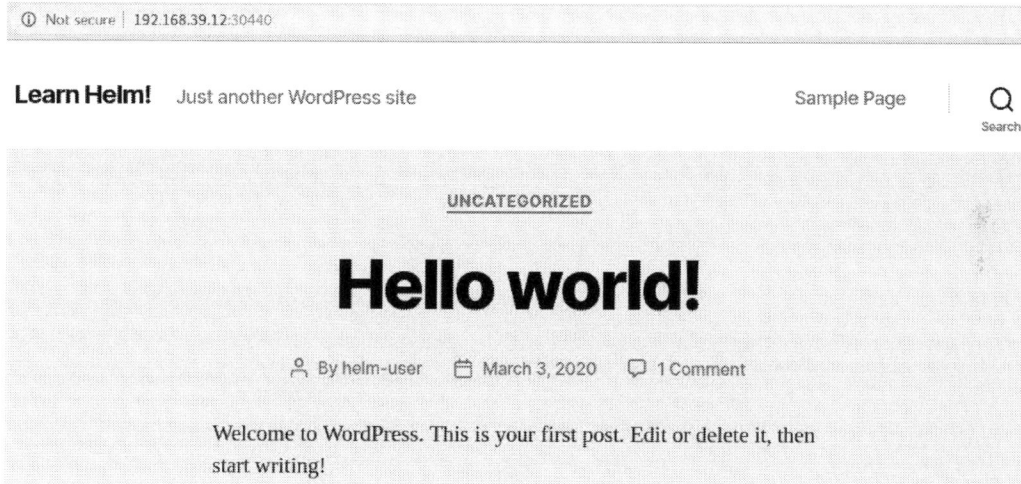

Figure 3.19 – The WordPress blog page

Several portions of this page may look familiar to you. First, notice that at the top-left corner of the screen the title of the blog is called **Learn Helm**! Not only does this bear a resemblance to the title of this book, but it is also the string you gave the `wordpressBlogName` value previously during installation. You can also see this value included in the copyright statement at the bottom of the page, © **2020 Learn Helm!**.

Another value that affected the customization of the home page is `wordpressUsername`. Notice that the author of the **Hello world!** post that is included is **helm-user**. This is the name of the user that was provided to the `wordpressUsername` value and would appear differently if an alternative username was provided.

The other link provided in the previous set of commands is for the admin console. Paste the link from the second `echo` command into a browser and you should be presented with the following screen:

Figure 3.20: The WordPress admin console login page

To log in to the admin console, enter the `wordpressUsername` and `wordpressPassword` values that you provided during the installation. These values can be seen by reviewing your local `wordpress-values.yaml` file. They can also be retrieved by running the following commands instructed by the WordPress chart's notes:

```
$ echo Username: helm-user
$ echo Password: $(kubectl get secret --namespace chapter3
wordpress -o jsonpath='{.data.wordpress-password}' | base64
--decode)
```

Once authenticated, the admin console dashboard is displayed, as shown:

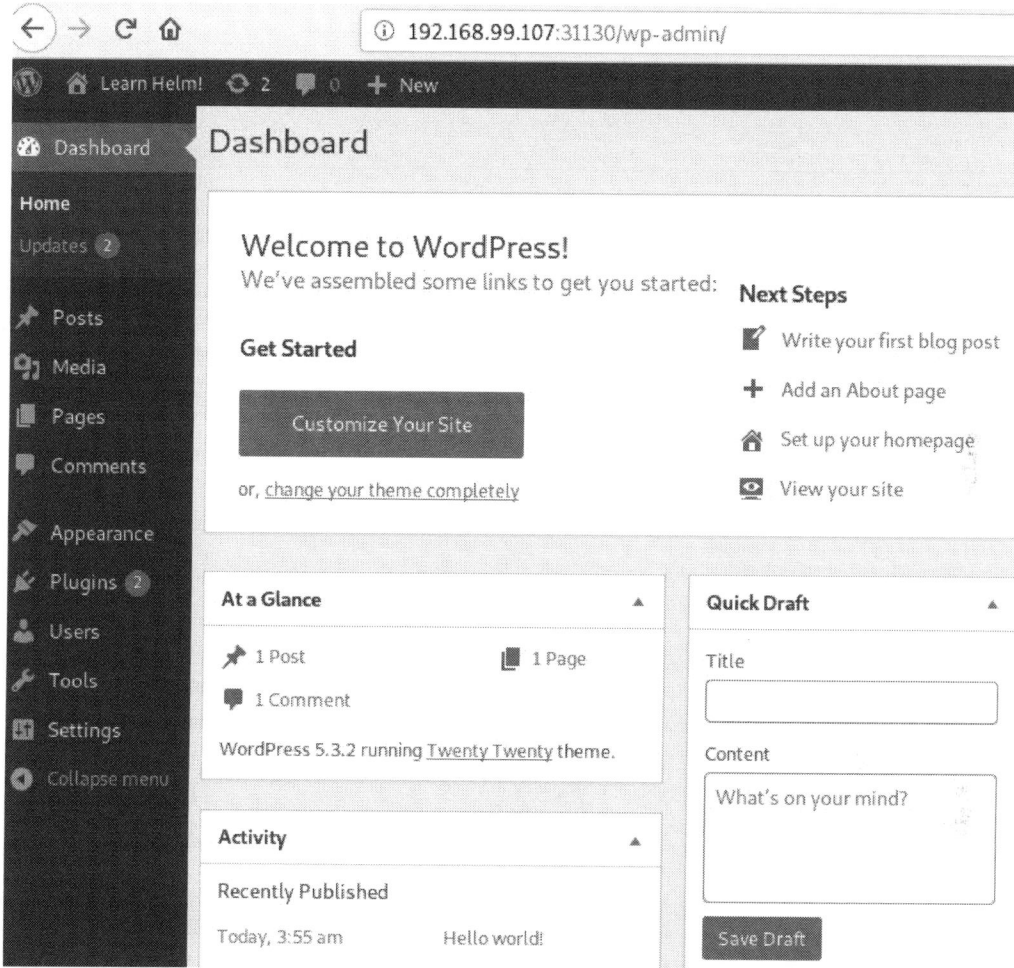

Figure 3.21 – The WordPress admin console page

If you're in charge of managing this WordPress site, this is where you can configure your site, write posts, and manage plugins. If you click on the top-right link that says **Howdy, helm-user**, you will be directed to the `helm-user` profile page. From there, you can see several of the other values that you provided during the installation, as shown:

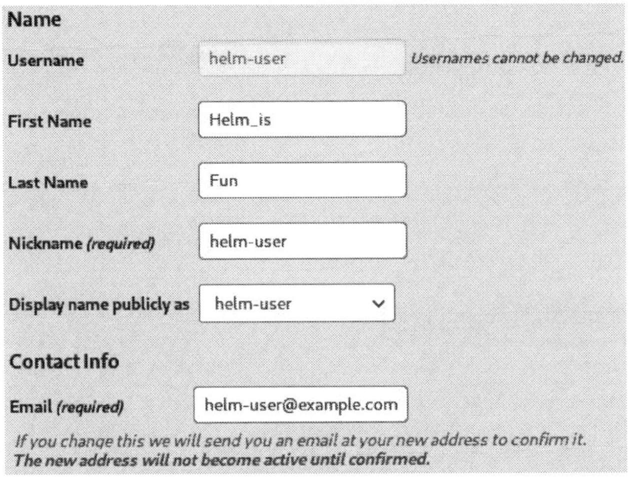

Figure 3.22 – The WordPress profile page

The **First Name**, **Last Name**, and **Email** fields refer to their corresponding `wordpressFirstname`, `wordpressLastname`, and `wordpressEmail` Helm values.

Feel free to continue exploring your WordPress instance. Once complete, continue to the next section to learn how to perform an upgrade on a Helm release.

Upgrading the WordPress release

Upgrading a release refers to the process of modifying the values that a release was installed with or upgrading to a newer version of the chart. In this section, we will upgrade the WordPress release by configuring additional values around the WordPress replica and resource requirements.

Modifying the Helm values

It is common for Helm charts to expose values to configure the number of instances of an application and their related set of resources. The following screenshots illustrate several portions of the `helm show values` command that relate to the values used for this purpose.

The first value, `replicaCount`, is straightforward to set. Since `replica` is a Kubernetes term that describes the number of Pods needed to deploy an application, it's implied that `replicaCount` is used to specify the number of application instances that are deployed as part of a release:

```
replicaCount: 1
```

Figure 3.23 – `replicaCount` in the `helm show values` command

Add the following line to your `wordpress-values.yaml` file to increase the number of replicas from `1` to `2`:

```
replicaCount: 2
```

The second value that we need to define refers to a set of values under the `resources` YAML stanza:

```
## Configure resource requests and limits
## ref: http://kubernetes.io/docs/user-guide/compute-resources/
##
resources:
  requests:
    memory: 512Mi
    cpu: 300m
```

Figure 3.24 – The values under the resources stanza

Values can be indented, as in the `resources` stanza, to provide a logical grouping. Under the `resources` stanza is a `requests` stanza, which is used to configure the `memory` and `cpu` values that Kubernetes will allocate to the WordPress application. Let's modify these values during the upgrade by decreasing the memory request to `256Mi` (256 mebibytes) and the `cpu` request to `100m` (100 millicores). Add these modifications to the `wordpress-values.yaml` file, as shown:

```
resources:
  requests:
    memory: 256Mi
    cpu: 100m
```

After defining these two new values, your entire `wordpress-values.yaml` file will appear as follows:

```
wordpressUsername: helm-user
wordpressPassword: my-pass
wordpressEmail: helm-user@example.com
```

```
wordpressFirstName: Helm
wordpressLastName: User
wordpressBlogName: Learn Helm!
service:
  type: NodePort
replicaCount: 2
resources:
  requests:
    memory: 256Mi
    cpu: 100m
```

Once the values file has been updated with these new values, you can run the helm upgrade command to upgrade the release, as we will discuss in the next section.

Running the upgrade

The helm upgrade command is almost identical to helm install in basic syntax, as you can see in the following example:

```
helm upgrade [RELEASE] [CHART] [flags]
```

While helm install expects you to provide a name for a new release, helm upgrade expects you to provide the name of an already-existing release that should be upgraded.

Values defined in a values file can be provided using the --values flag, identical to that of the helm install command. Run the following command to upgrade the WordPress release with a new set of values:

```
$ helm upgrade wordpress bitnami/wordpress --values wordpress-
values.yaml -n chapter3 --version 8.1.0
```

Once the command is executed, you should see an output similar to that of helm install depicted in an earlier section:

```
Release "wordpress" has been upgraded. Happy Helming!
NAME: wordpress
LAST DEPLOYED: Sun Dec 22 13:05:10 2019
NAMESPACE: chapter3
STATUS: deployed
REVISION: 2
NOTES:
1. Get the WordPress URL:

  export NODE_PORT=$(kubectl get --namespace chapter3 -o jsonpath="{.spec.port
s[0].nodePort}" services wordpress)
  export NODE_IP=$(kubectl get nodes --namespace chapter3 -o jsonpath="{.items
[0].status.addresses[0].address}")
  echo "WordPress URL: http://$NODE_IP:$NODE_PORT/"
  echo "WordPress Admin URL: http://$NODE_IP:$NODE_PORT/admin"

2. Login with the following credentials to see your blog

  echo Username: helm-user
  echo Password: $(kubectl get secret --namespace chapter3 wordpress -o jsonpa
th="{.data.wordpress-password}" | base64 --decode)
```

Figure 3.25 – The output for `helm upgrade`

You should also see the `wordpress` Pods restarting with by running the following command:

```
$ kubectl get pods -n chapter3
```

In Kubernetes, new Pods are created when a deployment is modified. The same behavior can be observed in Helm. The values that were added during the upgrade introduced a configuration change of the WordPress deployment and new WordPress Pods were created, as a result, with the updated configuration. These changes can be observed using the same `helm get manifest` and `kubectl get deployment` commands that were used earlier after the installation.

In the next section, we'll perform a couple more upgrades to demonstrate how values can sometimes behave differently during an upgrade.

Reusing and resetting values during an upgrade

The `helm upgrade` command includes two additional flags that are used to manipulate values that are not present in the `helm install` command.

Let's look at these flags now:

- `--reuse-values`: When upgrading, reuse the last release's values.
- `--reset-values`: When upgrading, reset the values to the chart defaults.

If an upgrade is performed without providing values with the `--set` or `--values` flags, the `--reuse-values` flag is added by default. In other words, the same values that were used by the previous release will be used again during the upgrade if no values are provided:

1. Run another `upgrade` command without specifying any values:

```
$ helm upgrade wordpress bitnami/wordpress -n chapter3
--version 8.1.0
```

2. Run the `helm get values` command to inspect the values used in the upgrade:

```
$ helm get values wordpress -n chapter3
```

Notice that the values displayed are identical to the previous upgrade:

```
USER-SUPPLIED VALUES:
replicaCount: 2
resources:
  requests:
    cpu: 100m
    memory: 256Mi
service:
  type: NodePort
wordpressBlogName: Learn Helm!
wordpressEmail: helm-user@example.com
wordpressFirstName: Helm_is
wordpressLastName: Fun
wordpressPassword: my-pass
wordpressUsername: helm-user
```

Figure 3.26 – The output of the `helm get values`

Different behavior can be observed when values are provided from the command line during an upgrade. If values are passed via the `--set` or `--values` flags, all of the chart's values that are not provided are reset to default.

3. Run another upgrade by providing a single value with `--set`:

```
$ helm upgrade wordpress bitnami/wordpress --set
replicaCount=1 -n chapter3 --version 8.1.0
```

4. After the upgrade, run the `helm get values` command:

```
$ helm get values wordpress -n chapter3
```

The output will declare that the only user-supplied value was the value for `replicaCount`:

```
USER-SUPPLIED VALUES:
replicaCount: 1
```

Figure 3.27 – The output for `replicaCount`

When at least one value is provided during an upgrade, Helm automatically applies the `--reset-values` flag. This causes all of the values to be set back to their default values, except for the individual properties provided with the `--set` or `--values` flags.

Users can manually provide the `--reset-values` or `--reuse-values` flags to explicitly determine the behavior of values during an upgrade. Use the `--reset-values` flag if you would like the next upgrade to reset each value to its default before overriding it from the command line. Provide the `--reuse-values` flag if you would like to reuse each of the values from a previous revision while setting different values from the command line. To help simplify the management of values during an upgrade, try to keep your values in a file that can be used to declaratively set values for each upgrade.

If you have been following along with each of the commands provided in this chapter, you should now have four revisions of the WordPress release. This fourth revision is not quite in the way we want the application to be configured, as it only specifies the `replicaCount` value because most of the values were set back to their defaults. In the next section, we will explore how the WordPress release can be rolled back to the stable version that contains the set of desired values.

Rolling back the WordPress release

While moving forward is preferred, there are some occasions where it makes more sense to return to a previous version of the application. The `helm rollback` command exists to satisfy this use case. Let's roll back the WordPress release to a previous state.

Inspecting the WordPress history

Every Helm release has a history of **revisions**. A revision is used to track the values, Kubernetes resources, and chart version that were used in a particular release version. A new revision is created when a chart is installed, upgraded, or rolled back. Revision data is saved in Kubernetes secrets by default (other options are ConfigMap or local memory, determined by the `HELM_DRIVER` environment variable). This allows your Helm release to be managed and interacted with by different users on the Kubernetes cluster, provided they have the **Role-Based Access Control** (**RBAC**) that allows them to view or modify resources in your namespace.

The revision secrets can be observed by using `kubectl` to get the secrets from the `chapter3` namespace:

```
$ kubectl get secrets -n chapter3
```

This will return all of the secrets, but you should see these four in the output:

```
sh.helm.release.v1.wordpress.v1
Sh.helm.release.v1.wordpress.v2
sh.helm.release.v1.wordpress.v3
sh.helm.release.v1.wordpress.v4
```

Each of these secrets corresponds with an entry of the release's revision history, which can be viewed by running the `helm history` command:

```
$ helm history wordpress -n chapter3
```

This command will display a table of each revision, similar to the following (some columns have been omitted for readability):

REVISION	...	STATUS	...	DESCRIPTION
1		superseded		Install complete
2		superseded		Upgrade complete
3		superseded		Upgrade complete
4		deployed		Upgrade complete

In this output, each revision has a number, along with the time it was updated, the status, the chart, the app version of the upgrade, and the description of the upgrade. Revisions that have a status of `superseded` were upgraded. The revision that says `deployed` is the currently-deployed revision. Other statuses include `pending` and `pending_upgrade`, which means the installation or upgrade is currently in progress. `failed` refers to a particular revision that has failed to install or be upgraded and `unknown` corresponds to a revision that had an unknown state. It's unlikely you will ever encounter a release with a state of `unknown`.

The `helm get` commands described previously can be used against a revision number by specifying the `--revision` flag. For this rollback, let's determine the release that had the full set of desired values. As you may recall, the current revision, `revision 4`, only contains the `replicaCount` value, but `revision 3` should contain the desired values.

This can be verified by running the `helm get values` command with the `--revision` flag:

```
$ helm get values wordpress --revision 3 -n chapter3
```

The full list of values is presented by inspecting this revision:

```
USER-SUPPLIED VALUES:
replicaCount: 2
resources:
  requests:
    cpu: 100m
    memory: 256Mi
service:
  type: NodePort
wordpressBlogName: Learn Helm!
wordpressEmail: helm-user@example.com
wordpressFirstName: Helm_is
wordpressLastName: Fun
wordpressPassword: my-pass
wordpressUsername: helm-user
```

Figure 3.28 – The output of checking a specific revision

It is possible to run the other `helm get` commands against a revision number to perform a further inspection. If necessary, the `helm get manifest` command can also be executed against `revision 3` to check the state of the Kubernetes resources that would be restored.

In the next section, we will execute the rollback.

Running the rollback

The `helm rollback` command has the following syntax:

```
helm rollback <RELEASE> [REVISION] [flags]
```

Users provide the name of the release and the desired revision number to roll a Helm release back to a previous point in time. Run the following command to execute the rollback of WordPress to `revision 3`:

```
$ helm rollback wordpress 3 -n chapter3
```

The `rollback` subcommand provides a simple output, printing the following message:

```
Rollback was a success! Happy Helming!
```

This rollback can be observed in the release history by running the `helm history` command:

```
$ helm history wordpress -n chapter3
```

In the release history, you will notice that a fifth revision was added with a status of `deployed` and a description of `Rollback to 3`. When an application is rolled back, it adds a new revision to the release history. This is not to be confused with an upgrade. The highest revision number simply denotes the currently deployed release. Be sure to check a revision's description to determine whether it was created by an upgrade or a rollback.

You can get this release's values to ensure that the rollback now uses the desired values by running `helm get values` again:

```
$ helm get values wordpress -n chapter3
```

The output will show the values from the latest stable release:

```
USER-SUPPLIED VALUES:
replicaCount: 2
resources:
  requests:
    cpu: 100m
    memory: 256Mi
service:
  type: NodePort
wordpressBlogName: Learn Helm!
wordpressEmail: helm-user@example.com
wordpressFirstName: Helm_is
wordpressLastName: Fun
wordpressPassword: my-pass
wordpressUsername: helm-user
```

Figure 3.29 – The values from the latest stable release

You may notice that we did not explicitly set the chart version or the release's values in the `rollback` subcommand. This is because the `rollback` subcommand is not designed to accept these inputs; it is designed to roll back a chart to a previous revision and leverage that revision's chart version and values. Note that the `rollback` subcommand should not be part of everyday Helm practices and that it should be reserved only for emergencies where the current state of an application is unstable and must be reverted to a previously stable point.

If you have successfully rolled back the WordPress release, you are nearing the end of this chapter's exercise. The final step is to remove the WordPress application from the Kubernetes cluster by leveraging the `uninstall` subcommand, which we will describe in the next section.

Uninstalling the WordPress release

Uninstalling a Helm release means deleting the Kubernetes resources that it manages. In addition, the `uninstall` command deletes the release's history. While this is often what we want, specifying the `--keep-history` flag will instruct Helm to retain the release history.

The syntax for the `uninstall` command is very simple:

```
helm uninstall RELEASE_NAME [...] [flags]
```

Uninstall the WordPress release by running the `helm uninstall` command:

```
$ helm uninstall wordpress -n chapter3
```

Once uninstalled, you will see the following message:

```
release 'wordpress' uninstalled
```

You will also notice that the `wordpress` release no longer exists in the `chapter3` namespace:

```
$ helm list -n chapter3
```

The output will be an empty table. You can also confirm that the release is no longer present by attempting to use `kubectl` to get the WordPress deployments:

```
$ kubectl get deployments -l app=wordpress -n chapter3
No resources found in chapter3 namespace.
```

As expected, there are no more WordPress deployments available.

```
$ kubectl get pvc -n chapter3
```

You will, however, notice that there is still a `PersistentVolumeClaim` command available in the namespace:

```
NAME                        STATUS   VOLUME
data-wordpress-mariadb-0    Bound    pvc-a721aeb7-d3df-4221-b3a0-a7f30a6d10c6
```

Figure 3.30 – Output showing `PersistentVolumeClaim`

This `PersistentVolumeClaim` resources was not deleted because it was created in the background by a `StatefulSet`. In Kubernetes, the `PersistentVolumeClaim` resources that are created by a `StatefulSet` are not automatically removed if the `StatefulSet` is deleted. During the `helm uninstall` process, the `StatefulSet` was deleted but the associated `PersistentVolumeClaim` was not. This is what we would expect. The `PersistentVolumeClaim` resource can be deleted manually with the following command:

```
$ kubectl delete pvc -l release=wordpress -n chapter3
```

Now that we've installed and uninstalled Wordpress, let's clean up your Kubernetes environment so that we have a clean setup for the exercises we will carry out in later chapters of this book.

Cleaning up your environment

To clean up your Kubernetes environment, you can remove this chapter's namespace by running the following command:

```
$ kubectl delete namespace chapter3
```

After the `chapter3` namespace is deleted, you can also stop the Minikube VM:

```
$ minikube stop
```

This will shut down the VM but will retain its state so that you can quickly begin working again in the next exercise.

Summary

In this chapter, you learned how to install a Helm chart and manage its life cycle. We began by searching Helm Hub for a WordPress chart to install. After locating a chart, the repository containing the chart was added by following the instructions from its Helm Hub page. We then proceeded to inspect the WordPress chart to create a set of values that overrides their defaults. These values were saved to a `values` file, which was then provided during the installation.

After the chart was installed, we used `helm upgrade` to upgrade the release by providing additional values. We performed a rollback after this with `helm rollback` to restore the chart to a previous state. Finally, we removed the WordPress release at the end of the exercise with `helm uninstall`.

This chapter taught you how to leverage Helm as an end user and chart consumer. You used Helm as a package manager to install a Kubernetes application to your cluster. You also managed the life cycle of the application by performing upgrades and a rollback. Understanding this workflow is essential to managing installations with Helm.

In the next chapter, we will explore the concept and structure of a Helm chart in greater detail to begin learning how charts can be created.

Further reading

To learn more about adding repositories locally, inspecting charts, and using the four life cycle commands used throughout this chapter (`install`, `upgrade`, `rollback`, and `uninstall`), go to `https://helm.sh/docs/intro/using_helm/`.

Questions

1. What is Helm Hub? How can a user interact with it to find charts and chart repositories?

2. What is the difference between the `helm get` and `helm show` sets of commands? When would you use one set of commands over the other?

3. What is the difference between the `--set` and `--values` flags in the `helm install` and `helm upgrade` commands? What are the benefits of using one over the other?

4. What command can be used to provide the list of revisions for a release?

5. What happens by default when you upgrade a release without providing any values? How does this behavior differ to when you do provide values for an upgrade?

6. Imagine you have five revisions of a release. What would the `helm history` command show after you roll back the release to `revision 3`?

7. Imagine you want to view all of the releases deployed to a Kubernetes namespace. What command should you run?

8. Imagine you run `helm repo add` to add a chart repository. What command can you run to list all of the charts under that repository?

Section 2: Helm Chart Development

In this section, you will learn how a Helm chart is structured. You will learn how to build a Helm chart from scratch and will learn techniques for debugging and testing your charts.

This section comprises the following chapters:

4
Understanding Helm Charts

In the previous chapter, you learned how to use Helm from an end user perspective, leveraging it as a package manager to install applications to Kubernetes. Using Helm in this fashion did not require any Kubernetes expertise or any deep understanding of the application since all of the resources and logic were included as part of a Helm chart. The only concept you needed to be familiar with were the values that the chart provided in order to customize your installation.

We will now shift gears from using Helm charts to understanding how they work and are created.

To do so, we will cover the following topics:

- Understanding the YAML format
- Understanding chart templates
- Understanding chart definitions
- Life cycle management
- Documenting a Helm chart

Technical requirements

This section requires the `helm` binary to be installed on your local machine. The installation and configuration of this tool are covered in *Chapter 2, Preparing a Kubernetes and Helm Environment.*

Understanding the YAML format

YAML Ain't Markup Language (YAML) is a file format used to create human-readable configuration. It is the file format most commonly used to configure Kubernetes resources and is also the format used for many of the files in Helm charts.

YAML files follow a key-value format to declare configuration. Let's explore the YAML key-value construct.

Defining key-value pairs

One of the most basic examples of a YAML key-value pair is shown here:

```
name: LearnHelm
```

In the preceding example, the `name` key is given a `LearnHelm` value. In YAML, keys and values are separated by a colon (:). Characters written to the left of the colon represent the key, while characters written to the right of the colon represent the value.

Spacing matters in YAML format. The following line does not constitute a key-value pair:

```
name:LearnHelm
```

Notice that a space is missing between the colon and the `LearnHelm` string. This would result in a parsing error. A space must exist between the colon and the value.

While the preceding example represents a simple key-value pair, YAML allows users to configure more complex pairings with nested elements or blocks. An example is shown here:

```
resources:
  limits:
    cpu: 100m
    memory: 512Mi
```

The preceding example demonstrates a resources object containing a map of two key-value pairs:

Key	Value
`resources.limits.cpu`	`100m`
`resources.limits.memory`	`512Mi`

Keys are determined by following the indentation under a YAML block. Each indentation adds a dot (.) separator to the name of the key. The value of the key has been reached when there are no longer any indentations remaining in the YAML block. By common practice, indentations in YAML should use two spaces, but users can provide as many spaces as they desire as long as the spacing is consistent throughout the document.

> **Important note:**
> **Tabs** are not supported by YAML and their use will result in a parsing error.

With an understanding of YAML key-value pairs, let's now explore some of the common types that values can be defined as.

Value types

Values in a YAML file can be of different types. The most common type is a string, which is a text value. Strings can be declared by wrapping a value in quotations, but this is not always required. If a value contains at least one alphabetical letter or special character, the value is considered a string, with or without quotation marks. Multi-line strings can be set by using the pipe (|) symbol, as shown:

```
configuration: |
  server.port=8443
  logging.file.path=/var/log
```

Values can also be integers. A value is an integer when it is a numeric character that is not wrapped in quotations. The following YAML declares an integer value:

```
replicas: 1
```

Compare this to the following YAML, which assigns replicas to a string value:

```
replicas: '1'
```

Boolean values are often used as well, which can be declared with either true or false:

```
ingress:
  enable: true
```

This YAML sets `ingress.enable` to the `true` Boolean value. Other acceptable Boolean values are `yes`, `no`, `on`, `off`, `y`, `n`, `Y`, and `N`.

Values can also be set to more complex types, such as lists. Items in a list in YAML are identified by the dash (-) symbol.

The following demonstrates a YAML list:

```
servicePorts:
  - 8080
  - 8443
```

This YAML sets `servicePorts` to the list of integers (such as `8080` and `8443`). This syntax can also be used to describe a list of objects:

```
deployment:
  env:
    - name: MY_VAR
      value: MY_VALUE
    - name: SERVICE_NAME
      value: MY_SERVICE
```

In this case, `env` is set to a list of objects containing the `name` and `value` fields. Lists are often used in both Kubernetes and Helm configuration and understanding them is valuable to using Helm to its fullest potential.

While YAML is more commonly used in the worlds of Kubernetes and Helm for its ease of readability, the **JavaScript Object Notation (JSON)** format can be used as well. Let's briefly describe this format.

The JSON format

YAML is a superset of another widely used format—JSON. JSON is a string of key-value pairs, similar to YAML. The key difference is that while YAML relies on spacing and indentation to properly configure key-value pairs, JSON relies on braces and brackets.

The following example converts the previous YAML example into JSON format:

```
{
  'deployment': {
    'env': [
      {
        'name': 'MY_VAR',
        'value': 'MY_VALUE'
      },
      {
        'name': 'SERVICE_NAME',
        'value': 'MY_SERVICE'
      }
    ]
  }
}
```

All of the keys in JSON are wrapped in quotation marks and positioned before a colon:

- Curly braces ({) denote a block in a similar way to how indentations denote a block in YAML.

- Square brackets ([) denote a list in a similar way to how dashes denote a list in YAML.

There are many more constructs to the YAML and JSON formats, but this introduction provides more than enough information to understand how they can be used in Helm charts.

In the next section, we will discuss the Helm chart file structure, which you may notice contains several YAML and JSON files.

The Helm chart structure

As you will recall from previous chapters, a Helm chart is a packaging of Kubernetes resources, allowing users to deploy applications of varying complexities to Kubernetes. In order to be considered a Helm chart, however, a certain file structure must be followed:

```
my-chart/
  # chart files and directories
```

It is best practice to name the top-level directory as the name of the Helm chart. This is not a technical requirement, but it makes identifying the name of a Helm chart much simpler. For the preceding example file structure, the Helm chart's name is likely to be `my-chart`.

Under the top-level directory are the files and directories that comprise the Helm chart. The following table shows each of these possible files and directories:

File/directory	Definition	Required?
`Chart.yaml`	A file that contains metadata about the Helm chart.	Yes.
`templates/`	A directory that contains Kubernetes resources in YAML format.	Yes, unless dependencies are declared in `Chart.yaml`.
`templates/NOTES.txt`	A file that can be generated to provide usage instructions during chart installation.	No.
`values.yaml`	A file that contains the chart's default values.	No, but every chart should contain this file as a best practice.
`.helmignore`	A file that contains a list of files and directories that should be omitted from the Helm chart's packaging.	No.
`charts/`	A directory that contains charts that the Helm chart depends on.	Does not need to be explicitly provided as Helm's dependency management system will automatically create this directory.
`Chart.lock`	A file used to save the previously applied dependency versions.	Does not need explicitly provided as Helm's dependency management system will automatically create this file.
`crds/`	A directory that contains Custom Resource Definition (CRD) YAML resources to be installed before resources under `templates/`.	No.
`README.md`	A file that contains installation and usage information about the Helm chart.	No, but every Helm chart should contain this file.
`LICENSE`	A file that contains the chart's license.	No.
`values.schema.json`	A file that contains the chart's values schema in JSON format.	No.

Throughout this chapter, we will explore each of these files to understand how a Helm chart is created. We'll first begin by understanding how chart templates work to allow Kubernetes resources to be dynamically generated.

Understanding chart templates

The primary purpose of a Helm chart is to create and manage the Kubernetes resources that make up an application. This is accomplished through chart templates, with values serving as parameters to customize those templates. In this section, we will discuss how Helm templates and values function.

Helm charts must contain a `templates/` directory that defines the Kubernetes resources to be deployed (although this directory is not strictly required if the chart declares dependencies). The contents under the `templates/` directory are YAML files that are made up of Kubernetes resources. The contents of a `templates/` directory may appear similar to the following:

```
templates/
  configmap.yaml
  deployment.yaml
  service.yaml
```

The `configmap.yaml` resource may then look as follows:

```
apiVersion: v1
kind: ConfigMap
metadata:
  name: {{ .Release.Name }}
data:
  configuration.txt: |-
    {{ .Values.configurationData }}
```

You may question whether the prior example is a valid YAML syntax. It is because the `configmap.yaml` file is actually a Helm template that will modify the configuration of this resource based on a certain set of values to produce a valid YAML resource. The opening and closing curly braces represent input text for a **Golang (Go)** template that will be removed during an installation or upgrade.

Let's learn more about Go templates and how they can be used to generate Kubernetes resource files.

Go templating

Go is a programming language that was developed by Google in 2009. It is the programming language used by Kubernetes, Helm, and many other tools in the Kubernetes and container community. A core component of the Go programming language is templates, which can be leveraged to generate files of different formats. In the case of Helm, Go templates are used to generate Kubernetes YAML resources under a Helm chart's `templates/` directory.

Go template controls structures and processing begin with two opening curly braces (`{{`) and ends with two ending curly braces (`}}`). While these punctuation marks may appear in a local file under the `templates/` directory, they are removed during the processing that takes place during an installation or upgrade.

We will dive deeper into Go templating in *Chapter 5*, *Building Your First Helm Chart*, where you will build your own Helm chart. In this chapter, we will discuss common capabilities of Go templating as an introduction to this feature before getting some hands-on practice. We'll start our discussion with a list of capabilities that Go templating provides, beginning with parameterization.

Parameterizing fields with values and built-in objects

Helm charts contain a `values.yaml` file in their chart directories. This file declares all of a chart's default values, which are referenced by Go templates and processed by Helm to dynamically generate Kubernetes resources.

A chart's `values.yaml` file may have values defined as follows:

```
## chapterNumber lists the current chapter number
chapterNumber: 4
## chapterName gives a description of the current chapter
chapterName: Understanding Helm Charts
```

Lines that begin with the pound symbol (#) are comments (which are ignored during execution) and should provide details about the values they describe so that the user understands how they should be applied. Comments can also include the name of the value to allow comments to appear when a value is searched upon. Other lines in the file represent key-value pairs. An introduction to the YAML format is described at the beginning of this chapter.

Go templates beginning with `.Values` will reference values defined in a `values.yaml` file or passed in using the `--set` or `--values` flags during an installation or upgrade.

The following example represents a template before it is processed:

```
env:
  - name: CHAPTER_NUMBER
    value: {{ .Values.chapterNumber }}
  - name: CHAPTER_NAME
    values: {{ .Values.chapterName }}
```

After the template is processed, a snippet of a YAML resource is rendered as in the following:

```
env:
  - name: CHAPTER_NUMBER
    value: 4
  - name: CHAPTER_NAME
    values: Understanding Helm Charts
```

The `.Values` construct used to refer to a chart's values is a built-in object that can be used for parameterization. A full list of built-in objects can be found in the Helm documentation (`https://helm.sh/docs/chart_template_guide/builtin_objects/`), but the most common objects are described in the following table:

Object	Definition
`.Release.Name`	The name of the release provided for the installation.
`.Release.Namespace`	The namespace that the release was installed to.
`.Release.Revision`	The revision number of the installation or upgrade.
`.Values`	Used to refer to values in the `values.yaml` file or values that were provided by the user.
`.Chart.Name`, `.Chart.Version`, `.Chart.AppVersion`, and so on	Used to refer to fields in the `Chart.yaml` file. Refer to these fields by following the convention `Chart.$Field`.
`.Files.Get`	Used to get a file in a chart directory.
`.Files.AsSecrets`	Returns a file as a Base64-encoded string to create `secret` data from files in a chart directory.
`.Files.AsConfig`	Returns file bodies as a YAML map to create ConfigMap data from files in a chart directory.
`.Capabilities.APIVersions`	Returns a list of the API versions available in the Kubernetes cluster.
`.Template.Name`	Returns the relative file path to the template that this object uses.

The dot (`.`) prefixed to each object represents the object scope. A dot followed by an object name limits the scope to that object. For example, the `.Values` scope only makes a chart's values visible; the `.Release` scope only makes fields under the `Release` object visible; and the `.` scope represents global scope, making all of these objects visible, plus the common objects defined in the preceding table.

The values.schema.json file

While on the topic of values and parameterization, let's take a moment to discuss the `values.schema.json` file, which is one of the files that may be included in a chart's directory. The `values.schema.json` file is used to enforce a particular schema in a `values` file. This schema can be used to validate the provided values during an installation or an upgrade.

The following snippet shows what the `values.schema.json` file looks like:

```
{
    '$schema': 'https://json-schema.org/draft-07/schema#',
    'properties': {
      'replicas': {
          'description': 'number of application instances to
  deploy',
          'minimum': 0
          'type' 'integer'
      },
        . . .
    'title': 'values',
    'type': 'object'
}
```

With this schema file in place, the `replicas` value should be set to `0` as a minimum. Additional values added to this file place additional restrictions on the values that can be provided. This file is a good way of ensuring users only provide the values that are supported as parameters in the chart's templates.

While Go templates allow chart developers to parameterize Helm charts, they also allow developers to provide conditional logic into a YAML file. We will explore this feature next.

Fine-grained template processing with flow control

While parameterization allows chart developers to substitute fields with certain values, Go templating also provides developers with the ability to control the flow and structure of their templates. This can be accomplished using the following keywords (referred to as `actions` in Go):

Action	Definition
if/else	Used to conditionally include or exclude sections of a file
with	Used to modify the scope of the values that are referenced
range	Used to loop over a list of values

There are some occasions during chart templating where it may be necessary to include or exclude certain Kubernetes resources or certain parts of a resource. The if...else actions can be used for this purpose. The following snippet from a deployment template includes a conditional block:

```
readinessProbe:
{{- if .Values.probeType.httpGet }}
  httpGet:
    path: /healthz
    port: 8080
    scheme: HTTP
{{- else }}
  tcpSocket:
    port: 8080
{{- end }}
  initialDelaySeconds: 30
  periodSeconds: 10
```

The if block is used to conditionally set the readinessProbe stanza. If the probeType.httpGet value evaluates to true or is non-null, the httpGet readinessProbe will be templated. Otherwise, the readinessProbe that is created will be a tcpSocket readinessProbe type. The dashes used in the curly braces are used to indicate that whitespace should be removed after processing. Dashes used after the opening braces remove whitespace before the braces and dashes used immediately before the closing braces remove whitespace after the braces.

Chart developers can also use the `with` action to modify the scope of the values. This action is useful when a block of values that are referenced are deeply nested. It can simplify the readability and maintainability of a template file by reducing the amount of characters required to reference a deeply nested value.

The following code describes a `values` file, which includes deeply nested values:

```
application:
  resources:
    limits:
      cpu: 100m
      memory: 512Mi
```

Without the `with` action, these values would be referenced in a `template` file, as follows:

```
cpu: {{ .Values.application.resources.limits.cpu }}
memory: {{ .Values.application.resources.limits.memory }}
```

The `with` action allows a developer to modify the scope of these values and reference them with a shortened syntax:

```
{{- with .Values.application.resources.limits }}
cpu: {{ .cpu }}
memory: {{ .memory }}
{{- end }}
```

Finally, developers can perform repetitive actions using the `range` action. This action allows developers to loop over a list of values. Imagine that a chart has the following values:

```
servicePorts:
  - name: http
    port: 8080
  - name: https
    port: 8443
  - name: jolokia
    port: 8778
```

The preceding code provides a list of `servicePorts`, which can be looped over, shown in the following example:

```
spec:
  ports:
{{- range .Values.servicePorts }}
  - name: {{ - name }}
    port: {{ .port }}
{{- end }}
```

The `with` and `range` actions limit the scope to the object that is provided. In the `range` example, the `range` acts on the `.Values.servicePorts` object, limiting the scope of the dot (.) symbol to values defined under this object. To enact a global scope under `range` where all the values and built-in objects are referenced, developers should prefix references with the dollar sign ($) symbol, as shown:

```
{{- range .Values.servicePorts }}
  - name: {{ $.Release.Name }}-{{ .name }}
    port: {{ .port }}
{{- end }}
```

In addition to a chart's values, developers can also create variables to help render resources. We will explore this in the next section.

Template variables

Although they are not as commonly used as other templating features, chart developers can create variables in their chart templates to provide additional processing options. A common use for this approach is flow control, but template variables can serve other use cases as well.

A variable in a chart template is defined as follows:

```
{{ $myvar := 'Hello World!' }}
```

This sets the `myvar` variable to the `Hello World!` string. Variables can be assigned to objects as well, such as a chart's values:

```
{{ $myvar := .Values.greeting }}
```

A variable that is set is then referenced later in the template in the following way:

```
data:
    greeting.txt: |
      {{ $myvar }}
```

One of the best cases for using variables is in a range block, where variables are set to capture the index and value of list iterations:

```
data:
    greetings.txt: |
  {{- range $index, $value := .Values.greetings }}
      Greeting {{ $index }}: {{ $value }}
  {{- end }}
```

The result can be rendered as follows:

```
data:
    greetings.txt: |
      Greeting 0: Hello
      Greeting 1: Hola
      Greeting 2: Hallo
```

Variables can also simplify the processing of map iterations, as shown:

```
data:
    greetings.txt: |
  {{- range $key, $val := .Values.greetings }}
      Greeting in {{ $key }}: {{ $val }}
  {{- end }}
```

A possible result may be as follows:

```
data:
    greetings.txt: |
      Greeting in English: Hello
      Greeting in Spanish: Hola
      Greeting in German: Hallo
```

Finally, variables can be used to refer to a value outside of the current scope.

Consider the following `with` block:

```
{{- with .Values.application.configuration }}
My application is called {{ .Release.Name }}
{{- end }}
```

A template such as this one would fail to process since `.Release.Name` is not under the scope of `.Values.application.configuration`. One way this can be remedied is by setting a variable to `.Release.Name` above the `with` block:

```
{{ $appName := .Release.Name }}
{{- with .Values.application.configuration }}
My application is called {{ $appName }}
{{- end }}
```

While this is a possible solution to this problem, the approach of using a dollar sign to refer to the global scope is preferred as it requires less lines to configure and is easier to read as chart complexity increases.

Flow control and variables are powerful concepts that allow resources to be dynamically generated. In addition to flow control, chart developers can also leverage functions and pipelines to assist in resource rendering and formatting.

Complex processing with functions and pipelines

Go provides the concepts of functions and pipelines to enable complex processing of data within a template.

A Go template function is similar to other functions you may have encountered in other languages and constructs. Functions contain logic designed to consume certain inputs and provide an output based on the inputs that were provided.

For Go templates, functions are called by using the following syntax:

```
functionName arg1 arg2 . . .
```

One Go function that is commonly used is the `indent` function. This function is used to indent a string of a specified number of characters to ensure strings are properly formatted since YAML is a whitespace-sensitive markup language. The `indent` function takes the number of spaces to indent as input, as well as the string that should be indented.

The following template illustrates this:

```
data:
    application-config: |-
{{ indent 4 .Values.config }}
```

This example indents the string contained in the config value by 4 spaces to ensure the string is properly indented under the application-config YAML key.

The other construct Helm provides is pipelines. A pipeline is a concept borrowed from **UNIX** where the output of one command is fed as input to a different command:

```
cat file.txt | grep helm
```

The preceding example displays a UNIX pipeline. On the left side of the pipe (|) is the first command and on the right side is the second command. The first command, cat file.txt, prints the contents of a file named file.txt and passes it as input to the grep helm command, which filters the first command's output for the word helm.

Go pipelines work in a similar way. This can again be demonstrated with the indent function:

```
data:
    application-config: |-
{{ .Values.config | indent 4 }}
```

This will also indent the config value by 4 spaces. Pipelines are best used to chain multiple commands together. A third command can be added to the pipeline, called quote, which quotation quote marks around the final templated product:

```
data:
    application-config: |-
{{ .Values.config | indent 4 | quote }}
```

Because this is written as a pipeline, it is easy and natural to read.

There are many different Go template functions that can be used in a Helm chart. These functions can be found in the Go documentation at `https://golang.org/pkg/text/template/#hdr-Functions` and in the Sprig template library at `http://masterminds.github.io/sprig/`. Some common Go template functions that you may use during chart development are as follows:

- `date`: To format a date
- `default`: Set a default value
- `fail`: To fail template rendering
- `include`: To execute a Go template and return the results
- `nindent`: Similar to indent, except prepends a new line before indenting
- `indent`: To indent text by a set number of spaces
- `now`: To display the current date/time
- `quote`: To wrap a string in quotation marks
- `required`: To require user input
- `splitList`: To split a string into a list of strings
- `toYaml`: To convert a string into YAML format

The Go template language also consists of the following Boolean operators that can be used in `if` actions to further control the generation of YAML resources:

- `and`
- `or`
- `not`
- `eq` (short for equal)
- `ne` (short for not equal)
- `lt` (short for less than)
- `le` (short for less than or equal to)
- `gt` (short for greater than)
- `ge` (short for greater than or equal to)

In addition to generating Kubernetes resources, Go templates can also be used to create functions that can be reused in YAML resources that have repetitive templating. This can be accomplished by creating named templates, described in the next section.

Enabling code reuse with named templates

When creating template files, there may be boilerplate or repetitive blocks of YAML in a Kubernetes resource.

One example of this is the labels of a resource, which can be specified as follows:

```
labels:
  'app.kubernetes.io/instance': {{ .Release.Name }}
  'app.kubernetes.io/managed-by': {{ .Release.Service }}
```

For consistency, each of these labels can be added to each resource in a Helm chart. If the chart contains many different Kubernetes resources, it can be cumbersome to include the desired labels in each file, especially if a label needs to be modified or if a new label needs to be added to each resource in the future.

Helm provides a construct called named templates that allows chart developers to create reusable templates that can be applied to reduce boilerplate. Named templates are defined under the `templates/` directory and are files that begin with underscores and end with the `.tpl` file extension. Many charts are created with a file called `_helpers.tpl` that contains the named templates, although the file does not need to be called `helpers`.

To create a named template in the `tpl` file, developers can leverage the `define` action. The following example creates a named template that can be used to encapsulate resource labels:

```
{{- define 'mychart.labels' }}
labels:
  'app.kubernetes.io/instance': {{ .Release.Name }}
  'app.kubernetes.io/managed-by': {{ .Release.Service }}
{{- end }}
```

The `define` action takes a template name as an argument. In the preceding example, the template name is called `mychart.labels`. The common convention for naming a template is $CHART_NAME.$TEMPLATE_NAME, where $CHART_NAME is the name of the Helm chart and $TEMPLATE_NAME is a short, descriptive name that describes the purpose of the template.

The `mychart.labels` name implies that the template is native to the `mychart` Helm chart and will generate labels to resources that it is applied to.

To use a named template in a Kubernetes YAML template, you can use the `include` function, which has the following usage:

```
include [TEMPLATE_NAME] [SCOPE]
```

The `TEMPLATE_NAME` parameter is the name of the named template that should be processed. The `SCOPE` parameter is the scope of values and built-in objects that should be processed. Most of the time, this parameter is a dot (`.`) to denote the current top-level scope, but the dollar sign (`$`) symbol should be used if the named template references values outside of the current scope.

The following example demonstrates how the `include` function is used to process a named template:

```
metadata:
  name: {{ .Release.Name }}
  {{- include 'mychart.labels' . | indent 2 }}
```

This example begins by setting the name of the resource to the name of the release. It then uses the `include` function to process the labels and indents each line by two spaces, as declared by the pipeline. When processing is finished, a resource within a release called `template-demonstration` may appear as follows:

```
metadata:
  name: template-demonstration
  labels:
    'app.kubernetes.io/instance': template-demonstration
    'app.kubernetes.io/managed-by': Helm
```

Helm also provides a `template` action that can also expand named templates. This action has the same usage as `include`, but with one major limitation—it cannot be used in a pipeline to provide additional formatting and processing. The `template` action is used to simply display data inline. Because of this limitation, chart developers should use the `include` function over the `template` action since `include` has feature parity with `template` but also provides the additional benefit of pipeline processing.

In the next section, we will learn how named templates can be used to reduce boilerplate across multiple different charts.

Library charts

Helm charts have a `type` field defined in the `Chart.yaml` file that is set to either `application` or `library`. Application charts are used to deploy full applications to Kubernetes. This is the most common type of chart and is the default setting. However, charts can also be defined as library charts. This type of chart is not used to deploy applications but instead to provide named templates that may be used across multiple different charts. An example of this use case is the `labels` example defined in the previous section. Developers can maintain multiple different charts whose resources have the same labels. Rather than defining the same named templates in each chart's `_helpers.tpl` file, developers can declare a library chart that provides the named template for generating resource labels as a dependency.

While Helm is most commonly used to create traditional Kubernetes resources, it can also create **Custom Resources (CRs)**, which we will explain in the next section.

Templating CRs

CRs are used to create resources that are not native to the Kubernetes API. You may want to use this functionality to augment the abilities that Kubernetes provides. CRs can be created using Helm templates such as native Kubernetes resources, but there must first be a **Custom Resource Definition (CRD)** that defines the CR. If the CRD is not present before the CR is created, the installation will fail.

Helm charts can include a `crds/` folder, which consists of the CRDs that must be presented before templates are installed. An example `crds/` folder is shown here:

```
crds/
    my-custom-resource-crd.yaml
```

The file `my-custom-resource-crd.yaml` may have the following contents:

```
apiVersion: apiextensions.k8s.io/v1
kind: CustomResourceDefinition
metadata:
  name: my-custom-resources.learnhelm.io
spec:
  group: learnhelm.io
  names:
    kind: MyCustomResource
    listKind: MyCustomResourceList
```

```
plural: MyCustomResources
singular: MyCustomResource
scope: Namespaced
version: v1
```

The templates/ directory can then contain an instance of the MyCustomResource resource.

```
templates/
  my-custom-resource.yaml
```

A file structure such as this will ensure that the MyCustomResource CRD is installed before the CR defined under the templates/ directory.

> **Important note:**
> This capability requires the user to be a cluster administrator as creating CRDs requires escalated privileges. If you are not a cluster administrator, it may be better to ask an admin to create your CRDs beforehand. If you do so, the crds/ folder would not need to be included in your chart because the CRDs would already be present in the cluster.

By now, we have covered Helm templates in a large amount of detail. To summarize, Helm templates are the 'brains' of your Helm chart and are used to generate Kubernetes resources. We will get hands-on experience with writing Helm templates, along with other topics discussed in this chapter, in *Chapter 5, Building Your First Helm Chart*.

For now, let's continue our discussion on Helm chart fundamentals with a topic of equal importance to chart templates—the Chart.yaml file.

Understanding chart definitions

The Chart.yaml file, also known as the chart definition, is a resource that declares different metadata about a Helm chart. This file is required and if it is not included in a chart's file structure, you'll receive the following error:

```
Error: validation: chart.metadata is required
```

In *Chapter 3, Installing Your First Helm Chart*, we explored the chart definition of **Bitnami's WordPress chart** by running the `helm show chart` command. Recall this chart definition by running this command again. We will assume that the Bitnami chart repository has already been added since this task was performed in *Chapter 3, Installing Your First Helm Chart*:

```
$ helm show chart bitnami/wordpress --version 8.1.0
```

Below lists the chart definition of the wordpress chart.

```
apiVersion: v1
appVersion: 5.3.2
dependencies:
- condition: mariadb.enabled
  name: mariadb
  repository: https://kubernetes-charts.storage.googleapis.com/
  tags:
  - wordpress-database
  version: 7.x.x
description: Web publishing platform for building blogs and websites.
home: http://www.wordpress.com/
icon: https://bitnami.com/assets/stacks/wordpress/img/wordpress-stack-220x234.png
keywords:
- wordpress
- cms
- blog
- http
- web
- application
- php
maintainers:
- email: containers@bitnami.com
  name: Bitnami
name: wordpress
sources:
- https://github.com/bitnami/bitnami-docker-wordpress
version: 8.1.0
```

Figure 4.1 – The chart definition of the wordpress chart.

The chart definition, or the `Chart.yaml` file, can contain many different fields. Some of the fields are required while most of the other fields are optional and can be provided only if necessary.

Now that we have a basic understanding of the `Chart.yaml` file, we will explore the file's required fields in the next section.

Required fields

A chart definition must contain the following fields that contain crucial chart metadata:

Field	Description
apiVersion	The chart API version
name	The name of the Helm chart
version	The version of the Helm chart

Let's explore each of these required fields in more detail:

- The apiVersion field can be set to one of two different values:

  v1

  v2

- If the apiVersion field is set to v1, this means that the chart follows a legacy chart structure. This is the apiVersion value that was used before the release of Helm 3, where an additional requirement.yaml file was supported in the chart structure and the type field in the chart definition was not supported. Helm 3 is backward-compatible with the apiVersion value v1, but new charts should be set to the apiVersion value v2 to avoid deprecated features being used.

- The name field is used to define the name of the Helm chart. This value should be equal to the name of the top-level directory containing the Helm chart's files. The name of the Helm chart appears in the search results from the helm search command, as well as the helm list command, to return the name of the chart used for a release. The value of this field should be concise yet descriptive, describing the application installed by the chart in a short name such as wordpress or redis-cluster. Kebab case, or separating words with dashes, is the common convention when distinguishing different words in a name. Sometimes, names will be written as one word, such as rediscluster.

- The version field is used to determine the version of the Helm chart. Versions must follow the **Semantic Versioning (SemVer)** 2.0.0 format to be a valid chart version. SemVer describes a version based on a Major.Minor.Patch format, where the Major version should increase when a breaking change is introduced, the Minor version should increase when a backward-compatible feature is released, and the Patch version should increase when a bug is fixed. When the Minor version is increased, the Patch version is set back to 0. When the Major version is increased, both the Minor and Patch versions are reset to 0. Chart developers should take special care when incrementing chart versions as they are used to indicate when breaking changes, new features, and bug fixes are released.

While these three fields are the only fields required in the `Chart.yaml` file, there are many more optional fields that can be included to add additional metadata to the chart.

Let's take a look at the other possible `Chart.yaml` fields.

Optional metadata

In addition to the required fields, there are many optional fields that can be used to provide additional details about a chart, described in the following table:

Field	Description
appVersion	The version of the application deployed with the Helm chart. This does not need to be SemVer.
dependencies	A list of charts that the chart defined by Chart.yaml is dependent on.
deprecated	Indicates whether the Helm chart has been deprecated.
description	A short description of the Helm chart.
home	The URL to the project's home page.
icon	An icon in SVG or PNG format used to represent the Helm chart. Displayed on the chart's page on Helm Hub.
keywords	A list of keywords used to describe the project that is used to search with the helm search command.
kubeVersion	A range of compatible Kubernetes versions in SemVer.
maintainers	A list of maintainers for the Helm chart.
sources	A list of URLs that link to the Helm chart's or the application's source code.
type	The type of Helm chart that should be defined.

Some of these fields provide simple metadata to display information to a user about the Helm chart. Other fields, however, are used to modify the behavior of the Helm chart. The first of these fields is the `type` field, which can be set to either `application` or `library`. If set to `application`, the chart deploys Kubernetes resources. If set to `library`, the chart provides functions to other charts through the form of helper templates.

The second field that can modify the behavior of the Helm chart is the `dependencies` field, which is discussed in the next section.

Managing chart dependencies

Chart dependencies are used to install other charts' resources that a Helm chart may depend on. An example of this is the `wordpress` chart, which declared the `mariaDB` chart as a dependency to save backend data. By using the `mariadb` dependency, the WordPress chart did not need to define its resources from scratch.

Dependencies are declared in the `Chart.yaml` file by populating the `dependencies` field. The following is the relevant snippet from the `wordpress` chart's definition:

```
dependencies:
- condition: mariadb.enabled
  name: mariadb
  repository: https://kubernetes-charts.storage.googleapis.com/
  tags:
  - wordpress-database
  version: 7.x.x
```

Figure 4.2 – The mariadb dependency declared in the wordpress Helm chart.

While this example displays a single dependency, `mariadb`, the dependencies block can define a list of multiple dependencies.

A `dependencies` block contains many different fields that can be applied to modify the behavior of a chart's dependency management. These fields are defined in the following table:

Field	Definition	Required?
name	The name of the dependency chart	Yes
repository	Where the dependency chart resides	Yes
version	The version of the dependency chart to include	Yes
alias	An alternative name to give a dependency	No
condition	A Boolean value that determines whether the dependency should be included or not	No
import-values	Propogate values from a dependency chart to the parent chart	No
tags	A list of Boolean values that determine whether the chart should be included or not	No

The minimum required fields under the dependencies blocks are the name, repository, and version fields. As shown in the preceding wordpress dependency snippet, the name of the dependency is mariadb and the repository can be found at https://kubernetes-charts.storage.googleapis.com/. This searches the provided repository for a Helm chart whose name field in the Chart.yaml file is mariadb. The version field of a dependencies block specifies the version of the chart that should be included. This can be pinned to a specific version, such as 7.0.0, or it can specify a wildcard version. The dependency listed in the preceding example provides a wildcard version, 7.x.x, which instructs Helm to download the latest version of the chart that matches the wildcard.

Now, with an understanding of the required dependencies fields, let's learn how the declared dependencies can be downloaded.

Downloading dependencies

Dependencies can be downloaded using the `helm dependency` subcommand listed in the following table:

Command	Definition
`helm dependency build`	Rebuilds the charts/ directory based on the Chart.lock file. If a Chart.lock file is not found, this command will mirror the behavior of the "helm dependency update" command
`helm dependency list`	Lists the dependencies for the given chart
`helm dependency update`	Updates the charts/ directory based on the contents of Chart.yaml and generate a Chart.lock file.

To download dependencies for the first time, you can run the `helm dependency update` command, which downloads each dependency into the `charts/` directory of the given Helm chart:

```
$ helm dependency update $CHART_PATH
```

The `helm dependency update` command downloads dependencies from repositories in the form of GZip archives with the `.tgz` file extension. This command also generates a file called `Chart.lock`. The `Chart.lock` file is similar to the `Chart.yaml` file. However, while the `Chart.yaml` file contains the desired state of the chart dependencies, the `Chart.lock` file defines the actual state of the dependencies that were applied.

An example of a `Chart.lock` file can be seen here:

```
dependencies:
- name: mariadb
  repository: https://charts.bitnami.com
  version: 7.3.1
digest: sha256:8bb0797aa542ddb22c41cf39d599264ebbe3665c95a22421ffd57fdb99bdb740
generated: "2020-01-01T22:39:38.439294071-05:00"
```

Figure 4.3 – A `Chart.lock` file

Compare this to a simple corresponding `Chart.yaml` file:

```
apiVersion: v2
version: 0.0.1
name: dependencies-demonstration
dependencies:
  - name: mariadb
    version: 7.x.x
    repository: https://charts.bitnami.com
```

Figure 4.4 – A corresponding Chart.yaml file

In the Chart.yaml file, you can see that the version of the specified mariadb dependency was version 7.x.x, but the version in the Chart.lock file is version 7.3.1. This is because the Chart.yaml file instructed Helm to download the latest version of the 7.x.x release, and the actual version that was downloaded was version 7.3.1.

With the Chart.lock file in place, Helm is able to redownload the exact dependencies that were originally downloaded in the event that the charts/ directory is removed or needs to be rebuilt. This can be done by running the helm dependency build command against a chart:

```
$ helm dependency build $CHART_PATH
```

Because you can download dependencies using the helm dependency build command, it is possible to omit the charts/ directory from source control to reduce the size of repositories.

Over time, newer versions under the 7.x.x release will be available. The helm dependency update command can be run again to reconcile this dependency, meaning the latest available version will be downloaded and the Chart.lock file will regenerate. If in the future you want to download from the 8.x.x release or would like to pin the dependency to a specific release, such as 7.0.0, you can set this in the Chart.yaml file and run helm dependency update.

The helm dependency list command can be used to view the downloaded dependencies of a Helm chart saved to your local machine:

```
$ helm dependency list $CHART_NAME
```

You'll see an output similar to the following:

```
NAME      VERSION REPOSITORY                    STATUS
mariadb 7.x.x    https://charts.bitnami.com     ok
```

Figure 4.5 – "helm dependency list" output

The STATUS column determines whether the dependency has been successfully downloaded to the charts/ directory. It has been downloaded if the status reads ok. If the status reads as missing, the dependency has not been downloaded yet.

By default, every declared dependency in the Chart.yaml file will be downloaded, but this can be modified by providing the condition or tags fields of the dependencies block, which we will discuss in the next section.

Conditional dependencies

The condition and flags fields can be leveraged to conditionally include dependencies during an installation or upgrade. Consider an example dependencies block in the Chart.yaml file:

```
dependencies:
  - name: dependency1
    repository: https://example.com
    version: 1.x.x
    condition: dependency1.enabled
    tags:
      - monitoring
  - name: dependency2
    repository: https://example.com
    version: 2.x.x
    condition: dependency2.enabled
    tags:
      - monitoring
```

Notice the inclusion of the `condition` and `tags` fields. The `condition` field lists a value that should be provided by the user or set in the chart's `values.yaml` file. If it evaluates to `true`, the `condition` field causes the chart to be included as a dependency. If `false`, the dependency will not be included. Multiple conditions can be defined by separating each condition with a comma, as follows:

```
condition: dependency1.enabled, global.dependency1.enabled
```

The best practice around setting a condition is to follow a `chartname.enabled` value format, where each dependency has a unique condition set depending on the dependency's chart name. This allows users to enable or disable individual charts by following an intuitive value schema. If the condition values are not included in the chart's `values.yaml` file or are not provided by the user, this field is ignored.

While the `condition` field is used to enable or disable individual dependencies, the `tags` field is used to enable or disable groups of dependencies. In the preceding `dependencies` block, both dependencies list a tag called `monitoring`. This means that if the `monitoring` tag is enabled, both dependencies are included. If the `monitoring` tag is set to `false`, the dependency is omitted. Tags are enabled or disabled by setting them under a `tags` YAML object in the parent chart's `values.yaml` file, as follows:

```
tags:
  monitoring: true
```

A dependency can define multiple tags in the `Chart.yaml` file by following the YAML syntax for lists. Only one tag needs to be evaluated to `true` for the dependency to be included.

> **Important note:**
> If all of a dependency's tags are ignored, the dependency will be included by default.

In this section, we discussed how dependencies can be declared conditionally. Next, we will discuss how values from a dependency can be overridden and referenced.

Overriding and referencing values from a child chart

By default, the values belonging to a dependency chart (also referred to as a **child chart**) can be overridden or referenced by wrapping them in a map with a name set to the same as the child chart. Imagine a child chart called my-dep that supports the following values:

```
replicas: 1
servicePorts:
  - 8080
  - 8443
```

When this chart is installed as a dependency, these values can be overridden by setting them in a my-dep YAML object of the parent chart, as shown:

```
my-dep:
  replicas: 3
  servicePorts:
    - 8080
    - 8443
    - 8778
```

The preceding example overrides the replicas and servicePorts values defined in my-dep to set 3 for replicas and add 8778 to servicePorts. These values can be referenced in the parent chart's templates by following dot notation—for example, my-dep.replicas. In addition to overriding and referencing values, you can directly import dependency values by defining the import-values field, explained in the next section.

Importing values with import-values

The dependencies block of the Chart.yaml file supports an import-values field that can be used to import a child chart's default values. This field works in a couple of ways. The first way is to provide a list of keys to import from the child chart. In order for this to work, the child chart must have values declared under an exports block, as follows:

```
exports:
  image:
    registry: 'my-registry.io'
    name: learnhelm/my-image
```

```
        tag: latest
```

The parent chart can then define the import-values field in the Chart.yaml file:

```
dependencies:
  - name: mariadb
    repository: https://charts.bitnami.com/bitnami
    version: 7.x.x
    import-values:
      - image
```

This allows default values under exports.image in the child chart to be referenced as follows in the parent chart:

```
registry: 'my-registry.io'
name: learnhelm/my-image
tag: latest
```

Notice that this has removed the image map and left only the key-value pairs that were underneath it. If you don't want this to happen, the import-values field can retain the image map by following what is referred to as the child-parent format. This allows chart developers to specify the values that should be imported from the child chart and provides the name that they should be referred to as in the parent chart. The child-parent format allows this to be done without the need for values in an exports block in the child chart. The following dependencies block demonstrates an example of this:

```
dependencies:
  - name: mariadb
    repository: https://charts.bitnami.com/bitnami
    version: 7.x.x
    import-values:
      - child: image
        parent: image
```

This example takes each value under the image block in the child chart and imports it under an image block in the parent chart.

> **Important note:**
> The values imported using the `import-values` field cannot be overridden in the parent chart. If you need to override values in the child chart, you should not use the `import-values` field and should instead override the desired values by prefixing each one with the name of the child chart.

In this section, we covered how dependencies can be managed in the `Chart.yaml` file. Now, let's learn about how life cycle management hooks can be defined in a Helm chart.

Life cycle management

One of the primary benefits of Helm charts and their associated releases is the ability to manage complex applications on Kubernetes. A release undergoes multiple phases during its life span. To provide additional management capabilities around the life cycle of a release, Helm features a `hooks` mechanism so that actions can be undertaken at different points in time within a release cycle. In this section, we will explore the different phases of a release's life span and introduce how `hooks` can be used to provide capabilities for interacting not only with the release but also the entire Kubernetes environment.

In *Chapter 3, Installing Your First Helm Chart*, we encountered several phases that encompass the overall life span of a Helm release, including its installation, upgrade, removal, and rollback. Given that Helm charts can be complex, as they manage one or more applications that will be deployed to Kubernetes, there is often the need to perform additional actions besides just deploying resources. These can include the following:

- Completing prerequisites that are needed by the application, such as managing certificates and secrets
- Database management as part of a chart upgrade to either perform a backup or restoration
- Cleaning up assets before the removal of a chart

The list of potential options can be long and it is important to first understand the basics of Helm hooks as well as when they can be executed, which we will describe in the next section.

The basics of a Helm hook

A hook executes as a one-time action at a designated point in time during the life span of a release. A hook, as with the majority of the features within Helm, is implemented as yet another Kubernetes resource and, more specifically, within a container. While the majority of workloads within Kubernetes are designed to long-living processes, such as an application serving API requests, workloads can also be made up of a single task or set of tasks executed using a script that indicates either success or failure once completed.

Two options that are typically used in a Kubernetes environment to create short-lived tasks are to make use of either a bare **pod** or a **job**. A bare pod is a pod that runs until completion and then terminates, but will not be rescheduled if the underlying node fails. For this reason, it may be preferred to run life cycle hooks as jobs, which reschedules the hook if the node fails or becomes unavailable.

Since hooks are simply defined as Kubernetes resources, they are also placed in the templates/ folder and annotated with the helm.sh/hook annotation. The designation of this annotation ensures they are not rendered with the rest of the resources that are applied to a Kubernetes environment during standard processing. Instead, they are rendered and applied based on the value specified within the helm.sh/hook annotation, which determines when it should be executed within Kubernetes as part of the Helm release life cycle.

Here's an example of how a hook can be defined as a job:

```
apiVersion: batch/v1
kind: Job
metadata:
  name: helm-auditing
  annotations:
    'helm.sh/hook': pre-install,post-install
spec:
  template:
    metadata:
      name: helm-auditing
    spec:
      restartPolicy: Never
      containers:
      - name: helm-auditing
        command: ["/bin/sh", "-c", "echo Hook Executed at
```

```
$(date)"]
        image: alpine
```

This trivial example prints out the current date and time in the container before sleeping for 10 seconds. Helm executes this hook before and after installing the chart, as noted by the value of the 'helm.sh/hook' annotation. A use case for this type of hook is to tie into an auditing system that tracks the installation of applications to a Kubernetes environment. A similar hook can be added after the installation completes to track the total time it took to complete the chart installation process.

Now that we have explained the basics of Helm hooks, let's discuss how hooks can be defined in a Helm chart.

Hook execution

As you saw in the `job` hook in the previous section, the value of the `helm.sh/hook` annotation was `pre-install`. `pre-install` is one of the points during the life span of a Helm chart where a hook can be executed.

The following table denotes the available options for the `helm.sh/hook` annotation, indicating when the hook is executed. The descriptions for each hook references the official Helm documentation, which can be found at `https://helm.sh/docs/topics/charts_hooks/#the-available-hooks`:

Annotation value	Description
pre-install	Executes after templates are rendered but before any resources are created in Kubernetes
post-install	Executes after all resources are loaded into Kubernetes
pre-delete	Executes on a deletion request before any resources are deleted from Kubernetes
post-delete	Executes on a deletion request after all of the release's resources have been deleted
pre-upgrade	Executes on an upgrade request after templates are rendered but before any resources are updated
post-upgrade	Executes on an upgrade after all resources have been upgraded
pre-rollback	Executes on a rollback request after templates are rendered but before any resources are rolled back
post-rollback	Executes on a rollback request after all resources have been modified
test	Executes when the `helm test` subcommand is invoked, which is discussed further in Chapter 6, *Testing Helm Charts* (replaces the `test-success` and `test-failure` options from previous versions of Helm)

The `helm.sh/hook` annotation can contain multiple values indicating that the same resource is executed at different points in time within a chart's release cycle. For example, for a hook to be executed before and after a chart installation, the following annotation can be defined on either the pod or job:

```
annotations:
  'helm.sh/hook': pre-install,post-install
```

It is useful to understand how and when hooks are executed in order to determine the desired phase in a charts' life cycle that needs to be selected. As described in the previous example, when a hook is denoted to run in the `pre-install` and `post-install` portions of an execution of the `helm install` command, the following actions take place:

1. The user installs a Helm chart (by running, for example, `helm install bitnami/wordpress --version 8.1.0`).

2. The Helm API is invoked.

3. CRDs in the `crds/` folder are loaded to the Kubernetes environment.

4. Verification of the chart templates is performed and the resources are rendered.

5. The `pre-install` hooks are ordered by weight, then are rendered and loaded to Kubernetes.

6. Helm waits until the hooks are ready.

7. Template resources are rendered and applied to the Kubernetes environment.

8. The `post-install` hooks are executed.

9. Helm waits until the `post-install` hooks are complete.

10. The results of the `helm install` command are returned.

With an understanding of the basics of Helm hook execution, let's cover some of the more advanced topics around Helm hooks.

Advanced hook concepts

While minimal effort is needed to transform a standard Helm template resource into a hook, there are additional options that aid in chart execution and resource removal.

There is no limit to the number of hooks that can be executed during the life span of a Helm chart and there may be cases where multiple hooks are configured for the same life cycle phase. When this scenario arises, hooks, by default, are ordered alphabetically by name. However, you can define the order by specifying the weight of each hook using the `helm.sh/weight` annotation. Weights are sorted in ascending order, but if multiple hooks contain the same weight value, the default logic of sorting alphabetically by name is used.

While hooks present a useful mechanism for life cycle management, you should keep in mind that hooks, unlike regular template resources, are not removed with the rest of the chart during an invocation of the `helm uninstall` command as they are not tracked or managed by Helm. Instead, a couple of strategies can be employed to remove hooks during a release's life cycle, such as configuring a deletion policy and setting a TTL on a job.

First, the `helm.sh/hook-delete-policy` annotation can be specified on the pod or job associated with the hook. This annotation determines when Helm should act on removing the resource from Kubernetes. The following options are available (the descriptions reference the Helm documentation, which can be found at `https://helm.sh/docs/topics/charts_hooks/#hook-deletion-policies`):

Annotation value	Description
before-hook-creation	Deletes the previous resources before the hook is launched (a default action)
hook-succeeded	Deletes the resources after the hook is successfully executed
hook-failed	Deletes the resources if the hook failed during execution

Additionally, Kubernetes provides the option of defining a **Time-To-Live (TTL)** mechanism to limit the amount of time a resource is retained for after completion using the `ttlSecondsAfterFinished` property of the job, as shown:

```
apiVersion: batch/v1
kind: Job
metadata:
  name: ttl-job
  annotations:
    'helm.sh/hook': post-install
spec:
  ttlSecondsAfterFinished: 60
```

In this example, the resources are removed in 60 seconds upon completion or failure.

The final stage of a release's life cycle is its deletion, and although standard chart templates are removed during the invocation of the `helm uninstall` command you may want certain resources to be retained so that Helm doesn't take action on them. A common use case for this is when a new persistent volume via a `PersistentVolumeClaim` command is created at the beginning of a release's life cycle but should not be removed alongside other resources at the end so that the volume's data is retained. This option is enabled through the use of the `helm.sh/resource-policy` annotation, as shown:

```
'helm.sh/resource-policy': keep
```

Helm will no longer consider removing this resource during the execution of the `helm uninstall` command. It is important to note that when a resource is no longer managed, it becomes orphaned once the remainder of the resources is removed. This can cause challenges if the `helm install` command is used as it may cause resource-naming conflicts with the existing resource that was not previously removed. The orphaned resource can be deleted manually by using the `kubectl delete` command.

This section discussed how you can write hooks and automation to manage a chart's life cycle. In the next section, we will discuss how you can properly document a Helm chart to ensure its users have a smooth experience.

Documenting a Helm chart

As with any other software that users interact with, a Helm chart should be properly documented so that users know how to interact with it. The Helm chart structure supports a `README.md` file for documenting usage, a `LICENSE` file for covering usage and distribution rights, and a `templates/NOTES.txt` file for generating usage instructions during chart installation.

The README.md File

README is a file commonly used in software development to describe the installation, usage, and other details of a product. A Helm chart's README file often contains the following details:

- **Prerequisites**: A common example of a prerequisite is creating a `secret` or a set of secrets to the Kubernetes cluster before a chart is installed. for the purpose of mounting to a Kubernetes deployment. Users can be made aware of this requirement by referencing the README file.

- **Values**: Charts often consist of many different values, each of which should be described in a table in the README file. The table should specify the name of the value, its description or function, and its default value. You may also find it helpful to denote whether or not the value needs to be provided during an installation or upgrade.

- **Application-specific information**: Once an application is installed using the Helm chart, you may need additional information on the application itself, such as how it can be accessed or how the application functions. These details can be provided in the README file as well.

Helm READMEs are written using the **Markdown** formatting language. Markdown is commonly used in GitHub projects and open source software and is a way of easily codifying text that can be displayed in an elegant format. Markdown can be explored further on the **Markdown Guide** website, located at `https://www.markdownguide.org/`.

The LICENSE file

Apart from the technical instructions contained in a README file, chart maintainers may find it necessary to include a license that indicates the permissions users have around chart usage and distribution. These details can be composed in a file called LICENSE under the chart directory.

The LICENSE file is a plaintext file containing a software license. The license may be custom-written or it can be a copy of a license commonly used in open source software, such as the Apache License 2.0 or the MIT License. Understanding the differences between licenses as well as the legality in using and distributing software is beyond the scope of this book, but you can begin exploring these details at the **Choose a License** website (`https://choosealicense.com/`), which will assist you in selecting an appropriate license for your Helm chart.

The templates/NOTES.txt file

Similar to the README.md file, the templates/NOTES.txt file is used to provide usage instructions for the application once installed using Helm. The difference is that while the README.md file is static, the NOTES.txt file can be dynamically generated using Go templating.

Imagine that a Helm chart has the following value configured in its `values.yaml` file:

```
## serviceType can be set to NodePort or LoadBalancer
serviceType: NodePort
```

Depending on the type of service that is set, the instructions to access the application will differ. If the service is a `NodePort` service, access will be gained by using a certain port number set on each Kubernetes node. If the service is set to `LoadBalancer`, the application will be accessed using the URL of a load balancer provisioned automatically on the creation of the service. Understanding how to access the application based on the type of service being used may be difficult for less experienced Kubernetes users, so the maintainer of this chart should provide a `NOTES.txt` file under the `templates/` directory that provides instructions on how the application can be accessed.

The following example illustrates how a `templates/NOTES.txt` file can be used for this purpose:

```
Follow these instructions to access your application.
{{- if eq .Values.serviceType 'NodePort' }}
export NODE_PORT=$(kubectl get --namespace {{ .Release.
Namespace }} -o jsonpath='{.spec.ports[0].nodePort}' services
{{.Release.Name }})

export NODE_IP=$(kubectl get nodes --namespace {{ .Release.
Namespace }} -o jsonpath='{.items[0].status.addresses[0].
address}')

echo "URL: http://$NODE_IP:$NODE_PORT"
{{- else }}
export SERVICE_IP=$(kubectl get svc --namespace {{ .Release.
Name }} wordpress --template '{{ range (index .status.
loadBalancer.ingress 0) }}{{.}}{{ end }}')

echo "URL: http://$SERVICE_IP"
{{- end }}
```

This file will be generated and displayed during the application's install, upgrade, and rollback phases and can be recalled by running the `helm get notes` command. By providing this file, users will get a better understanding of how to use the application.

We have described the majority of the assets that comprise a Helm chart so far in this chapter, except for the actual packaging, which allows a chart to be easily distributable. This concept will be described in the next section.

Packaging a Helm chart

While Helm charts follow a common file structure, they should be packaged in order to be easily distributed. Charts are packaged in `tgz` archives. While this archives can be manually created by using the `tar` bash utility or an archive manager, Helm provides the `helm package` command to simplify this task. The syntax of the `helm package` command is shown here:

```
$ helm package [CHART_NAME] [...] [flags]
```

The `helm package` command is run against a local chart directory. If this command is successful, it will generate a `tgz` archive with the following file format:

```
$CHART_NAME-$CHART_VERSION.tgz
```

The archive can then be distributed by pushing to a chart repository, which is a task that is explored further in *Chapter 5, Building Your First Helm Chart*.

The `helm package` command includes every file under a chart directory. While this is often the preferred behavior, it may not always be desired if the directory contains files that are not essential to Helm. One example of a directory where this commonly occurs is the `.git/` directory, which is present in projects managed by **Git SCM**. If this file is packaged into the chart's `tgz` archive, it will not serve any purpose and will only increase the size of the archive. Helm supports a file called `.helmignore` that can be used to omit certain files and folders from the Helm archive. The following describes an example `.helmignore` file:

```
# Ignore git directories and files
.git/
.gitignore
```

The preceding file indicates that if the `.git/` directory or the `.gitignore` files appear in a chart's directory, they will be ignored by the `helm package` command, meaning they will not be present in the resulting `tgz` archive. Lines that begin with the pound symbol (#) in this file serve as comments. Be sure to include a `.helmignore` file in your Helm charts if your chart's directory contains files and folders that are not necessary to the overall function of the chart.

Summary

A Helm chart is a set of files, written primarily in the YAML format, that follows a certain file structure. The `Chart.yaml` file is used to set chart metadata and declare dependencies. The `templates/` directory is used to contain Kubernetes YAML resources that are Go-templated, allowing them to be dynamically generated. Kubernetes resources defined under the `templates/` directory can also contain certain hooks to configure stages in an application's life cycle. To provide documentation to users, charts can contain the `README.md` and `templates/NOTES.txt` files and can also contain the `LICENSE` file to declare chart usage and distribution rights. Finally, charts can contain a `.helmignore` file, which is used to omit declared files from the final packaged product.

In this chapter, you learned about the structure of a Helm chart and how to configure key chart components. With the knowledge from this chapter under your belt, you now have an understanding of the basic concepts of how to write your first Helm chart from scratch, which we will do in *Chapter 5, Building Your First Helm Chart*.

Further reading

To learn more about the basics behind creating Helm charts, consult the Chart Template Guide page on the Helm documentation at `https://helm.sh/docs/chart_template_guide/`. The Charts section at `https://helm.sh/docs/topics/charts/` also describes many of the topics discussed throughout this chapter, including chart file structure, dependencies, and the `Chart.yaml` file.

Questions

1. What is the file format that is most commonly used in Kubernetes and Helm?

2. What are the three required fields in the `Chart.yaml` file?

3. How can the values from a chart dependency be referenced or overridden?

4. Imagine you want to take a data snapshot of a database deployed with Helm. What can you do to ensure that a data `snapshot` is taken before upgrading the database to a newer version?

5. What files can you, as a chart developer, create to provide documentation and simplify the chart installation process for the end user?

6. What Helm templating construct can you take advantage of to generate repeating YAML portions?

7. How does the `Chart.yaml` file differ from the `Chart.lock` file?

8. What is the name of the annotation that defines a resource as a hook?

9. What is the purpose of functions and pipelines in chart templates? What are some common functions that can be used?

5

Building Your First Helm Chart

In the previous chapter, you learned about the various aspects that comprise a Helm chart. Now, it is time to put this knowledge to the test by building a Helm chart. Learning to build a Helm chart will allow you to package a complex Kubernetes application in a way that makes it simple to deploy.

In this chapter, you will learn how to build a Helm chart that deploys the `guestbook` application, a common quickstart application used throughout the Kubernetes community. This chart will be built by following best practices around Kubernetes and Helm chart development, to provide a well-written and easily maintainable piece of automation. Throughout the process of developing this chart, you will learn many different skills that you can apply toward building your own Helm charts. At the end of the chapter, you will learn how to package your Helm chart and deploy it to a chart repository, where it can be easily accessible to end users.

Here are the main topics covered in this chapter:

- Understanding the Guestbook application
- Creating a Guestbook Helm chart
- Improving the Guestbook Helm chart
- Publishing the Guestbook chart to a chart repository

Technical requirements

This chapter requires the following technologies:

- `minikube`
- `kubectl`
- `helm`

In addition to the preceding tooling, you will find the GitHub repository for this book located at `https://github.com/PacktPublishing/-Learn-Helm`. We will reference the `helm-charts/charts/guestbook` folder contained in this chapter.

It is recommended that you have your own GitHub account in order to complete the final section of this chapter, *Creating a chart repository*. Instructions on how to create your own account will be provided in that section.

Understanding the Guestbook application

In this chapter, you will create a Helm chart to deploy the Guestbook tutorial application provided by the Kubernetes community. This application is introduced in the Kubernetes documentation at the following page: `https://kubernetes.io/docs/tutorials/stateless-application/guestbook/`

The Guestbook application is a simple **PHP: Hypertext Preprocessor (PHP)** frontend designed to persist messages to a Redis backend. The frontend consists of a dialog box and a **Submit** button, as illustrated in the following screenshot:

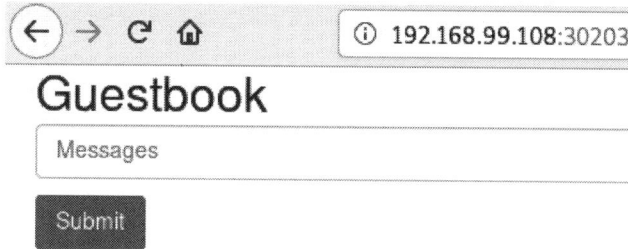

Figure 5.1: The Guestbook PHP frontend

To interact with this application, users can follow these next steps:

1. Type a message in the **Messages** dialog box.

2. Click the **Submit** button.

3. When the **Submit** button is clicked, the message will be saved to a Redis database.

Redis is an in-memory, key-value data store that, in this chapter, will be clustered for data replication. The cluster will consist of one master node that the Guestbook frontend will write to. Once written to, the master node will replicate the data across multiple slave nodes, from which the Guestbook frontend will read.

The following diagram describes how the Guestbook frontend interacts with the Redis backend:

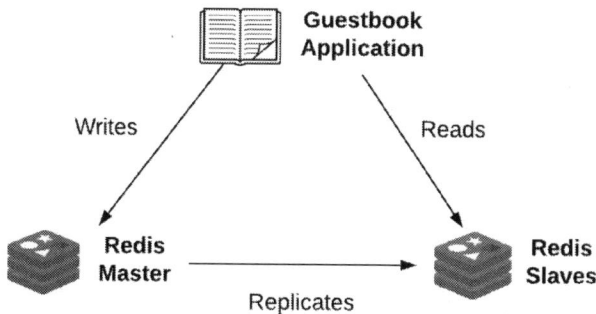

Figure 5.2: Guestbook frontend and Redis interaction

With a basic understanding of how the Guestbook frontend and Redis backend interact, let's set up a Kubernetes environment to begin developing a Helm chart. Before we begin, let's first start minikube and create a dedicated namespace for this chapter.

Setting up the environment

In order to see your chart in action, you'll need to create your minikube environment by following these steps:

1. Start minikube by running the `minikube start` command, as follows:

    ```
    $ minikube start
    ```

2. Create a new namespace called `chapter5`, like this:

    ```
    $ kubectl create namespace chapter5
    ```

We'll use this namespace when the Guestbook chart is deployed. Now that the environment is prepared, let's begin writing the chart.

Creating a Guestbook Helm chart

In this section, we will create a Helm chart to deploy the Guestbook application. The final chart has been published under the `helm-charts/charts/guestbook` folder of the Packt repository. Feel free to reference this location as you follow along with the examples.

We will begin development by first scaffolding the Guestbook Helm chart to create the chart's initial file structure.

Scaffolding the initial file structure

As you may recall from *Chapter 4*, *Understanding Helm Charts*, Helm charts must follow a particular file structure in order to be considered valid. Namely, a chart must contain the following required files:

*   `Chart.yaml`: Used to define chart metadata
*   `values.yaml`: Used to define default chart values
*   `templates/`: Used to define chart templates and Kubernetes resources to be created

We provided a list of each of the possible files a chart can contain in *Chapter 4*, *Understanding Helm Charts*, but the three preceding files are the files that are necessary in order to begin developing a new chart. While these three files can be created from scratch, Helm provides a `helm create` command that can be used to more quickly scaffold a new chart.

In addition to creating the files listed previously, the `helm create` command will also generate many different boilerplate templates that can be leveraged to more quickly write your Helm chart. Let's use this command to scaffold out a new Helm chart called `guestbook`.

The `helm create` command takes the name of the Helm chart (`guestbook`) as an argument. Run the following command on your local command line to scaffold this chart:

```
$ helm create guestbook
```

Upon running this command, you will see a new directory on your machine called `guestbook/`. This is the directory that contains your Helm chart. Inside the directory, you will see the following four files:

- `charts/`
- `Chart.yaml`
- `templates/`
- `values.yaml`

As you can see, the `helm create` command created a `charts/` directory, in addition to the required `Chart.yaml`, `values.yaml`, and `templates/` files. The `charts/` directory is currently blank, but will later become automatically populated when we declare a chart dependency. You may also notice that the other mentioned files have been automatically populated with default settings. We will leverage many of these defaults throughout this chapter while developing the `guestbook` chart.

If you explore the contents underneath the `templates/` directory, you will find that many different template resources have been included by default. These resources will save time that would have otherwise been spent creating these from scratch. While many useful templates were generated, we will remove the `templates/tests/` folder. This folder is used to contain the tests for your Helm chart, but we will focus on writing your own tests in *Chapter 6, Testing Helm Charts*. Run the following command to remove the `templates/tests/` folder:

```
$ rm -rf guestbook/templates/tests
```

Now that the `guestbook` chart has been scaffolded, let's proceed by evaluating the `Chart.yaml` file that has been generated.

Evaluating the chart definition

The chart definition, or `Chart.yaml` file, is used to contain the metadata of a Helm chart. We discussed each of the possible options of a `Chart.yaml` file in *Chapter 4, Understanding Helm Charts*, but let's recap on some of the primary settings contained within a typical chart definition, as follows:

- `apiVersion`: Set to either the `v1` or `v2` (`v2` is the preferred option for Helm 3)

- `version`: The version of the Helm chart. This should be a version that adheres to **Semantic Versioning specifications (SemVer)**.

- `appVersion`: The version of the application being deployed by the Helm chart

- `name`: The name of the Helm chart

- `description`: A brief description of the Helm chart and what it is designed to deploy

- `type`: Set to either `application` or `library`. `Application` charts are used to deploy a specific application. `Library` charts contain a set of helper functions (also called 'named templates') that can be used across other charts to reduce boilerplate.

- `dependencies`: A list of charts that the Helm chart depends on

If you observe your scaffolded `Chart.yaml` file, you will notice that each of these fields (except for dependencies) has already been set. This file can be seen in the following screenshot:

```
apiVersion: v2
name: guestbook
description: A Helm chart for Kubernetes

# A chart can be either an 'application' or a 'library' chart.
#
# Application charts are a collection of templates that can be
# to be deployed.
#
# Library charts provide useful utilities or functions for the
# a dependency of application charts to inject those utilities
# pipeline. Library charts do not define any templates and the
type: application

# This is the chart version. This version number should be inc
# to the chart and its templates, including the app version.
version: 0.1.0

# This is the version number of the application being deployed
# incremented each time you make changes to the application.
appVersion: 1.16.0
```

Figure 5.3: The scaffolded Chart.yaml file

We will leave each of the settings contained within this file at their defaults for now (though feel free to write a more creative description if you would like). We'll update a couple of these default values when they become relevant, later on in the chapter.

An additional setting that is not included in the default chart definition, but should be considered, is `dependencies`. We will discuss this in greater detail in the next section, where a Redis dependency will be added to simplify the development effort.

Adding a Redis chart dependency

As mentioned in the *Understanding the Guestbook application* section, this Helm chart must be able to deploy a Redis database that will be used to save the state of the application. If you were creating this chart completely from scratch, you would need to have a proper understanding of how Redis works and how it can be properly deployed to Kubernetes. You would also need to create the corresponding chart templates required to deploy Redis.

Alternatively, by including a Redis dependency that already contains the logic and required chart templates, you can greatly reduce the amount of effort involved in creating the `guestbook` Helm chart. Let's modify the scaffolded `Chart.yaml` file by adding a Redis dependency to simplify chart development.

The process to add a Redis chart dependency can be performed by following these steps:

1. Search the Helm Hub repository for Redis charts by running the following command:

    ```
    $ helm search hub redis
    ```

2. One of the charts that will be displayed is Bitnami's Redis chart. This is the chart we will use as the dependency. If you have not already added the `bitnami` chart repository in *Chapter 3, Installing Your First Helm Chart,* add this chart repository now by using the `helm add repo` command. Note that the repository **Uniform Resource Locator (URL)** was retrieved from the Redis chart's page in the Helm Hub repository. The code can be seen in the following snippet:

    ```
    $ helm add repo bitnami https://charts.bitnami.com/
    bitnami
    ```

3. Determine the version of the Redis chart you would like to use. A list of version numbers can be found by running the following command:

```
$ helm search repo redis --versions
```

NAME	CHART VERSION	APP VERSION
bitnami/redis	10.5.14	5.0.8
bitnami/redis	10.5.13	5.0.8
bitnami/redis	10.5.12	5.0.8
bitnami/redis	10.5.11	5.0.8

The version that you must select is a chart version, not an app version. The app version only describes the Redis version, while the chart version describes the version of the actual Helm chart.

Dependencies allow you to choose a particular chart version, or a wildcard such as 10.5.x. Using a wildcard allows you to easily keep your chart updated with the latest Redis version matching that wildcard (which, in this case, is version 10.5.14). In this example, we will use version 10.5.x.

4. Add the dependencies field to the Chart.yaml file. For the guestbook chart, we will configure this field with the following minimum required fields (additional fields are discussed in *Chapter 4, Understanding Helm Charts*):

name: The name of the dependency chart

version: The version of the dependency chart

repository: The repository URL of the dependency chart

Add the following **YAML Ain't Markup Language (YAML)** code to the end of your Chart.yaml file, providing the information you have gathered about the Redis chart to configure the dependency's settings:

```yaml
dependencies:
  - name: redis
    version: 10.5.x
    repository: https://charts.bitnami.com/bitnami
```

Once you have added your dependency, your full `Chart.yaml` file should appear as follows (comments and empty lines have been removed for brevity):

```
apiVersion: v2
name: guestbook
description: A Helm chart for Kubernetes
type: application
version: 0.1.0
appVersion: 1.16.0
dependencies:
  - name: redis
    version: 10.5.x
    repository: https://charts.bitnami.com/bitnami
```

This file can also be reviewed in the Packt repository at `https://github.com/PacktPublishing/-Learn-Helm/blob/master/helm-charts/charts/guestbook/Chart.yaml` (be aware that the version and `appVersion` fields may differ, as we will modify these later in the chapter).

Now that your dependency has been added to the chart definition, let's download this dependency to ensure that it has been configured properly.

Downloading the Redis chart dependency

When downloading a dependency for the first time, you should use the `helm dependency update` command. This command will download your dependency to the `charts/` directory and will generate the `Chart.lock` file, which specifies metadata about the chart that was downloaded.

Run the `helm dependency update` command to download your Redis dependency. The command takes as an argument the location of your Helm chart, and can be seen in the following snippet:

```
$ helm dependency update guestbook
Hang tight while we grab the latest from your chart
repositories...
...Successfully got an update from the 'bitnami' chart
repository
Update Complete.  Happy Helming!
Saving 1 charts
```

```
Downloading redis from repo https://charts.bitnami.com/
bitnami
Deleting outdated charts
```

You can validate the fact that the download was successful by ensuring that the Redis chart appears under the `charts/` folder, as illustrated here:

```
$ ls guestbook/charts
redis-10.5.14.tgz
```

Now that the Redis dependency has been included, let's proceed by modifying the `values.yaml` file. Here, we will override values specific to configuring Redis, as well as the Guestbook frontend application.

Modifying the values.yaml file

A Helm chart's `values.yaml` file is used to provide a set of default parameters that are referenced throughout the chart's templates. When users interact with the Helm chart, they can override these defaults if necessary, using the `--set` or `--values` flags. In addition to providing a set of default parameters, a well-written Helm chart should be self-documenting, containing intuitive names for each value and comments that explain difficult values to implement. Writing a self-documenting `value.yaml` file allows users and maintainers alike to simply refer to this file if they need to understand the chart's values.

The `helm create` command generates a values file that contains many boilerplate values commonly used throughout Helm chart development. Let's finish configuring the Redis dependency by adding a few additional values at the end of this file. Afterward, we'll focus on modifying some of the boilerplate values to configure the Guestbook frontend resources.

Adding values to configure the Redis chart

Although adding a dependency prevents you from needing to create its chart templates, you may still need to override some of its values in order to configure it. In this case, it will be necessary to override a few of the Redis chart's values to allow it to work seamlessly with the rest of the `guestbook` chart.

Let's begin by first learning about the Redis chart's values. This can be done by running the `helm show values` command against the downloaded Redis chart, as follows:

```
$ helm show values charts/redis-10.5.14.tgz
```

Be sure to modify the command to match the Redis chart version that you downloaded. With a list of values displayed, let's identify those that will need to be overridden, as follows:

1. The first value that will need to be overridden in the Redis chart is `fullnameOverride`. This value appears in the `helm show values` output, as follows:

    ```
    ## String to fully override redis.fullname template
    ##
    # fullnameOverride:
    ```

    Charts often use this value in a named template called `$CHART_NAME.fullname` to easily generate their Kubernetes resource names. When `fullnameOverride` is set, the named template will evaluate to this value. Otherwise, the result of this template will be based on the `.Release.Name` object, or the name of the Helm release provided at installation.

    The Redis dependency uses the `redis.fullname` template to help set the Redis master and Redis slave service names.

    The following snippet shows an example of how the Redis master service name is generated in the Redis chart:

    ```
    name: {{ template 'redis.fullname' . }}-master
    ```

    The Guestbook application requires the Redis services to be named `redis-master` and `redis-slave`. As a result, the `fullnameOverride` value should be set to `redis`.

If you are interested in learning more about how the redis.fullname template works and how it is applied throughout the Redis chart, you can unarchive the Redis dependency under the charts/ folder. In that folder, you will find the redis.fullname template in the templates/_helpers.tpl file and note its invocations throughout each YAML template. (It turns out that your generated guestbook chart also contains a similar template in the _helpers.tpl file, but in general, it's safer to refer to the dependency's resources in case their maintainer customized the template.)

If you are interested in learning more about how the Guestbook application works, the source code can be found on GitHub. The following file defines the required Redis service names:

```
https://github.com/kubernetes/examples/blob/master/
guestbook/php-redis/guestbook.php
```

2. The next value that needs to be overridden from the Redis chart is usePassword. The following code snippet shows what this value looks like in the helm show values output:

```
## Use password authentication
usePassword: true
```

The Guestbook application has been written for unauthenticated access to the Redis database, so we will want to set this value to false.

3. The final value that we need to override is configmap. Here is how this value appears in the helm show values output:

```
## Redis config file
## ref: https://redis.io/topics/config
##
configmap: |-
   # Enable AOF https://redis.io/topics/
persistence#append-only-file
   appendonly yes
   # Disable RDB persistence, AOF persistence already
enabled.
   save ''
```

The default `configmap` value will enable both types of persistence that Redis can employ, **Append Only File (AOF)** and **Redis Database File (RDF)** persistence. AOF persistence in Redis works by adding new data entries to a changelog-style file to provide a history of changes. RDF persistence works by copying data to a file on certain intervals, so as to create data snapshots.

Later in this chapter, we will create simple life cycle hooks that allow users to back up and restore the Redis database to a previous snapshot. Because only RDB persistence works with snapshot files, we will overwrite the `configmap` value to read `appendonly no`, which will disable AOF persistence.

With each Redis value identified, add these values to the end of your chart's `values.yaml` file, as shown in the following code block:

```
redis:
  # Override the redis.fullname template
  fullnameOverride: redis
  # Enable unauthenticated access to Redis
  usePassword: false
  # Disable AOF persistence
  configmap: |-
    appendonly no
```

Remember from *Chapter 4, Understanding Helm Charts,* that values overridden from a chart dependency must be scoped underneath that chart name. That is why each of these values will be added underneath a `redis:` stanza.

You can check that you have configured your Redis values properly by referencing the `values.yaml` file located at `https://github.com/PacktPublishing/-Learn-Helm/blob/master/helm-charts/charts/guestbook/values.yaml` in the Packt repository.

> **Important note**
> Some values unrelated to Redis may differ from your `values.yaml` file, as we will be modifying these in the next section.

With the Redis dependency's values configured, let's proceed to modify the default values generated by `helm create` to deploy the Guestbook frontend.

Modifying values to deploy the Guestbook frontend

When you ran the `helm create` command at the beginning of the chapter, some of the items that it created were default templates under the `templates/` directory and default values in the `values.yaml` file.

Here is a list of the default templates that were created:

- `deployment.yaml`: Used to deploy the Guestbook application to Kubernetes.
- `ingress.yaml`: Provides one option to access the Guestbook application from outside the Kubernetes cluster.
- `serviceaccount.yaml`: Used to create a dedicated `serviceaccount` for the Guestbook application.
- `service.yaml`: Used to load-balance between multiple instances of the Guestbook application. Can also provide an option to access the Guestbook application from outside the Kubernetes cluster.
- `_helpers.tp`: Provides a set of common templates used throughout the Helm chart.
- `NOTES.txt`: Provides a set of instructions used to access the application after it is installed.

Each of these templates is configured by the chart's values. While the `helm create` command gave a great starting point toward deploying the Guestbook application, it did not provide each of the default values needed. In order to replace the defaults with their required values, we can observe the generated chart templates and modify their parameters accordingly.

Let's walk through the template locations that indicate where modifications need to be made.

The first location is in the `deployment.yaml` chart template. Within that file, there is a line that indicates the container image to deploy, as illustrated here:

```
image: '{{ .Values.image.repository }}:{{ .Chart.AppVersion }}'
```

As you can see, the image is determined by the `image.repository` value and the `AppVersion` chart setting. If you look in your `values.yaml` file, you can see that the `image.repository` value is currently configured to deploy the `nginx` image by default, as illustrated here:

```
image:
  repository: nginx
```

Similarly, if you look in the `Chart.yaml` file, you can see that the `AppVersion` is currently set to `1.16.0`, as illustrated here:

```
appVersion: 1.16.0
```

Since the Guestbook application originated as a Kubernetes tutorial, you can find the specific image that needs to be deployed in the Kubernetes documentation at `https://kubernetes.io/docs/tutorials/stateless-application/guestbook/#creating-the-guestbook-frontend-deployment`. In the documentation, you can see that the image must be specified as follows:

```
image: gcr.io/google-samples/gb-frontend:v4
```

As a result, in order for the image field to be properly generated, the `image.repository` value must be set to `gcr.io/google-samples/gb-frontend`, and the `AppVersion` chart setting must be set to `v4`.

The second location where a modification must be made is in the `service.yaml` chart template. In this file, there is a line that determines the service type, as illustrated here:

```
type: {{ .Values.service.type }}
```

According to the `service.type` value, this service will default to having a `ClusterIP` service type, shown in the `values.yaml` file as follows:

```
service:
  type: ClusterIP
```

For the `guestbook` chart, we will modify this value to instead create a `NodePort` service. This will allow the application to be accessed easier in a minikube environment by exposing a port on the minikube **virtual machine** (**VM**). Once connected to the port, we can access the Guestbook frontend.

Note that while `helm create` generated an `ingress.yaml` template that would also allow access, `NodePort` services are more commonly recommended when working in minikube environments because add-ons or enhancements are not required. Luckily, the generated chart disables the ingress resource creation by default, so no action is required to disable this feature.

Now that we have determined the default settings that need to be changed, let's proceed by first updating the `values.yaml` file, as follows:

1. Replace the `image.repository` value so that it is set to `gcr.io/google-samples/gb-frontend`. The entire `image:` stanza should now read as follows:

```
image:
  repository: gcr.io/google-samples/gb-frontend
  pullPolicy: IfNotPresent
```

2. Replace the `service.type` value so that it is set to `NodePort`. The entire `service:` stanza should now read as follows:

```
service:
  type: NodePort
  port: 80
```

3. You can verify that your `values.yaml` file has been modified correctly by referring to the file in the Packt repository at `https://github.com/PacktPublishing/-Learn-Helm/blob/master/helm-charts/charts/guestbook/values.yaml`.

Next, let's update the `Chart.yaml` file so that the correct Guestbook application version is deployed, as follows:

1. Replace the `appVersion` field so that it is set to v4. The `appVersion` field should now read as follows:

```
appVersion: v4
```

2. You can verify that your `Chart.yaml` file has been modified correctly by referring to the file in the Packt repository at `https://github.com/PacktPublishing/-Learn-Helm/blob/master/helm-charts/charts/guestbook/Chart.yaml`.

Now that the chart has been updated with the proper values and settings, let's see this chart in action by deploying it to the minikube environment.

Installing the Guestbook chart

To install your `guestbook` chart, run the following command outside of your `guestbook/` directory:

```
$ helm install my-guestbook guestbook -n chapter5
```

The following message will be displayed if the installation was successful:

```
NAME: my-guestbook
LAST DEPLOYED: Sun Apr 26 09:57:52 2020
NAMESPACE: chapter5
STATUS: deployed
REVISION: 1
NOTES:
1. Get the application URL by running these commands:
   export NODE_PORT=$(kubectl get --namespace chapter5 -o
jsonpath='{.spec.ports[0].nodePort}' services my-guestbook)
   export NODE_IP=$(kubectl get nodes --namespace chapter5 -o
jsonpath='{.items[0].status.addresses[0].address}')
   echo http://$NODE_IP:$NODE_PORT
```

While the installation was successful, you may find that the Guestbook and Redis pods are not immediately in the `Ready` state. When a Pod is not ready, it cannot be accessed yet.

You can also force Helm to wait until these pods become ready by passing in the `--wait` flag. The `--wait` flag can be accompanied by the `--timeout` flag to increase the amount of time in seconds that Helm will wait for pods to become ready. The default is set to 5 minutes, which would be more than enough time for this application.

You can ensure that all pods are ready without the `--wait` flag by checking each Pod's status, as follows:

```
$ kubectl get pods -n chapter5
```

When each Pod is ready, you will be able to observe that each Pod reports `1/1` under the READY column, as illustrated here:

```
NAME                                READY   STATUS    RESTARTS
my-guestbook-55ffc69c6f-tc27h       1/1     Running   0
redis-master-0                      1/1     Running   0
redis-slave-0                       1/1     Running   0
redis-slave-1                       1/1     Running   0
```

Figure 5.4: Output of kubectl get pods –n chapter5 when each Pod is ready

Once the pods are ready, you can run the commands that were displayed by the release notes. If necessary, they can be displayed again by running the following code:

```
$ helm get notes my-guestbook -n chapter5

NOTES:

1. Get the application URL by running these commands:

   export NODE_PORT=$(kubectl get --namespace chapter5 -o jsonpath='{.spec.ports[0].nodePort}' services my-guestbook)

   export NODE_IP=$(kubectl get nodes --namespace chapter5 -o jsonpath='{.items[0].status.addresses[0].address}')

   echo http://$NODE_IP:$NODE_PORT
```

Copy and paste the Guestbook URL (output from the `echo` command) into your browser, and the Guestbook **user interface (UI)** should be displayed, as illustrated in the following screenshot:

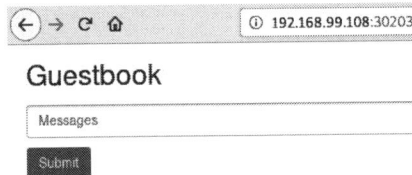

Figure 5.5: The Guestbook frontend

Try to type a message in the dialog box and click **Submit**. The Guestbook frontend will display the message under the **Submit** button, which indicates that the message has been saved to the Redis database, as illustrated in the following screenshot:

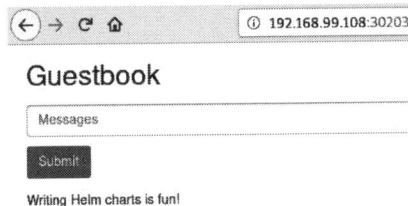

Figure 5.6: The Guestbook frontend displaying a previously sent message

If you are able to write a message and see it displayed on your screen, then you have successfully built and deployed your first Helm chart! If you are not able to see your messages, your Redis dependency may not have been set up correctly. In that case, make sure that your Redis values have been configured properly and that your Redis dependency has been properly declared in the `Chart.yaml` file.

When you are ready, uninstall this chart with the `helm uninstall` command, like this:

```
$ helm uninstall my-guestbook -n chapter5
```

You will also need to manually remove the Redis **PersistentVolumeClaims** (**PVCs**), since the Redis dependency made the database persistent by using `StatefulSet` (which does not automatically remove PVCs when deleted).

Run the following command to remove the Redis PVCs:

```
$ kubectl delete pvc -l app=redis -n chapter5
```

In the next section, we will explore ways in which the `guestbook` chart can be improved.

Improving the Guestbook Helm chart

The chart created in the previous section was able to successfully deploy the Guestbook application. However, as is the case with any type of software, the Helm chart can always be improved. In this section, we will focus on the following two features that will improve the `guestbook` chart:

- Life cycle hooks to back up and restore the Redis database
- Input validation to ensure only valid values are provided

Let's focus first on adding life cycle hooks.

Creating pre-upgrade and pre-rollback life cycle hooks

In this section, we will create two life cycle hooks, as follows:

1. The first hook will occur in the `pre-upgrade` life cycle phase. This phase takes place immediately after the `helm upgrade` command is run, but before any Kubernetes resources become modified. This hook will be used to take a data snapshot of the Redis database before performing the upgrade, ensuring that the database is backed up in case the upgrade is errant.

2.   The second hook will occur in the `pre-rollback` life cycle phase. This phase takes place immediately after the `helm rollback` command is run but before any Kubernetes resources are reverted. This hook will restore the Redis database to a previously taken data snapshot and will ensure that the Kubernetes resource configuration is reverted to match the way it was at the point the snapshot was taken.

By the end of this section, you will become more familiar with life cycle hooks and some of the powerful capabilities that can be performed with them. Be sure to keep in mind that the hooks created in this section are very simple and are only there for exploring the basic capabilities of Helm hooks. It is not advised to try to use these hooks verbatim in a production environment.

Let's walk through how the `pre-upgrade` life cycle hook can be created.

Creating the pre-upgrade hook to take a data snapshot

In Redis, data snapshots are contained inside a `dump.rdb` file. We can back this file up by creating a hook that first creates a new PVC in the Kubernetes namespace. The hook can then create a `job` resource that copies the `dump.rdb` file to the new `PersistentVolumeClaim`.

While the `helm create` command generates some powerful resource templates that allow the initial `guestbook` chart to be created quickly, it does not scaffold out any hooks that can be used for this task. As a result, you can create the pre-upgrade hook from scratch by following these steps:

1.   First, you should create a new folder to contain the hook templates. While this is not a technical requirement, it does help keep your hook templates separate from the regular chart templates. It also allows you to group the hook templates by function.

     Create a new folder called `templates/backup` in your `guestbook` file structure, as follows:

     ```
     $ mkdir guestbook/templates/backup
     ```

2.   Next, you should scaffold the two templates required to perform the backup. The first template required is a `PersistentVolumeClaim` template that will be used to contain the copied `dump.rdb` file. The second template will be a job template that will be used to perform the copy.

Create two empty template files to serve as placeholders, as follows:

```
$ touch guestbook/templates/backup/persistentvolumeclaim.
yaml
$ touch guestbook/templates/backup/job.yaml
```

3. You can double-check your work by referencing the Packt repository. Your file structure should appear identical to the structure found at `https://github.com/PacktPublishing/-Learn-Helm/tree/master/helm-charts/charts/guestbook/templates/backup`.

4. Next, let's create the `persistentvolumeclaim.yaml` template. Copy the contents of the file below to your `backup/persistentvolumeclaim.yaml` file (this file can also be copied from the Packt repository at `https://github.com/PacktPublishing/-Learn-Helm/blob/master/helm-charts/charts/guestbook/templates/backup/persistentvolumeclaim.yaml`. Keep in mind that whitespace consists of `spaces`, not tabs, as per valid YAML syntax. The contents of the file can be seen here:

```
1   {{- if .Values.redis.master.persistence.enabled }}
2   apiVersion: v1
3   kind: PersistentVolumeClaim
4   metadata:
5     name: redis-data-{{ .Values.redis.fullnameOverride }}-master-0-backup-{{ sub .Release.Revision 1 }}
6     labels:
7       {{- include "guestbook.labels" . | nindent 4 }}
8     annotations:
9       "helm.sh/hook": pre-upgrade
10      "helm.sh/hook-weight": "0"
11  spec:
12    accessModes:
13      - ReadWriteOnce
14    resources:
15      requests:
16        storage: {{ .Values.redis.master.persistence.size }}
17  {{- end }}
```

Figure 5.7: The backup/persistentvolumeclaim.yaml template

Before proceeding, let's walk through part of the `persistentvolumeclaim.yaml` file to help understand how it was created.

Lines 1 and *17* of this file consist of an `if` action. Since the action encapsulates the whole file, it indicates that this resource will only be included if the `redis.master.persistence.enabled` value is set to `true`. This value defaults to `true` in the Redis dependency chart and can be observed using the `helm show values` command.

Line 5 determines the name of the new PVC backup. Its name is based on the name given to the Redis master PVC created by the Redis dependency chart, which is `redis-data-redis-master-0`, so that it is obvious which PVC this is designed to be a backup of. Its name is also based on the revision number. Because this hook is run as a pre-upgrade hook, it will try to use the revision number being upgraded to. The `sub` function is used to subtract `1` from this revision number, so it is obvious that this PVC contains the data snapshot of the previous revision.

Line 9 creates an annotation to declare this resource as a `pre-upgrade` hook. *Line 10* creates a `helm.sh/hook-weight` annotation to determine the order in which this resource should be created compared to other pre-upgrade hooks. Weights are run in ascending order, so this resource will be created before other pre-upgrade resources.

5. After the `persistentvolumeclaim.yaml` file is created, we will create the final pre-upgrade template, `job.yaml`. Copy the following content to your `backup/job.yaml` file (this file can also be copied from the Packt repository at `https://github.com/PacktPublishing/-Learn-Helm/blob/master/helm-charts/charts/guestbook/templates/backup/job.yaml`):

```
 1  {{- if .Values.redis.master.persistence.enabled }}
 2  apiVersion: batch/v1
 3  kind: Job
 4  metadata:
 5    name: {{ include "guestbook.fullname" . }}-backup
 6    labels:
 7      {{- include "guestbook.labels" . | nindent 4 }}
 8    annotations:
 9      "helm.sh/hook": pre-upgrade
10      "helm.sh/hook-delete-policy": before-hook-creation,hook-succeeded
11      "helm.sh/hook-weight": "1"
12  spec:
13    template:
14      spec:
15        containers:
16          - name: backup
17            image: redis:alpine3.11
18            command: ["/bin/sh", "-c"]
19            args: ["redis-cli -h {{ .Values.redis.fullnameOverride }}-master save && cp /data/dump.rdb /backup/dump.rdb"]
20            volumeMounts:
21              - name: redis-data
22                mountPath: /data
23              - name: backup
24                mountPath: /backup
25        restartPolicy: Never
26        volumes:
27          - name: redis-data
28            persistentVolumeClaim:
29              claimName: redis-data-{{ .Values.redis.fullnameOverride }}-master-0
30          - name: backup
31            persistentVolumeClaim:
32              claimName: redis-data-{{ .Values.redis.fullnameOverride }}-master-0-backup-{{ sub .Release.Revision 1 }}
33  {{- end }}
```

Figure 5.8: The backup/job.yaml template

Let's walk through part of this `job.yaml` template to understand how it was created.

Line 9 once again defines this template to be a pre-upgrade hook. *Line 11* sets the hook weight to `1`, indicating that this resource will be created after the other pre-upgrade `PersistentVolumeClaim`.

Line 10 sets a new annotation to determine when this job should be deleted. By default, Helm does not manage hooks beyond their initial creation, meaning that they will not be deleted when the `helm uninstall` command is run. The `helm.sh/hook-delete-policy` annotation is used to determine the conditions in which a resource should be deleted. This job contains the `before-hook-creation` delete policy, which indicates it will be removed during a `helm upgrade` command if it already exists in the namespace, allowing a fresh job to be created in its place. This job will also have the `hook-succeeded` delete policy, which will result in its deletion if it is run successfully.

Line 19 performs the backup of the `dump.rdb` file. It connects to the Redis master, saves the state of the database, and copies the file to the backup PVC.

Lines 29 and *32* define the Redis master PVC and backup PVC, respectively. These PVCs are mounted by the job in order to copy the dump.rdb file.

If you have followed along with each of the preceding steps, then you have created your pre-upgrade hooks for your Helm chart. Let's continue to the next section to create the pre-rollback hook. Afterward, we will redeploy the guestbook chart to see these hooks in action.

Creating the pre-rollback hook to restore the database

Whereas the pre-upgrade hook was written to copy the dump.rdb file from the Redis master PVC to the backup PVC, the pre-rollback hook can be written to perform the reverse action to restore the database to a previous snapshot.

Follow these steps to create the pre-rollback hook:

1. Create the templates/restore folder, which will be used to contain the pre-rollback hook, as follows:

    ```
    $ mkdir guestbook/templates/restore
    ```

2. Next, scaffold an empty job.yaml template, which will be used to restore the database, as follows:

    ```
    $ touch guestbook/templates/restore/job.yaml
    ```

3. You can check that you have created the correct structure by referencing the Packt repository at https://github.com/PacktPublishing/-Learn-Helm/tree/master/helm-charts/charts/guestbook/templates/restore.

4. Next, let's add content to the job.yaml file. Copy the following content to your restore/job.yaml file (this file can also be copied from the Packt repository at https://github.com/PacktPublishing/-Learn-Helm/blob/master/helm-charts/charts/guestbook/templates/restore/job.yaml):

```
1   {{- if .Values.redis.master.persistence.enabled }}
2   apiVersion: batch/v1
3   kind: Job
4   metadata:
5     name: {{ include "guestbook.fullname" . }}-restore
6     labels:
7       {{- include "guestbook.labels" . | nindent 4 }}
8     annotations:
9       "helm.sh/hook": pre-rollback
10      "helm.sh/hook-delete-policy": before-hook-creation,hook-succeeded
11  spec:
12    template:
13      spec:
14        containers:
15          - name: restore
16            image: redis:alpine3.11
17            command: ["/bin/sh", "-c"]
18            args: ["cp /backup/dump.rdb /data/dump.rdb &&
19              redis-cli -h {{ .Values.redis.fullnameOverride }}-master debug restart || true"]
20            volumeMounts:
21              - name: redis-data
22                mountPath: /data
23              - name: backup
24                mountPath: /backup
25        restartPolicy: Never
26        volumes:
27          - name: redis-data
28            persistentVolumeClaim:
29              claimName: redis-data-{{ .Values.redis.fullnameOverride }}-master-0
30          - name: backup
31            persistentVolumeClaim:
32              claimName: redis-data-{{ .Values.redis.fullnameOverride }}-master-0-backup-{{ .Release.Revision }}
33  {{- end }}
```

Figure 5.9: The rollback/job.yaml template

Line 7 of this template declares this resource as a `pre-rollback` hook.

The actual data restore is performed on *lines 18* and *19*. *Line 18* copies the `dump.rdb` file from the backup PVC to the Redis master PVC. Once copied, *line 19* restarts the database so that the snapshot can be reloaded. The command used to restart the Redis database will return a failed exit code because the connection to the database will be terminated unexpectedly, but this can be resolved by appending `|| true` to the command, which will negate the exit code.

Line 29 defines the Redis master volume, and *line 32* defines the desired backup volume, which is determined by the revision that it is being rolled back to.

With the pre-upgrade and pre-rollback life cycle hooks created, let's see them in action by running them in the minikube environment.

Executing the life cycle hooks

In order to run the life cycle hooks you created, you must first install your chart again by running the `helm install` command, as follows:

```
$ helm install my-guestbook guestbook -n chapter5
```

When each Pod reports the `1/1 Ready` state, access your Guestbook application by following the displayed release notes. Note that the port to access the application will be different than it was previously.

Write a message once you access the Guestbook frontend. An example message can be seen in the following screenshot:

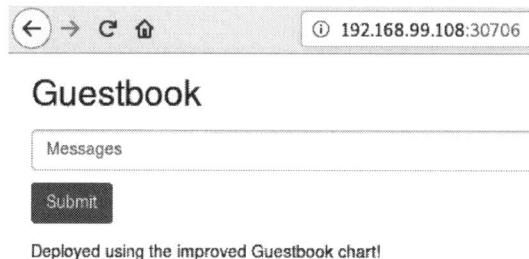

Figure 5.10: The Guestbook frontend upon installing the Guestbook chart and entering a message

Once a message has been written and its text is displayed under the **Submit** button, run the `helm upgrade` command to trigger the pre-upgrade hook. The `helm upgrade` command will hang briefly until the backup has finished, and can be seen here:

```
$ helm upgrade my-guestbook guestbook -n chapter5
```

When the command returns, you should find the Redis master PVC along with a new PVC created, called `redis-data-redis-master-0-backup-1`, which can be seen here:

```
$ kubectl get pvc -n chapter5
```

NAME	STATUS
redis-data-redis-master-0	Bound
redis-data-redis-master-0-backup-1	Bound

This PVC contains a data snapshot that can be used to restore the database during the pre-rollback life cycle phase.

Let's now proceed to add an additional message to the Guestbook frontend. You should have two messages appear under the **Submit** button, as illustrated in the following screenshot:

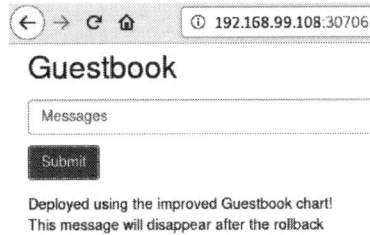

Figure 5.11: Guestbook messages before running the rollback

Now, run the `helm rollback` command to revert back to the first revision. This command will hang briefly until the restore process is finished, and can be seen here:

```
$ helm rollback my-guestbook 1 -n chapter5
```

When this command returns, refresh your Guestbook frontend in the browser. You will see the message you added after the upgrade disappear because it did not exist before the data backup was taken, as illustrated in the following screenshot:

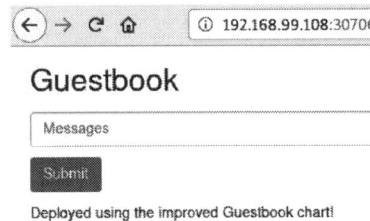

Figure 5.12: The Guestbook frontend after the pre-rollback life cycle phase is complete

While this backup-and-restore scenario served as a simple use case, it demonstrates one of many possibilities that adding Helm life cycle hooks to your charts can provide.

> **Important note**
>
> Hooks can be skipped by adding the `--no-hooks` flag to the corresponding life cycle command (`helm install`, `helm upgrade`, `helm rollback`, or `helm uninstall`). The command to which this command is applied will skip the hooks for that life cycle.

We will now focus on user input validation and how the Guestbook chart can be further improved upon to help prevent improper values from being provided.

Adding input validation

When working with Kubernetes and Helm, input validation is automatically performed by the Kubernetes **application programming interface** (**API**) server when a new resource is created. This means that if an invalid resource is created by Helm, an error message will be returned by the API server, resulting in a failed installation. Although Kubernetes performs native input validation, there may still be cases in which chart developers will want to perform validation before the resources reach the API server.

Let's begin exploring how input validation can be performed by using the `fail` function in the `guestbook` Helm chart.

Using the fail function

The `fail` function is used to immediately fail template rendering. This function can be used in cases where users have provided a value that is invalid. In this section, we will implement an example use case to restrict user input.

Your `guestbook` chart's `values.yaml` file contains a value called `service.type`, which is used for determining the type of service that should be created for the frontend. This value can be seen here:

```
service:
  type: NodePort
```

We set this value to default to `NodePort`, but technically, other service types can be used. Imagine you wanted to restrict the service type to only `NodePort` and `ClusterIP` services. This action can be performed by using the `fail` function.

Follow these steps to restrict the service type in your `guestbook` chart:

1. Locate the `templates/service.yaml` service template. This file contains a line that sets the service type depending on the `service.type` value, as illustrated here:

    ```
    type: {{ .Values.service.type }}
    ```

We should check that the `service.type` value first equals `ClusterIP` or `NodePort` before setting the service type. This can be done by setting a variable to the list of proper settings. Then, a check can be performed to ascertain that the `service.type` value is included in the list of valid settings. If it is, then proceed to set the service type. Otherwise, chart rendering should be halted and an error message should be returned to the user, notifying them of the valid `service.type` inputs.

2. Copy the `service.yaml` file illustrated next to implement the logic described in *Step 1*. This file can also be copied from the Packt repository at `https://github.com/PacktPublishing/-Learn-Helm/blob/master/helm-charts/charts/guestbook/templates/service.yaml`:

```
1   apiVersion: v1
2   kind: Service
3   metadata:
4     name: {{ include "guestbook.fullname" . }}
5     labels:
6       {{- include "guestbook.labels" . | nindent 4 }}
7   spec:
8   {{- $serviceTypes := list "ClusterIP" "NodePort" }}
9   {{- if has .Values.service.type $serviceTypes }}
10    type: {{ .Values.service.type }}
11  {{- else }}
12    {{- fail "value 'service.type' must be either 'ClusterIP' or 'NodePort'" }}
13  {{- end }}
14    ports:
15      - port: {{ .Values.service.port }}
16        targetPort: http
17        protocol: TCP
18        name: http
19    selector:
20      {{- include "guestbook.selectorLabels" . | nindent 4 }}
```

Figure 5.13: The service.type validation implemented in the service.yaml template

Lines 8 through *13* represent the input validation. *Line 8* creates a variable called `serviceTypes` that equals a list of proper service types. *Lines 9* through *13* represent an `if` action. The `has` function in *line 9* will check whether the `service.type` value is included in `serviceTypes`. If it is, then rendering will proceed to *line 10* to set the service's type. Otherwise, rendering will proceed to *line 12*. *Line 12* uses the `fail` function to halt template rendering and displays a message to the user about the valid service types.

Attempt to upgrade your `my-guestbook` release by providing an invalid service type (if you have uninstalled your release, an installation will suffice as well). To do so, run the following command:

```
$ helm upgrade my-guestbook . -n chapter5 --set service.type=LoadBalancer
```

If your changes in the preceding *Step 2* were successful, you should see a message similar to the following:

```
Error: UPGRADE FAILED: template: guestbook/templates/service.
yaml:12:6: executing 'guestbook/templates/service.yaml' at
<fail 'value 'service.type' must be either 'ClusterIP' or
'NodePort''>: error calling fail: value 'service.type' must be
either 'ClusterIP' or 'NodePort'
```

While validating a user's input with `fail` is a good way to ensure that provided values fit within a certain set of constraints, there are also occasions where you need to ensure that users have even provided certain values in the first place. This can be accomplished by using the `required` function, explained in the next section.

Using the required function

The `required` function, like `fail`, is also used to halt template rendering. The difference is that, unlike `fail`, the `required` function is used to ensure that a value is not left blank when the chart's templates are rendered.

Recall that your chart contains a value called `image.repository`, as illustrated here:

```
image:
  repository: gcr.io/google-samples/gb-frontend
```

This value is used to determine the image that will be deployed. Given this value's importance to the Helm chart, we can back it with the `required` function to ensure that it always has a value when the chart is installed. Although we provide a default in this chart currently, adding the `required` function would allow you to remove this default if you wanted to ensure that users always provided their own container image.

Follow these steps to implement the `required` function against the `image.repository` value:

1. Locate the `templates/deployment.yaml` chart template. The file contains a line that sets the container image based on the `image.repository` value (the `appName` chart setting also helps to set the container image, but for this example, we will focus only on `image.repository`), as illustrated here:

    ```
    image: '{{ .Values.image.repository }}:{{ .Chart.
    AppVersion }}'
    ```

2. The `required` function takes the following two arguments:

*   An error message to display whether the value is provided
    The value that must be provided

Given these two arguments, modify the `deployment.yaml` file so that the `image.repository` value is required.

To add this validation, you can copy from the following code snippet or reference the Packt repository at `https://github.com/PacktPublishing/-Learn-Helm/blob/master/helm-charts/charts/guestbook/templates/deployment.yaml`:

```
24    containers:
25      - name: {{ .Chart.Name }}
26        securityContext:
27          {{- toYaml .Values.securityContext | nindent 12 }}
28        image: "{{ required "value 'image.repository' is required" .Values.image.repository }}:{{ .Chart.AppVersion }}"
29        imagePullPolicy: {{ .Values.image.pullPolicy }}
30        ports:
31          - name: http
32            containerPort: 80
33            protocol: TCP
```

Figure 5.14: The deployment.yaml snippet that uses the required function on line 28

3. Attempt to upgrade your `my-guestbook` release by providing an empty `image.repository` value, as follows:

```
$ helm upgrade my-guestbook . -n chapter5 --set image.
repository=''
```

If your changes were successful, you should see an error message similar to the following:

```
Error: UPGRADE FAILED: execution error at (guestbook/
templates/deployment.yaml:28:21): value 'image.
repository' is required
```

At this point, you have successfully written your first Helm chart, complete with life cycle hooks and input validation!

In the next section, you will learn how to create a simple chart repository using GitHub Pages, which can be used to make your `guestbook` chart available to the world.

Publishing the Guestbook chart to a chart repository

Now that you have completed the development of the Guestbook chart, the chart can be published to a repository so that it is easily accessible for other users. Let's begin by first creating the chart repository.

Creating a chart repository

Chart repositories are servers containing two different components, as follows:

- Helm charts, packaged as `tgz` archives

- An `index.yaml` file, containing metadata about the charts contained in the repository

Basic chart repositories require maintainers to generate their own `index.yaml` files, while more complex solutions such as the Helm community's `ChartMuseum` tool dynamically generate the `index.yaml` file when new charts are pushed to the repository. In this example, we will create a simple chart repository using GitHub Pages. GitHub Pages allows maintainers to create a simple static hosting site out of a GitHub repository, which can be used to create a basic chart repository to serve Helm charts.

You will need to have a GitHub account to create a GitHub Pages chart repository. If you already have a GitHub account, you can log in at `https://github.com/login`. Otherwise, you can create a new account at `https://github.com/join`.

Once you have logged in to GitHub, follow these steps to create your chart repository:

1. Follow the `https://github.com/new` link to access the **Create a new repository** page.

2. Provide a name for your chart repository. We suggest the name `Learn-Helm-Chart-Repository`.

3. Select the checkbox next to **Initialize this repository with a README**. This is required because GitHub does not allow you to create a static site if it does not contain any content.

4. You can leave the rest of the settings at their default values. Note that in order to leverage GitHub Pages, you must leave the privacy setting set to **Public** unless you have a paid GitHub Pro account.

5. Click the **Create Repository** button to finish the repository creation process.

6. Although your repository has been created, it is not ready to serve Helm charts until GitHub Pages is enabled. Click the **Settings** tab within your repository to access your repository settings.

7. Locate the **GitHub Pages** section of the **Settings** page (and **Options** tab). It appears toward the bottom of the page.

8. Under **Source**, select the option in the drop-down list called **master branch**. This will allow GitHub to create a static site that serves the contents of your master branch.

9. If you have successfully configured GitHub Pages, you will receive a message at the top of the screen that says **GitHub Pages source saved**. You will also be able to see the URL to your static site, as displayed in the following example screenshot:

GitHub Pages

GitHub Pages is designed to host your personal, organization, or project pages from a GitHub repository.

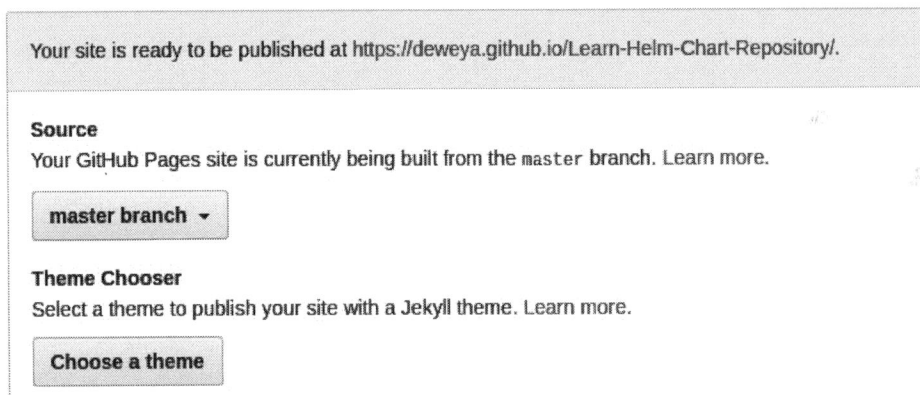

Your site is ready to be published at https://deweya.github.io/Learn-Helm-Chart-Repository/.

Source
Your GitHub Pages site is currently being built from the master branch. Learn more.

[master branch ▾]

Theme Chooser
Select a theme to publish your site with a Jekyll theme. Learn more.

[Choose a theme]

Figure 5.15: The GitHub Pages settings and example URL

Once you have configured your GitHub repository, you should clone it to your local machine. Follow these steps to clone your repository:

1. Navigate to the root of your repository by selecting the **Code** tab at the top of the page.

2. Select the green **Clone or download** button. This will reveal the URL to your GitHub repository. Note that this URL is not the same as your GitHub Pages static site.

You can use the following example screenshot as a reference to find your GitHub repository URL, if necessary:

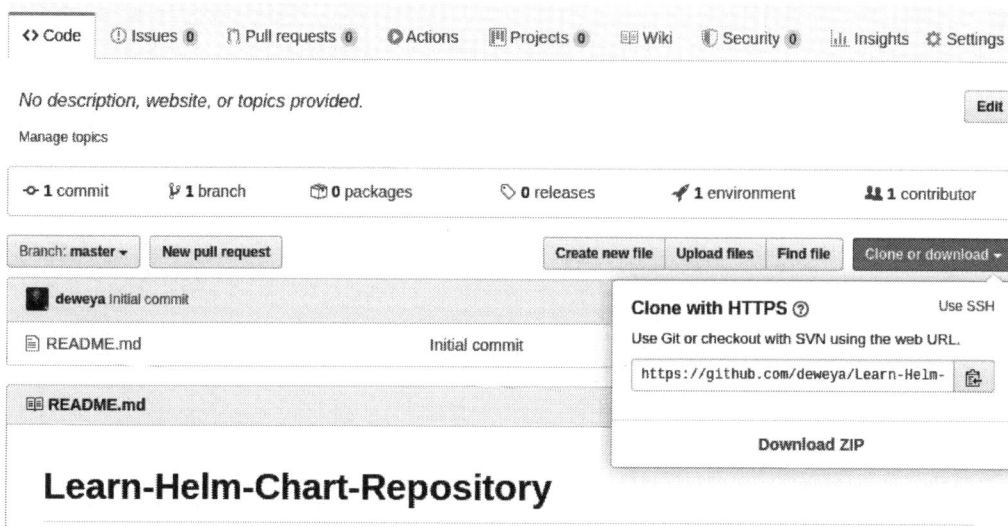

Figure 5.16: Your GitHub repository URL can be found by clicking the Clone or download button

3. Once you have acquired your repository's `git` reference, clone the repository to your local machine. Make sure you are not inside your `guestbook` directory when running the following command, as we want this repository to be separate from the `guestbook` chart:

```
$ git clone $REPOSITORY_URL
```

Once you have cloned the repository, continue to the next section to publish your `guestbook` chart to your chart repository.

Publishing the Guestbook Helm chart

Helm provides a couple of different commands to make publishing a Helm chart a simple task. However, before running these commands, you may find it necessary to increment your chart's `version` field in the `Chart.yaml` file. Versioning your charts is an important part of the release process, as is the case in other types of software.

Modify the version field in your chart's `Chart.yaml` file to 1.0.0, as follows:

```
version: 1.0.0
```

Once your `guestbook` chart's version has been incremented, you can proceed by packaging your chart into a `tgz` archive. This can be accomplished using the `helm package` command. Run this command from one level above your local `guestbook` directory, as follows:

```
$ helm package guestbook
```

If successful, this will create a file called `guestbook-1.0.0.tgz`.

> **Important note**
>
> When working with charts that contain dependencies, the `helm package` command requires those dependencies to be downloaded to the `charts/` directory in order to successfully package the chart. If your `helm package` command failed, check that your Redis dependency has been downloaded to the `charts/` directory. If it has not, you can add the `--dependency-update` flag to `helm package`, which will download the dependency and package your Helm chart in the same command.

Once your chart is packaged, the resulting `tgz` file should be copied to the clone of your GitHub chart repository by running the following command:

```
$ cp guestbook-1.0.0.tgz $GITHUB_CHART_REPO_CLONE
```

When this file is copied, you can use the `helm repo index` command to generate the `index.yaml` file for your Helm repository. This command takes as an argument the location of your chart repository clone. Run the following command to generate your `index.yaml` file:

```
$ helm repo index $GITHUB_CHART_REPO_CLONE
```

This command will succeed quietly, but you will see the new `index.yaml` file inside the `Learn-Helm-Chart-Repository` folder. The contents of this file provide the `guestbook` chart metadata. If there were other charts contained in this repository, their metadata would appear in this file as well.

Your Helm chart repository should now contain the `tgz` archive and the `index.yaml` file. Push these files to GitHub by using the following `git` commands:

```
$ git add --all
$ git commit -m 'feat: adding the guestbook helm chart'
$ git push origin master
```

You may be prompted to enter your GitHub credentials. Once provided, your local contents will be pushed to the remote repository, and your `guestbook` Helm chart will be served from the GitHub Pages static site.

Next, let's add your chart repository to your local Helm client.

Adding your chart repository

Similar to the process for other chart repositories, you must first know the URL to your GitHub Pages chart repository in order to add it locally. This URL was displayed in the **Settings** tab, as described in the *Creating a chart repository* section.

Once you know your chart repository's URL, you can add this repository locally with the `helm repo add` command, as follows:

```
$ helm repo add learnhelm $GITHUB_PAGES_URL
```

This command will allow your local Helm client to interact with your repository with the name `learnhelm`. You can verify that your chart was published by searching for the `guestbook` chart against your locally configured repos. This can be done by running the following command:

```
$ helm search repo guestbook
```

You should find the `learnhelm/guestbook` chart returned in the search output.

With your `guestbook` chart successfully published, let's finish by cleaning up your minikube environment.

Cleaning up

You can clean up your environment by deleting the `chapter5` namespace, as follows:

```
$ kubectl delete namespace chapter5
```

If you have finished working, you can also stop your minikube cluster with the `minikube stop` command.

Summary

In this chapter, you learned how to build a Helm chart from scratch by writing a chart to deploy the Guestbook application. You began by creating a chart that deployed the Guestbook frontend and a Redis dependency chart, and you later improved upon this chart by writing life cycle hooks and adding input validation. You concluded this chapter by building your own chart repository with GitHub Pages and publishing your guestbook chart to this location.

In the next chapter, you will learn strategies around testing and debugging a Helm chart, to enable you to further strengthen your chart development skills.

Further reading

For additional information on the Guestbook application, please refer to the *Deploying PHP Guestbook application with Redis* tutorial from the Kubernetes documentation, at `https://kubernetes.io/docs/tutorials/stateless-application/guestbook/`.

To learn more about developing Helm chart templates, please refer to the following links:

- *Chart Development Guide from the Helm documentation*: `https://helm.sh/docs/chart_template_guide/getting_started/`

- *List of best practices from the Helm documentation*: `https://helm.sh/docs/topics/chart_best_practices/conventions/`

- Additional information on chart hooks: `https://helm.sh/docs/topics/charts_hooks/`

- Information on chart repositories: `https://helm.sh/docs/topics/chart_repository/`

Questions

1. Which command can be used to scaffold a new Helm chart?

2. Which key advantages did declaring a Redis chart dependency provide when developing the guestbook chart?

3. What annotation can be used to set the execution order of hooks for a given life cycle phase?

4. What are the common use cases for using the `fail` function? What about the `required` function?

5. Which Helm commands are involved in order to publish a Helm chart to a GitHub Pages chart repository?

6. What is the purpose of the `index.yaml` file in a chart repository?

6
Testing Helm Charts

Testing is a common task that engineers must perform during software development. Testing is performed to validate the functionality of a product as well as to prevent regressions as a product evolves over time. Well-tested software is easier to maintain over time and allows developers to more confidently provide new releases to end users.

A Helm chart should be properly tested in order to ensure that it delivers its features to the level of quality expected. In this chapter, we will discuss the ways that robust Helm chart testing can be achieved, including the following topics:

- Setting up your environment
- Verifying Helm templating
- Testing in a live cluster
- Improving chart tests with the chart testing project
- Cleaning up

Technical requirements

This chapter will use the following technologies:

- `minikube`

- `kubectl`

- `helm`

- `git`

- `yamllint`

- `yamale`

- `chart-testing(ct)`

In addition to these tools, you can follow along with the samples in the Packt GitHub repository located at `https://github.com/PacktPublishing/-Learn-Helm`, which will be referenced throughout this chapter. In many of the example commands used throughout this chapter, we will reference the Packt repository, so you may find it helpful to clone this repository by running the `git clone` command:

```
$ git clone https://github.com/PacktPublishing/-Learn-Helm
Learn-Helm
```

Now, let's proceed with setting up your local `minikube` environment.

Setting up your environment

In this chapter, we will create and run a series of tests for the `Guestbook` chart created in the previous chapter. Run the following steps to set up your `minikube` environment, where we will test the Guestbook chart:

1. Start `minikube` by running the `minikube start` command:

   ```
   minikube start
   ```

2. Then, create a new namespace called `chapter6`:

   ```
   kubectl create namespace chapter6
   ```

With your `minikube` environment ready, let's begin by discussing how Helm charts can be tested. We will begin the discussion by outlining the methods you can use to verify your Helm templates.

Verifying Helm templating

In the previous chapter, we built a Helm chart from scratch. The final product was quite complex, containing parameterization, conditional templating, and life cycle hooks. Since one of the primary purposes of Helm is to create Kubernetes resources, you should ensure that your resource templates are generated properly before they are applied to a Kubernetes cluster. This can be done in a variety of ways, which we will discuss in the following section.

Validating template generation locally with helm template

The first way to validate your chart's templating is to use the `helm template` command, which can be used to render a chart template locally and display its fully rendered contents in the standard output.

The `helm template` command has the following syntax:

```
$ helm template [NAME] [CHART] [flags]
```

This command renders a template locally, using the `NAME` argument to satisfy the `.Release` built-in object and the `CHART` argument for the chart that contains the Kubernetes templates. The `helm-charts/charts/guestbook` folder in the Packt repository can be used to demonstrate the functionality of the `helm template` command. This folder contains the chart that was developed in the previous section as well as additional resources that will be used later in this chapter.

Render the `guestbook` chart locally by running the following command:

```
$ helm template my-guestbook Learn-Helm/helm-charts/charts/
guestbook
```

The result of this command will display each of the Kubernetes resources that would be created if they were applied to the cluster, as shown:

```
---
# Source: guestbook/charts/redis/templates/configmap.yaml
apiVersion: v1
kind: ConfigMap
metadata:
  name: my-guestbook-redis
  labels:
    app: redis
    chart: redis-10.3.5
    heritage: Helm
    release: my-guestbook
data:
  redis.conf: |-
    # User-supplied configuration:
    appendonly no
    save ""
  master.conf: |-
    dir /data
    rename-command FLUSHDB ""
    rename-command FLUSHALL ""
  replica.conf: |-
    dir /data
    slave-read-only yes
    rename-command FLUSHDB ""
    rename-command FLUSHALL ""
---
# Source: guestbook/charts/redis/templates/health-configmap.yaml
apiVersion: v1
kind: ConfigMap
```

Figure 6.1 – "helm template" output

The preceding screenshot displays the beginning portion of the output from the `helm template` command as executed against the Guestbook chart created in the previous chapter. As you can see, a fully rendered `ConfigMap` is shown along with the beginning of another `ConfigMap` that was created with the release. Rendering these resources locally provides you with an idea of the exact resources and specifications that would be created if the release was installed against a Kubernetes cluster.

During chart development, you may want to use the `helm template` command regularly to validate that your Kubernetes resources are being generated properly.

Some common aspects of chart development that you would want to validate include the following:

- That parameterized fields are successfully replaced by default or overridden values
- That control actions such as `if`, `range`, and `with` successfully generates YAML files based on the provided values
- That resources contain proper spacing and indentation
- That functions and pipelines are used correctly to properly format and manipulate the YAML file
- That functions such as `required` and `fail` properly validate values based on user input

With an understanding of how chart templates can be rendered locally, let's now dive into some of the specific aspects that you can test and validate by leveraging the `helm template` command.

Testing template parameterization

It is important to check that your template's parameters are successfully populated with values. This is important because your charts will likely consist of multiple different values. You can ensure that your charts are properly parameterized by making sure each value has a sensible default value or has validation that fails chart rendering if a value is not provided.

Imagine the following deployment:

```
apiVersion: apps/v1
kind: Deployment
<skipping>
  replicas: {{ .Values.replicas }}
<skipping>
        ports:
          - containerPort: {{ .Values.port }}
```

Sensible defaults for the `replicas` and `port` values should be defined in the chart's `values.yaml` file, as follows:

```
replicas: 1
port: 8080
```

Running the `helm template` command against this template resource renders the following deployment, replacing the `replicas` and `port` values with their defaults:

```
apiVersion: apps/v1
kind: Deployment
<skipping>
  replicas: 1
<skipping>
        ports:
          - containerPort: 8080
```

The output from `helm template` allows you to verify that your parameters are properly replaced by their default values. You can also verify that the provided values are overridden successfully by passing the `--values` or `--set` arguments to the `helm template` command:

```
$ helm template my-chart $CHART_DIRECTORY --set replicas=2
```

The resulting template reflects your provided values:

```
apiVersion: apps/v1
kind: Deployment
<skipping>
  replicas: 2
<skipping>
        ports:
          - containerPort: 8080
```

While values with the default settings defined are often simple to test with `helm template`, it is more important to test values that require validation as invalid values can prevent your chart from installing properly.

You should use `helm template` to ensure that values with restrictions, such as those that only allow particular inputs, are successfully validated with the `required` and `fail` functions.

Imagine the following deployment template:

```
apiVersion: apps/v1
kind: Deployment
<skipping>
  replicas: {{ .Values.replicas }}
<skipping>
    containers:
      - name: main
        image: {{ .Values.imageRegistry }}/{{ .Values.
imageName }}
        ports:
          - containerPort: {{ .Values.port }}
```

If this deployment belongs to a chart with the same `values` file defined in the previous code block and you expected users to provide the `imageRegistry` and `imageName` values to install the chart, if you then use the `helm template` command without providing these values, then the result is less than desirable, as you can see in the following output:

```
apiVersion: apps/v1
kind: Deployment
<skipping>
  replicas: 1
<skipping>
    containers:
      - name: main
        image: /
        ports:
          - containerPort: 8080
```

Since there was no gating in place, the rendered result is a deployment with an invalid image, /. Because we tested this with `helm template`, we know that we need to handle the case where these values are not defined. This can be done by using the `required` function to provide validation that these values are specified:

```
apiVersion: apps/v1
kind: Deployment
<skipping>
  replicas: {{ .Values.replicas }}
<skipping>
      containers:
        - name: main
          image: {{ required 'value 'imageRegistry' is
required' .Values.imageRegistry }}/{{ required 'value
'imageName' is required' .Values.imageName }}
          ports:
            - containerPort: {{ .Values.port }}
```

When the `helm template` command is applied to a chart with the updated deployment template, the result displays a message that instructs the user to provide the first missing value that is encountered by the templating engine:

```
$ helm template my-chart $CHART_DIRECTORY
Error: execution error at (test-chart/templates/deployment.
yaml:17:20): value 'imageRegistry' is required
```

You can further test this validation by providing the valid values files alongside the `helm template` command. For this example, we will assume the following values are provided in a user-managed `values` file:

```
imageRegistry: my-registry.example.com
imageName: learnhelm/my-image
```

This file can then be provided when executing the following command:

```
$ helm template my-chart $CHART_DIRECTORY --values my-values.
yaml
---
# Source: test-chart/templates/deployment.yaml
```

```
apiVersion: apps/v1
kind: Deployment
<skipping>
  replicas: 1
<skipping>
      containers:
        - name: main
          image: my-registry.example.com/learnhelm/my-image
          ports:
            - containerPort: 8080
```

As a general rule of thumb for parameterization, make sure you keep track of your values and ensure that each value is used in your chart. Set sensible defaults in the `values.yaml` file and use the `required` function in cases where defaults cannot be set. Use the `helm template` function to ensure that values are properly rendered and produce the desired Kubernetes resource configuration.

As an aside, you may also want to consider including the required values in your `values.yaml` file as empty fields with a comment noting that they are required. This allows users to view your `values.yaml` file and see all the values that your chart supports, including the values that they are required to provide for themselves. Consider the following `values` file after the `imageRegistry` and `imageName` values are added to it:

```
replicas: 1
port: 8080
## REQUIRED
imageRegistry:
## REQUIRED
imageName:
```

Although these values are written in your chart's `values.yaml` file, these values still evaluate to null when the `helm template` command runs, providing the same behavior as they would if they were not defined as in prior executions. The difference is that you can now explicitly see that these values are required, so you won't be taken by surprise when you attempt to install the chart for the first time.

Next, we will discuss how generating your chart templates locally can help you test your chart's control actions.

Testing the control actions

Besides basic parameterization, you should also consider using the `helm template` command to verify that control actions (specifically `if` and `range`) are handled properly to produce the desired results.

Consider the following deployment template:

```
apiVersion: apps/v1
kind: Deployment
<skipping>
{{- range .Values.env }}
        env:
          - name: {{ .name }}
            value: {{ .value }}
{{- end }}
{{- if .Values.enableLiveness }}
        livenessProbe:
          httpGet:
            path: /
            port: {{ .Values.port }}
          initialDelaySeconds: 5
          periodSeconds: 10
{{- end }}
        ports:
          containerPort: 8080
```

If the `env` and `enableLiveness` values are both `null`, you could test whether this rendering will still be successful by running the `helm template` command:

```
$ helm template my-chart $CHART_DIRECTORY --values my-values.
yaml

---
# Source: test-chart/templates/deployment.yaml
apiVersion: apps/v1
kind: Deployment
<skipping>
```

```
        ports:
        - containerPort: 8080
```

You will notice that both the `range` and `if` actions are not generated. Null or empty values do not have any entries acted on them by the `range` clause and these values are also evaluated as `false` when provided to the `if` action. You can verify that you have written your template to properly generate YAML using these actions by providing the `env` and `enableLiveness` values to `helm template`.

You can add these values to a `values` file, as shown:

```
env:
  - name: BOOK
    value: Learn Helm
enableLiveness: true
```

With these changes made, verify the desired results of the `helm template` command to demonstrate that the template is written properly to consume these values:

```
---
# Source: test-chart/templates/deployment.yaml
apiVersion: apps/v1
kind: Deployment
<skipping>
        env:
        - name: BOOK
          value: Learn Helm
        livenessProbe:
          httpGet:
            path: /
            port: 8080
          initialDelaySeconds: 5
          periodSeconds: 10
        ports:
        - containerPort: 8080
```

You should make sure you are in the habit of regularly rendering your templates with `helm template` when you add additional control structures to your charts as they can quickly make the chart development process more difficult, especially if control structures are numerous or complex.

Aside from checking that the control structures are properly generated, you should also check whether your functions and pipelines are working as designed, which we will discuss next.

Testing functions and pipelines

The `helm template` command is also useful for validating the rendering produced by functions and pipelines, which are often used to produce formatted YAML.

Take the following template as an example:

```
apiVersion: apps/v1
kind: Deployment
<skipping>
        resources:
{{ .Values.resources | toYaml | indent 12 }}
```

This template contains a pipeline that parameterizes and formats the `resources` value to specify the container's resource requirements. It would be wise to include a sensible default in your chart's `values.yaml` file to make sure the application has an appropriate limit to prevent over-utilization of cluster resources.

An example of the `resources` value for this template is shown here:

```
resources:
  limits:
    cpu: 200m
    memory: 256Mi
```

You need to run the `helm template` command to ensure that this value is properly converted into a valid YAML format and that the output is properly indented to produce a valid deployment resource.

Running the `helm template` command against this template results in the following output:

```
apiVersion: apps/v1
kind: Deployment
<skipping>
        resources:
          limits:
            cpu: 200m
            memory: 256Mi
```

Next, we will discuss how server-side validation can be enabled when rendering your resources with `helm template`.

Adding server-side validation to chart rendering

While the `helm template` command is important to the chart development process and should be used frequently to verify your chart rendering, it does have a key limitation. The main purpose of the `helm template` command is to provide client-side rendering, meaning it does not communicate with the Kubernetes API server to provide resource validation. If you would like to ensure that your resources are valid after they are generated, you can use the `--validate` flag to instruct `helm template` to communicate with the Kubernetes API server after the resources are generated:

```
$ helm template my-chart $CHART_DIRECTORY --validate
```

Any generated template that does not produce a valid Kubernetes resource provides an error message. Imagine, for example, a deployment template was used where the `apiVersion` value was set to `apiVersion: v1`. In order to produce a valid deployment, you must set the `apiVersion` value to `apps/v1` as that is the correct name of the API that serves the deployment resource. Simply setting this to `v1` will generate what appears to be a valid resource by the client-side rendering of `helm template` without the `--validation` flag, but with the `--validation` flag you would expect to see the following error:

```
Error: unable to build kubernetes objects from release
manifest: unable to recognize '': no matches for kind
'Deployment' in version 'v1'
```

The `--validate` flag is designed to catch errors in your generated resources. You should use this flag if you have access to a Kubernetes cluster and if you want to determine whether or not your chart is generating valid Kubernetes resources. Alternatively, you can use the `--dry-run` flag against the `install`, `upgrade`, `rollback`, and `uninstall` commands to perform validation.

An example of using this flag with the `install` command is shown here:

```
$ helm install my-chart $CHART --dry-run
```

This flag will generate the chart's templates and perform validation, similar to running the `helm template` command with the `--validate` flag. Using `--dry-run` will print each generated resource to the command line and will not create the resources in the Kubernetes environment. It is primarily used by end users to perform a sanity check before running an installation to ensure that they have provided the correct values and that the installation will produce the desired results. Chart developers can choose to use the `--dry-run` flag in this fashion to test chart rendering and validation, or they can choose to use `helm template` to generate your chart's resources locally and provide `--validate` to add additional server-side validation.

While it is necessary to verify that your templates are generated the way you intend, it is also necessary to ensure that your templates are generated in a way that follows best practices to simplify development and maintenance. Helm provides a command called `helm lint` that can be used for this purpose, which we will learn more about next.

Linting Helm charts and templates

Linting your charts is important to prevent errors in your chart's formatting or the chart's definition file and provide guidance on best practices when working with Helm charts. The `helm lint` command has the following syntax:

```
$ helm lint PATH [flags]
```

The `helm lint` command is designed to be run against a chart directory to ensure that the chart is valid and properly formatted.

> **Important note:**
> The `helm lint` command does not validate the rendered API schemas or perform linting on your YAML style, but simply checks that the chart consists of the appropriate files and settings that a valid Helm chart should have.

You can run the `helm lint` command against the Guestbook chart that you created in *Chapter 5, Building Your First Helm Chart*, or against the chart under the `helm-charts/charts/guestbook` folder in the Packt GitHub repository at `https://github.com/PacktPublishing/-Learn-Helm/tree/master/helm-charts/charts/guestbook`:

```
$ helm lint $GUESTBOOK_CHART_PATH
==> Linting guestbook/
[INFO] Chart.yaml: icon is recommended

1 chart(s) linted, 0 chart(s) failed
```

This output declares that the chart is valid, which is noted by the `1 chart(s) linted, 0 chart(s) failed` message. The `[INFO]` message recommends the chart include an `icon` field in the `Chart.yaml` file, but this is not required. Other types of messages include `[WARNING]`, which indicates that the chart breaks the chart conventions, and `[ERROR]`, which indicates that the chart will fail at installation.

Let's run through a few examples. Consider a chart with the following file structure:

```
guestbook/
  templates/
  values.yaml
```

Notice that there are issues with this chart structure. This chart is missing the `Chart.yaml` file that defines the chart's metadata. The linter run against a chart with this structure would produce the following error:

```
==> Linting .
Error unable to check Chart.yaml file in chart: stat Chart.
yaml: no such file or directory

Error: 1 chart(s) linted, 1 chart(s) failed
```

This error indicates that Helm cannot find the `Chart.yaml` file. If an empty `Chart.yaml` file is added to the chart to provide the correct file structure, an error will still ensue as the `Chart.yaml` file contains invalid contents:

```
guestbook/
  Chart.yaml  # Empty
```

```
  templates/
  values.yaml
```

Running the linter against this chart would produce the following errors:

```
==> Linting .
[ERROR] Chart.yaml: name is required
[ERROR] Chart.yaml: apiVersion is required. The value must be
either 'v1' or 'v2'
[ERROR] Chart.yaml: version is required
[INFO] Chart.yaml: icon is recommended
[ERROR] templates/: validation: chart.metadata.name is required

Error: 1 chart(s) linted, 1 chart(s) failed
```

This output lists the required fields that are missing from the Chart.yaml file. It indicates that the file must contain the name, apiVersion, and version fields, so these fields should be added to the Chart.yaml file to produce a valid Helm chart. The linter provides additional feedback on the apiVersion and version settings, checking that the apiVersion value is set to either v1 or v2 and that the version setting is a proper SemVer version.

The linter will also check for the existence of other required or recommended files, such as the values.yaml file and the templates directory. It will also make sure that files under the templates directory have a .yaml, .yml, .tpl, or .txt file extension. The helm lint command is great for checking whether your chart contains the appropriate contents, but it does not carry out extensive linting on your chart's YAML style.

To perform this linting, you can use another tool, called yamllint, which can be found at https://github.com/adrienverge/yamllint. This tool can be installed using the pip package manager, across a range of operating systems, using the following command:

```
pip install yamllint --user
```

It can also be installed with your operating system's package manager, as described in the yamllint quick-start instructions at https://yamllint.readthedocs.io/en/stable/quickstart.html.

In order to use `yamllint` on your chart's YAML resources, you must use it in combination with the `helm template` command to remove the Go templating and generate your YAML resources.

The following is an example of running this command against the guestbook chart from the Packt GitHub repository:

```
$ helm template my-guestbook Learn-Helm/helm-charts/charts/
guestbook | yamllint -
```

This command will generate the resources under the `templates/` folder and pipe the output to `yamllint`.

The result is shown here:

```
stdin
  59:81    error    line too long (109 > 80 characters)  (line-length)
  85:81    error    line too long (109 > 80 characters)  (line-length)
  129:3    error    wrong indentation: expected 4 but found 2  (indentation)
  149:3    error    wrong indentation: expected 4 but found 2  (indentation)
  178:3    error    wrong indentation: expected 4 but found 2  (indentation)
  272:81   error    line too long (89 > 80 characters)  (line-length)
  273:81   error    line too long (92 > 80 characters)  (line-length)
  274:81   error    line too long (89 > 80 characters)  (line-length)
  275:18   error    trailing spaces  (trailing-spaces)
```

Figure 6.2 – An example `yamllint` output

The line numbers provided reflect the entirety of the `helm template` output, which can make it difficult to determine which line from the `yamllint` output corresponds with which line from your YAML resources.

You can simplify this by redirecting the `helm template` output to determine its line numbers using the following command against the `guestbook` chart:

```
$ cat -n <(helm template my-guestbook Learn-Helm/helm-charts/
charts/guestbook)
```

`yamllint` will lint against many different rules, including the following:

- Indentation
- Line length
- Training spaces
- Empty lines
- Comment format

You can override the default rules by specifying your own by creating one of the following files:

- `.yamllint`, `.yamllint.yaml`, and `.yamllint.yml` in the current working directory
- `$XDB_CONFIG_HOME/yamllint/config`
- `~/.config/yamllint/config`

To override the indentation rule that is reported against the guestbook chart, you can create a `.yamllint.yaml` file in your current working directory with the following contents:

```
rules:
  indentation:
    # Allow      myList
    #              - item1
    #              - item2
    # Or
    #            myList
    #                - item1
    #                - item2
    indent-sequences: whatever
```

This configuration overrides `yamllint` so that it doesn't enforce one particular method of indentation when adding list entries. It is configured by the `indent-sequences: whatever` line. Creating this file and running the linter again against the guestbook will eliminate the indentation errors, that were seen previously seen previously:

```
$ helm template my-guestbook guestbook | yamllint -
```

In this section, we discussed how you can validate the local rendering of your Helm charts by using the `helm template` and `helm lint` commands. This, however, does not actually test your chart's functionality or the application's ability to function with the resources that your chart creates.

In the next section, we will learn how to create tests in a live Kubernetes environment to test your Helm chart.

Testing in a live cluster

Creating chart tests is an important part of developing and maintaining your Helm charts. Chart tests help verify that your chart is functioning as intended and they can help prevent regressions as features and fixes to your chart are added.

Testing consists of two different steps. First, you need to create pod templates under your chart's `templates/` directory that contain the `helm.sh/hook: test` annotation. These `pods` will run commands that test the functionality of your chart and application. Next, you need to run the `helm test` command, which initiates a `test` hook and creates resources with the aforementioned annotation.

In this section, we will learn how to test in a live cluster by adding tests to the Guestbook chart, continuing the development of the chart you created in the previous chapter. As a reference, the tests that you will create can be viewed in the Guestbook chart in the Packt repository, located at `https://github.com/PacktPublishing/-Learn-Helm/tree/master/helm-charts/charts/guestbook`.

Begin by adding the `test/frontend-connection.yaml` and `test/redis-connection.yaml` files under the `templates/` directory of your Guestbook chart. Be aware that chart tests do not have to be located under a `test` subdirectory, but keeping them there is a good way of keeping your tests organized and separated from the main chart templates:

```
$ mkdir $GUESTBOOK_CHART_DIR/templates/test
$ touch $GUESTBOOK_CHART_DIR/templates/test/frontend-connection.yaml
$ touch $GUESTBOOK_CHART_DIR/templates/test/backend-connection.yaml
```

In this section, we will populate these files with logic to validate their associated application components.

Let's begin writing the tests now that their placeholders have been added.

Creating the chart tests

As you recall, the Guestbook chart consists of a Redis backend and a PHP frontend. Users enter messages in a dialog box in the frontend, and the messages are persisted to the backend. Let's write a couple tests that ensure both the frontend and backend resources are available after an installation. We will begin with a test that checks the availability of the Redis backend. Add the following contents to the chart's templates/test/backend-connection.yaml file (this file can also be viewed in the Packt repository at https://github.com/PacktPublishing/-Learn-Helm/blob/master/helm-charts/charts/guestbook/templates/test/backend-connection.yaml):

```
1  apiVersion: v1
2  kind: Pod
3  metadata:
4    name: {{ include "guestbook.fullname" . }}-test-backend-connection
5    labels:
6      {{- include "guestbook.labels" . | nindent 4 }}
7    annotations:
8      "helm.sh/hook": test
9      "helm.sh/hook-delete-policy": before-hook-creation
10 spec:
11   containers:
12     - name: test-backend-connection
13       image: redis:alpine3.11
14       command: ["/bin/sh", "-c"]
15       args: ["redis-cli -h {{ .Values.redis.fullnameOverride }}-master MGET messages"]
16   restartPolicy: Never
```

Figure 6.3 - The backend connection test for the Guestbook Helm chart

This template defines a Pod that will be created during the test lifecycle hook. Also defined in this template is a hook delete policy that indicates when previous test pods should be removed. You could also add hook weights if the tests we will create needed to be run in any order.

The args field underneath the containers object displays the command that the test will be based on. It will use the redis-cli tool to connect to the Redis master and run the command MGET messages. The Guestbook frontend is designed to add messages entered by the user to a database key called messages. This simple test is designed to check that a connection to the Redis database can be made, and it will return the messages that a user has entered by querying the messages key.

The PHP frontend should also be tested for availability as well, as it is the user-facing component of the application. Add the following contents to the templates/test/frontend-connection.yaml file (these contents can also be seen in the Packt repository at https://github.com/PacktPublishing/-Learn-Helm/blob/master/helm-charts/charts/guestbook/templates/test/frontend-connection.yaml).

```
1 apiVersion: v1
2 kind: Pod
3 metadata:
4   name: {{ include "guestbook.fullname" . }}-test-frontend-connection
5   labels:
6     {{- include "guestbook.labels" . | nindent 4 }}
7   annotations:
8     "helm.sh/hook": test
9     "helm.sh/hook-delete-policy": before-hook-creation
10 spec:
11   containers:
12     - name: test-frontend-connection
13       image: curlimages/curl:7.68.0
14       command: ["/bin/sh", "-c"]
15       args: ["curl {{ include "guestbook.fullname" . }}"]
16   restartPolicy: Never
```

Figure 6.4 - The frontend connection test for the Guestbook Helm chart

This is a very simple test that runs an HTTP request to the Guestbook Service. Traffic sent to the Service will load-balance between Guestbook frontend instances. This test will check that the load balancing is being successfully performed and that the frontend is available.

Now, we have finished the templates needed for chart tests. Be advised that these templates can also be rendered locally by the helm template command and linted using helm lint and yamllint as described in earlier sections within this chapter. When developing your own Helm charts, you may find this to be useful for more advanced test cases.

Now that the tests are written, we will continue by running them in the Minikube environment.

Running the chart tests

In order to run a chart's tests, the chart must first be installed on a Kubernetes environment using the `helm install` command. Because the tests that are written are designed to run after the installation is complete, the `--wait` flag can be used when installing the chart so that it is easier to determine when pods are ready. Run the following command to install the Guestbook chart:

```
$ helm install my-guestbook $GUESTBOOK_CHART_DIR -n chapter6
--wait
```

Once the chart is installed, you can use the `helm test` command to execute the `test` life cycle hook and create the test resources. The syntax for the `helm test` command is shown here:

```
helm test [RELEASE] [flags]
```

Run the `helm test` command against the `my-guestbook` release:

```
$ helm test my-guestbook -n chapter6
```

If your test is successful, you will see the following results in the output:

```
TEST SUITE:      my-guestbook-test-frontend-connection
Last Started:    Tue Jan 28 18:50:23 2020
Last Completed:  Tue Jan 28 18:50:25 2020
Phase:           Succeeded
TEST SUITE:      my-guestbook-test-backend-connection
Last Started:    Tue Jan 28 18:50:25 2020
Last Completed:  Tue Jan 28 18:50:26 2020
Phase:           Succeeded
```

When running your tests, you can also use the `--logs` flag to print your logs to the command line from the execution of the tests.

Run the tests again using this flag:

```
$ helm test my-guestbook -n chapter6 --logs
```

You will see the same test summary as before, in addition to each test's associated container logs. The following is the first portion of the frontend connection test log output:

```
POD LOGS: my-guestbook-test-frontend-connection
   % Total     % Received % Xferd  Average Speed    Time      Time
Time   Current
                                   Dload   Upload    Total
Spent    Left   Speed
<html ng-app='redis'>
  <head>
    <title>Guestbook</title>
```

The following is the backend connection `test` log output:

```
POD LOGS: my-guestbook-test-backend-connection
```

The logs for this test will appear empty because you haven't yet entered any messages in the Guestbook frontend. You can run the test again after adding a message from the frontend to ensure the messages persist. Instructions to determine the URL of the Guestbook frontend are printed when you run both the installation and the `test` suites.

These instructions are again displayed here:

```
export IP=$(kubectl get nodes -o jsonpath='{.items[0].status.
addresses[0].address}')
export PORT=$(kubectl get svc my-guestbook -n chapter6 -o
jsonpath='{.spec.ports[0].nodePort}')
echo http://$IP:$PORT
```

Add a message from the Guestbook application once you have accessed the frontend from a browser.

An example is shown in the following screenshot:

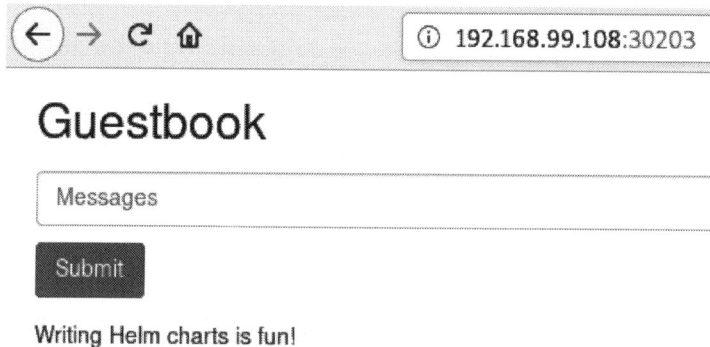

Figure 6.4-1 – The Guestbook application's frontend

Run the `test` suite again once a message is added, providing the `--logs` flag to display the logs from the tests. You should be able to verify that this message was added by observing the backend connection `test` log output:

```
$ helm test my-guestbook -n chapter6 --logs
```

The following is a snippet displaying the backend connection `test` log output. You can verify that the message was persisted to the Redis database:

```
POD LOGS: my-guestbook-test-backend-connection
,Writing Helm charts is fun!
```

In this section, we wrote simple tests that, as a whole, performed a smoke test on the installation of a chart. With these tests in place, we will feel more confident with making changes and adding features to this chart, provided that the chart tests run after each modification to ensure functionality is retained.

In the next section, we will discuss how the testing process can be improved by leveraging a tool called `ct`.

Improving chart tests with the chart testing project

The tests written in the previous section are sufficient enough to test whether the Guestbook application can be successfully installed. However, there are some key limitations that are inherent to the standard Helm testing process that need to be called out.

The first limitation to consider is the difficulty of testing the different permutations that can occur within a chart's values. Because the `helm test` command does not provide the ability to modify your release's values beyond those set at the time of an installation or upgrade, the following workflow must be followed when running `helm test` against different values settings:

1.   Install your chart with an initial set of values.

2.   Run `helm test` against your release.

3.   Delete your release.

4.   Install your chart with a different set of values.

5.   Repeat *steps 2* through *4* until a significant amount of value possibilities are tested.

In addition to testing different value permutations, you should also make sure regressions do not occur when making modifications to your charts. The best way to prevent regressions while also testing the newer version of your chart is to use the following workflow:

1.   Install a previous chart version.

2.   Upgrade your release to the newer chart version.

3.   Delete the release.

4.   Install the newer chart version.

This workflow should be repeated against each set of value permutations to ensure that there are no regressions or intended breaking changes.

These processes sound tedious but imagine the additional strain and maintenance on chart developers when maintaining multiple different Helm charts where careful testing should take place. When maintaining multiple Helm charts, chart developers tend to favor a `git` monorepo design. A repository is considered monorepo when multiple different artifacts or modules are contained in the same repository.

In the case of Helm charts, a monorepo could have the following file structure:

```
helm-charts/
  guestbook/
    Chart.yaml
    templates/
    README.md
    values.yaml
  redis/                # Contains the same file structure as
  'guestbook'
  wordpress/            # Contains the same file structure as
  'guestbook'
  README.md
```

Helm charts in a well-maintained monorepo should be tested when they are modified to ensure that intended breaking changes did not occur. When a chart is modified, its version field in its Chart.yaml file should also be increased according to the correct SemVer versioning to denote the type of change that was made. SemVer versions follow a MAJOR.MINOR.PATCH version numbering format.

Use the following list as guideline for how to increase a SemVer version:

- Increment the MAJOR version if you are making a breaking change to your chart. A breaking change is a change that is not backward-compatible with the previous chart version.

- Increment the MINOR version if you are adding a feature but you are not making a breaking change. You should increment this version if the change you are making is backward-compatible with the previous chart version.

- Increment the PATCH version if you are making a patch to a bug or a security vulnerability that will not result in a breaking change. This version should be incremented if the change is backward-compatible with the previous chart version.

Without well-written automation, it can become increasingly difficult to make sure charts are tested when modified and that their versions are incremented, especially if maintaining a monorepo with multiple Helm charts. This challenge prompted the Helm community to create a tool called ct to provide structure and automation around chart tests and maintenance. We will discuss this tool next.

Introducing the chart testing project

The chart testing project, which can be found at `https://github.com/helm/chart-testing`, is designed to be used against charts in a `git` monorepo to perform automated linting, validation, and testing. The automated testing is achieved by using `git` to detect charts that are changed against a target branch. Charts that are changed should undergo a testing process, while charts that are unchanged do not need to be tested.

The project's CLI, `ct`, provides four primary commands:

- `lint`: Lints and validates charts that have been modified
- `install`: Installs and tests charts that have been modified
- `lint-and-install`: Lints, installs, and tests charts that have been modified
- `list-changed`: Lists charts that have been modified

The `list-changed` command does not perform any validation or testing, while the `lint-and-install` command combines the `lint` and `install` commands to lint, install, and `test` modified charts. It also checks whether you have increased the modified charts' `version` fields in each of the charts' `Chart.yaml` files and fails testing for charts whose versions have not been increased but whose contents have been modified. This validation helps maintainers remain strict toward increasing their chart versions depending on the type of change made.

In addition to checking the chart versions, chart testing provides the ability to specify multiple values files per chart for testing purposes. During the invocation of the `lint`, `install`, and `lint-and-install` commands, chart testing loops through each test `values` file to override the chart's default values and to perform validation and testing based on the different values permutations provided. Test `values` files are written under a folder called `ci/` to keep these values separate from your chart's default `values.yaml` file, as in the following example file structure:

```
guestbook/
   Chart.yaml
   ci/
      nodeport-service-values.yaml
       ingress-values.yaml
   templates/
   values.yaml
```

Chart testing applies each `values` file under the `ci/` folder, regardless of the name used for the file. You may find it helpful to name each `values` file based on the values that are overridden so that the maintainers and contributors can understand the file contents.

The most common `ct` command you are likely to use is the `lint-and-install` command. The following lists the steps that this command uses to lint, install, and test charts that are modified in a `git` monorepo:

1. Detect the charts that have been modified.

2. Update the local Helm cache with the `helm repo update` command.

3. Download each modified chart's dependencies with the `helm dependency build` command.

4. Check whether each modified chart's version has been incremented.

5. For each chart that evaluates to `true` in *step 4*, lint the chart and each `values` file under the `ci/` folder.

6. For each chart that evaluates to `true` in *step 4*, perform the following additional steps:

    Install the chart in an automatically created namespace.

    Run tests by executing `helm test`.

    Delete the namespace.

    Repeat for each `values` file under the `ci/` folder.

As you can see, this command performs a variety of different steps to ensure that your charts are properly linted and tested by installing and testing each modified chart in a separate namespace, repeating the process for each `values` file defined under the `ci/` folder. However, by default, the `lint-and-install` command does not check for backward compatibility by performing an upgrade from an older version of the chart. This feature can be enabled by adding the `--upgrade` flag:

If a breaking change is not indicated, the `--upgrade` flag modifies *step 6* of the previous set of steps by running the following steps:

1. Install the older version of the chart in an automatically created namespace.

2. Run tests by executing `helm test`.

3. Upgrade the release to the modified version of the chart and run the tests again.

4. Delete the namespace.

5. Install the modified version of the chart in a new, automatically created namespace.

6. Run tests by executing `helm test`.

7. Upgrade the release again using the same chart version and rerun the tests.

8. Delete the namespace.

9. Repeat for each `values` file under the `ci/` folder.

It is recommended that you add the `--upgrade` flag to perform additional testing on Helm upgrades and to prevent possible regressions.

> **Important note:**
>
> The `--upgrade` flag will not take effect if you have incremented the `MAJOR` version of your Helm chart as this indicates that you made a breaking change and that an in-place upgrade on this version would not be successful.

Let's install the chart testing CLI and its dependencies locally so that we can later see this process in action.

Installing the chart testing tools

In order to use the chart testing CLI, you must have the following tools installed on your local machine:

- `helm`
- `git` (version `2.17.0` or later)
- `yamllint`
- `yamale`
- `kubectl`

Chart testing uses each of these tools in the testing process. `helm` and `kubectl` were installed in *Chapter 2, Preparing a Kubernetes and Helm Environment*, Git was installed in *Chapter 5, Building Your First Helm Chart*, and yamllint was installed at the beginning of this chapter. If you have followed along with this book so far, the only prerequisite tool you should need to install now is Yamale, which is a tool that chart testing uses to validate your charts' `Chart.yaml` files against a `Chart.yaml` schema file.

Yamale can be installed with the `pip` package manager, as shown:

```
$ pip install yamale --user
```

You can also install Yamale manually by downloading an archive from `https://github.com/23andMe/Yamale/archive/master.zip`.

Once downloaded, unzip the archive and run the setup script:

```
$ python setup.py install
```

Note that if you install the tool using a downloaded archive, you may need to run the `setup.py` script with elevated permissions, such as an administrator or as root on macOS and Linux.

Once you have the required tooling installed, you should download the chart testing tool from the project's GitHub releases page at `https://github.com/helm/chart-testing/releases`. Each release contains an *Assets* section with a list of archives.

Download the archive that corresponds with the platform type of your local machine. Version `v3.0.0-beta.1` was the version used for this book:

v3.0.0-beta.1

helm-bot released this on Dec 13, 2019

Changelog

ecd4546	Prepare release v3.0.0-beta.1 (#195)
62e23ac	Update docs for Helm 3 (#194)
b9d4ad0	List changed fixes (#190)
b857274	Add support for Helm 3 (#184)
5b7b21e	Migrate to Go modules (#183)

Docker images

- `docker pull quay.io/helmpack/chart-testing:v3.0.0-beta.1`
- `docker pull quay.io/helmpack/chart-testing:latest`

▼ Assets 7

chart-testing_3.0.0-beta.1_darwin_amd64.tar.gz	6.11 MB
chart-testing_3.0.0-beta.1_linux_amd64.tar.gz	6.2 MB
chart-testing_3.0.0-beta.1_linux_armv6.tar.gz	5.78 MB
chart-testing_3.0.0-beta.1_windows_amd64.zip	6.08 MB
checksums.txt	448 Bytes
Source code (zip)	
Source code (tar.gz)	

Figure 6.5 – The chart testing releases page on GitHub

Unarchive the chart testing release once you have downloaded the appropriate file from the GitHub releases page. Once unarchived, you will see the following contents:

```
LICENSE
README.md
etc/chart_schema.yaml
etc/lintconf.yaml
ct
```

You can remove the `LICENSE` and `README.md` files as they are not needed.

The `etc/chart_schema.yaml` and `etc/lintconf.yaml` files should be moved to either the `$HOME/.ct/` or the `/etc/ct/` location on your local machine. The `ct` file should be moved to somewhere that is managed by your system's `PATH` variable:

```
$ mkdir $HOME/.ct
$ mv $HOME/Downloads/etc/* $HOME/.ct/
$ mv $HOME/Downloads/ct /usr/local/bin/
```

Now, all of the required tooling is installed. For this example, we will make a change locally to the Packt repository and use chart testing to lint and install the modified charts.

If you have not yet cloned the repository to your local machine, you should do so now:

```
$ git clone https://github.com/PacktPublishing/-Learn-Helm
Learn-Helm
```

Once cloned, you may notice that this repository has a file in the top level called `ct.yaml` with the following contents:

```
chart-dirs:
  - helm-charts/charts
chart-repos:
  - bitnami=https://charts.bitnami.com/bitnami
```

The `chart-dirs` field of this file indicates to `ct` that the `helm-charts/charts` directory relative to the `ct.yaml` file is the root of the chart's monorepo. The `chart-repos` field provides a list of repositories that chart testing should run `helm repo add` against to ensure it is able to download dependencies.

There are a variety of other configurations that can be added to this file, which will not be discussed at this time but can be reviewed in the chart testing documentation at `https://github.com/helm/chart-testing`. Each invocation of the `ct` command references the `ct.yaml` file.

Now that the tooling is installed and the Packt repository has been cloned, let's test the `ct` tool out by executing the `lint-and-install` command.

Running the chart testing lint-and-install command

The `lint-and-install` command is used against the three Helm charts included under `Learn-Helm/helm-charts/charts`:

- `guestbook`: This is the Guestbook chart that you wrote in the previous chapter.

- `nginx`: This is an additional Helm chart that we have included for demonstration purposes. This chart, created by running the `helm create` command, is used to deploy the `nginx` reverse proxy.

To run the tests, first, navigate to the top level of the `Learn-Helm` repository:

```
$ cd $LEARN_HELM_LOCATION
$ ls
ct.yaml  guestbook-operator  helm-
charts  jenkins  LICENSE  nginx-cd  README.md
```

The `ct.yaml` file displays the location of the chart's monorepo via the `chart-dirs` field, so you can simply run the `ct lint-and-install` command from the top level:

```
$ ct lint-and-install
```

After running this command, you'll see the following message displayed at the end of the output:

```
All charts linted and installed successfully

No chart changes detected.
```

Figure 6.6 – The chart testing `lint-and-install` output when charts are not modified

Since none of the charts in this repository were modified, `ct` did not perform any actions on your charts. We should modify at least one of these charts to see the `lint-and-install` process take place. Modifications should take place in branches other than `master`, so a new branch called `chart-testing-example` should be created by executing the following command:

```
$ git checkout -b chart-testing-example
```

The modifications can be large or small; for this example, we will simply modify each chart's `Chart.yaml` file. Modify the `description` field of the `Learn-Helm/helm-charts/charts/guestbook/Chart.yaml` file to read as follows:

```
description: Used to deploy the Guestbook application
```

Previously, this value was `A Helm chart for Kubernetes`.

Modify the `description` field of the `Learn-Helm/helm-charts/charts/nginx/Chart.yaml` file to read as follows:

```
description: Deploys an NGINX instance to Kubernetes
```

Previously, this value was `A Helm chart for Kubernetes`. Verify that both charts have been modified from their last `git` commit by running the `git status` command:

```
On branch chart-testing-example
Changes not staged for commit:
  (use "git add <file>..." to update what will be committed)
  (use "git checkout -- <file>..." to discard changes in working directory)

        modified:   helm-charts/charts/guestbook/Chart.yaml
        modified:   helm-charts/charts/nginx/Chart.yaml

no changes added to commit (use "git add" and/or "git commit -a")
```

Figure 6.7 – The `git status` output after both charts have been modified

You should see a change in both the `guestbook` and `nginx` charts. With these charts modified, try running the `lint-and-install` command again:

```
$ ct lint-and-install
```

This time, `ct` determines whether changes have occurred to two of the charts in this monorepo, as in the following output:

```
Charts to be processed:
-----------------------------------------------------------------------
guestbook => (version: "1.0.0", path: "helm-charts/charts/guestbook")
nginx => (version: "1.0.0", path: "helm-charts/charts/nginx")
-----------------------------------------------------------------------
```

Figure 6.8 – Messages denoting changes to the `guestbook` and `nginx` charts

This process, however, will later fail because neither of the charts' versions were modified:

```
Linting chart 'guestbook => (version: "1.0.0", path: "helm-charts/charts/guestbook")'
Checking chart 'guestbook => (version: "1.0.0", path: "helm-charts/charts/guestbook")' for a version bump...
Old chart version: 1.0.0
New chart version: 1.0.0
Linting chart 'nginx => (version: "1.0.0", path: "helm-charts/charts/nginx")'
Checking chart 'nginx => (version: "1.0.0", path: "helm-charts/charts/nginx")' for a version bump...
Old chart version: 1.0.0
New chart version: 1.0.0
Error: Error linting and installing charts: Error processing charts
```

Figure 6.9 – The output when no chart changes have been made

This can be fixed by incrementing the guestbook and nginx chart versions. Since this change does not introduce new features, we will increment the PATCH version. Modify both chart versions to version 1.0.1 in their respective Chart.yaml files:

```
version: 1.1.0
```

Ensure that this change has been made to each chart by running the git diff command. If you see each version modification in the output, continue to run the lint-and-install command again:

```
$ ct lint-and-install
```

Now that the chart versions have been incremented, the lint-and-install command will follow the full chart testing workflow. You will see that each modified chart is linted and deployed to an automatically created namespace. Once the deployed application's pods are reported as ready, ct will automatically run the test cases of each chart as denoted by resources with the helm.sh/hook: test annotation. Chart testing will also print the logs of each test pod, as well as the namespace events.

You may notice, in the lint-and-install output, that the nginx chart is deployed twice, while the guestbook chart was only deployed and tested once. This is because the nginx chart has a ci/ folder, located at Learn-Helm/helm-charts/charts/nginx/ci/, that contains two different values files. The values files in the ci/ folder are iterated on by chart testing, which installs the chart as many times as there are values files to ensure that each combination of values results in a successful installation. The guestbook chart does not include a ci/ folder, so this chart was only installed once.

This can be observed in the following lines of the `lint-and-install` output:

```
Linting chart with values file 'nginx/ci/clusterip-values.
yaml'...
```
```
Linting chart with values file 'nginx/ci/nodeport-values.
yaml'...
```
```
Installing chart with values file 'nginx/ci/clusterip-values.
yaml'...
```
```
Installing chart with values file 'nginx/ci/nodeport-values.
yaml'...
```

While the command was useful for testing the functionality of both charts, it did not validate whether upgrades to the newer version will be successful.

To do this, we need to provide the `--upgrade` flag to the `lint-and-install` command. Try, once again, to run this command, but this time with the `--upgrade` flag:

```
$ ct lint-and-install --upgrade
```

This time, an in-place upgrade will occur for each `values` file under `ci/`. This can be seen in the output as follows:

```
Testing upgrades of chart 'guestbook => (version: '1.0.1',
path: 'guestbook')' relative to previous revision 'guestbook
=> (version: '1.0.0', path: 'ct_previous_revision216728160/
guestbook')'...
```

Recall that an in-place upgrade will only be tested if the MAJOR version between versions is the same. If you use the `--upgrade` flag but did change the MAJOR version, you will see a message similar to the following :

```
Skipping upgrade test of 'guestbook => (version: '2.0.0', path:
'helm-charts/charts/guestbook')' because: 1 error occurred:
        * 2.0.0 does not have same major version as 1.0.0
```

Now, with an understanding of how to perform robust testing on your Helm charts with chart testing, we will conclude by cleaning up your `minikube` environment.

Cleaning up

If you are finished with the examples described in this chapter, you can remove the `chapter6` namespace from your `minikube` cluster:

```
$ kubectl delete ns chapter6
```

Finally, shut down your `minikube` cluster by running `minikube stop`.

Summary

In this chapter, you learned about the different methods you can apply to test your Helm charts. The most basic way of testing a chart is to run the `helm template` command against a local chart directory to determine whether its resources are properly generated. You can also use the `helm lint` command to ensure that your chart follows the correct format and you can use the `yamllint` command to lint the YAML style used in your chart.

Apart from local templating and linting, you can also perform live tests on a Kubernetes environment with the `helm test` command and the `ct` tool. In addition to performing chart tests, chart testing also provides capabilities that make it easier for chart developers to maintain Helm charts in a monorepo.

In the next chapter, you will learn how Helm can be used in a **Continuous Integration/ Continuous Delivery (CI/CD)** and GitOps setting, from both the perspective of a chart developer that is building and testing Helm charts and from the perspective of an end user using Helm to deploy an application to Kubernetes.

Further reading

For additional information on the `helm template` and `helm lint` commands, please refer to the following resources:

- `helm template`: https://helm.sh/docs/helm/helm_template/
- `helm lint`: https://helm.sh/docs/helm/helm_lint/

The following pages from the Helm documentation discuss chart tests and the `helm test` command:

- Chart tests: https://helm.sh/docs/topics/chart_tests/
- The `helm test` command: https://helm.sh/docs/helm/helm_test/

- Finally, see the chart testing GitHub repository for more information about the `ct` CLI: `https://github.com/helm/chart-testing`.

Questions

1. What is the purpose of the `helm template` command? How does it differ from the `helm lint` command?

2. What can you do to validate your chart templates before installing them in Kubernetes?

3. What tool can be leveraged to lint the style of your YAML resources?

4. How is a chart test created? How is a chart test executed?

5. What additional value does the `ct` tool bring to Helm's built-in testing capabilities?

6. What is the purpose of the `ci/` folder when used with the `ct` tool?

7. How does the `--upgrade` flag change the behavior of the `ct lint-and-install` command?

Section 3: Adanced Deployment Patterns

This section will build upon the basic concepts explained thus far and will teach you about more advanced concepts and possibilities around application management with Helm.

This section comprises the following chapters:

Chapter 7, Automating Helm Processes Using CI/CD and GitOps

Chapter 8, Using Helm with the Operator Framework

Chapter 9, Helm Security Considerations

7
Automating Helm Processes Using CI/CD and GitOps

In this book, we have so far discussed two high-level processes. First, we explored using Helm as an end user, leveraging Helm as a package manager to deploy applications of varying complexities to Kubernetes. Second, we explored developing and testing Helm charts as a chart developer, which involved encapsulating Kubernetes complexities in Helm charts and performing tests on charts to ensure that the required features were delivered to end users successfully.

Both of these processes involve invoking various different Helm CLI commands. These Helm CLI commands, while effective in carrying out their respective tasks, require manual invocation from the command line. Manual invocation can serve as a pain point when managing multiple different charts or applications and can make it difficult for larger enterprises to scale. As a result, we should explore alternative options that provide additional automation on top of what Helm already provides. In this chapter, we will investigate concepts relating to **Continuous Integration** and **Continuous Delivery (CI/CD)** and `GitOps`, which are methodologies that can automatically invoke the Helm CLI along with other commands in order to perform automated workflows against the contents of a Git repository. These workflows can be used to automatically deploy applications using Helm and to build, test, and package Helm charts during the chart development life cycle.

In this chapter, we will cover the following topics:

- Understanding CI/CD and GitOps
- Setting up our environment
- Creating a CI pipeline to build Helm charts
- Creating a CD pipeline to deploy applications with Helm
- Cleaning up

Technical requirements

This chapter requires you to have the following technologies installed on your local machine:

- Minikube
- Helm
- kubectl
- Git

In addition to these tools, you should find the Packt repository containing resources associated with the examples used in this chapter on GitHub at `https://github.com/PacktPublishing/-Learn-Helm`. This repository will be referenced throughout this chapter.

Understanding CI/CD and GitOps

So far, we have addressed many of the key concepts that are inherent to Helm development—building, testing, and deploying. However, our exploration has been limited to manual configurations and invocations of the Helm CLI. While this is okay when getting started with Helm, as you look to move a chart into a production-like environment, there are several questions that you need to consider, including the following:

- How can I be sure that the best practices for chart development and deployment are enforced?

- What are the implications of collaborators participating in the development and deployment processes?

These points are applicable to any software project, not just to Helm chart development. While we have covered a lot of best practices so far, when taking on new collaborators, they may not have the same understanding of these topics or the discipline to perform these crucial steps. Through the use of automation and repeatable processes, concepts such as CI/CD have been established to address some of these challenges.

CI/CD

The need for an automated software development process that can be adhered to each time a software change occurs led to the creation of CI. CI not only ensures that best practices are adhered to, but it also helps eliminate the common challenges faced by many developers, as embodied in the phrase 'it works on my machine.' One factor that we discussed previously is the use of **version control systems**, such as `git`, to store source code. Often, each user would have their own independent copy of source code, which made maintaining the code base challenging to manage as additional contributors were brought on.

CI is properly enabled through the use of an automation tool, where source code is retrieved and undergoes a predetermined set of steps whenever changes occur. The need for a proper automation tool led to the rise of software specifically designed for this purpose. Several examples of CI tools include Jenkins, TeamCity, and Bamboo, along with a variety of **Software-as-a-Service (SaaS)**-based solutions. By offloading the responsibility of tasks onto a third-party component, developers are more likely to commit code frequently and project managers can feel confident in the skill of their teams and the robustness of their products.

One key feature that is found in most of these tools is the ability to provide timely notifications on the current state of a project. Instead of discovering a breaking change later in the software development cycle, through the use of CI, as soon as changes are incorporated, processes are executed and notifications to interested parties are transmitted. By making use of rapid notifications, it provides the user who introduced the change with the opportunity to resolve the issue while the area of interest is at the front of the mind, instead of later on in the delivery process when they may be occupied elsewhere.

The ability to apply many of CI's concepts throughout an entire software delivery life cycle as an application moves its way toward production led to the creation of CD. CD is a set of defined steps written to progress software through a release process (more commonly referred to as a pipeline). CI and CD are typically paired together as many of the same execution engines that perform CI can also implement CD. CD has gained acceptance and popularity among many organizations where proper change control is enforced and approvals are required in order for the software release process to progress to the next stage. As many of the concepts around CI/CD are automated in a repeatable fashion, teams can look to fully eliminate the need for the manual approval steps once they feel confident that they have a reliable framework in place.

The process of implementing a fully automated build, test, deployment, and release process without any human intervention is known as **continuous deployment**. While many software projects never fully achieve continuous deployment, by just implementing the concepts emphasized by CI/CD, teams are able to produce real business value faster. In the next section, we will introduce GitOps as a mechanism to improve the management of applications and their configuration.

Taking CI/CD to the next level using GitOps

Kubernetes is a platform that embraces the use of declarative configuration. In the same way that an application written in any programming language, such as Python, Golang, or Java traverses its way through a CI/CD pipeline, Kubernetes manifests can implement many of the same patterns. Manifests should also be stored in a source code repository, such as Git, and can undergo the same type of build, test, and deployment practices. The rise in popularity of managing the life cycle of Kubernetes cluster configuration within Git repositories and then applying these resources in an automated fashion led to the concept of GitOps. First introduced by the software company WeaveWorks in 2017, GitOps has increased in popularity ever since as a way to manage Kubernetes configurations. While GitOps is best known in the context of Kubernetes, its principles can be applied to any cloud-native environment.

Similar to CI/CD, tools have been developed to manage the GitOps process. These include **ArgoCD from Intuit** and **Flux by WeaveWorks**, the organization responsible for coining the term GitOps. You do not need to use a tool that is specifically designed for GitOps as any automation tool, particularly one designed for managing the CI/CD process, can be utilized. The key differentiator between a traditional CI/CD tool and a tool designed for GitOps is the ability for the GitOps tool to constantly observe the state of the Kubernetes cluster and apply the desired configurations whenever the current state does not match the desired state, as defined in the manifests stored in Git. These tools make use of the controller pattern that is fundamental to Kubernetes itself.

Since Helm charts are ultimately rendered as Kubernetes resources, they, too, can be used to participate in the GitOps process and many of the aforementioned GitOps tools natively support Helm. We will see how to make use of Helm charts using CI/CD and GitOps throughout the remainder of this chapter, leveraging Jenkins as the tool of choice for both CI and CD.

Setting up our environment

In this chapter, we will develop two different pipelines to demonstrate how different processes around Helm can be automated.

Take the following steps to begin setting up your local environment:

1. First, given the increased memory requirements of this chapter, you should delete your `minikube` cluster and recreate it with 4g of memory if it was not inititalized with 4g of memory in *Chapter 2, Preparing a Kubernetes and Helm Environment*. This can be done by running the following commands:

   ```
   $ minikube delete
   $ minikube start --memory=4g
   ```

2. Once Minikube starts, create a new namespace called `chapter7`:

   ```
   $ kubectl create namespace chapter7
   ```

You should, additionally, fork the Packt repository, which will allow you to make modifications against the repository based on the steps described in these exercises:

1. Create a fork of the Packt repository by clicking the **Fork** button on the Git repo:

Learn Helm, published by Packt

Figure 7.1 – Select the Fork button to fork the Packt repository

You must have a GitHub account to fork a repository. The process of creating a new account is described in *Chapter 5, Building Your First Helm Chart.*

2. After you create a fork of the Packt repository, clone this fork to your local machine by running the following command:

```
$ git clone https://github.com/$GITHUB_USERNAME/-Learn-
Helm.git Learn-Helm
```

In addition to creating a fork of the Packt repository, you may want to remove the `guestbook` chart from your Helm repository, served from your GitHub Pages repository, which we created in *Chapter 5, Building Your First Helm Chart.* While it is not strictly necessary, the examples in this chapter will assume a clean slate.

Use the following steps to remove this chart from your chart repository:

1. Navigate to the local clone of your Helm chart repository. As you will recall, the name we recommended for your chart repository was `Learn-Helm-Chart-Repository`, so we will use this name throughout this chapter to refer to your GitHub Pages-based chart repository:

```
$ cd $LEARN_HELM_CHART_REPOSITORY_DIR
$ ls
guestbook-1.0.0.tgz    index.yaml    README.md
```

2. Remove the `guestbook-1.0.0.tgz` and `index.yaml` files from your chart repository:

```
$ rm guestbook-1.0.0.tgz index.yaml
$ ls
README.md
```

3. Push these changes to your remote repository:

```
$ git add --all
$ git commit -m 'Preparing for chapter 7'
$ git push origin master
```

4. You should be able to confirm in GitHub that your chart and index files have been removed, leaving only the `README.md` file:

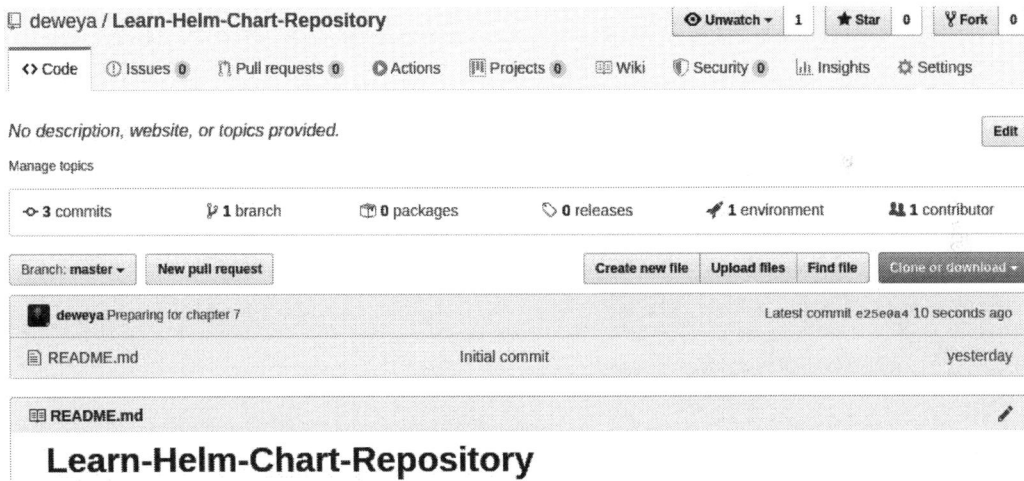

Figure 7.2 – The only file you should see in your chart repository is the README.md file

Now that you have started Minikube, created a fork of the Packt repository, and removed the Guestbook chart from `Learn-Helm-Chart-Repository`, let's begin learning how a CI pipeline can be created to release Helm charts.

Creating a CI pipeline to build Helm charts

The concept of CI can be applied to the perspective of a chart developer who builds, tests, packages, and releases Helm charts to a chart repository. In this section, we will describe what using an end-to-end CI pipeline to streamline this process may look like, as well as walk you through how to build an example pipeline. The first step is to design the components required for the example pipeline.

Designing the pipeline

In the previous chapters, developing Helm charts was largely a manual process. While Helm provides automation for creating `test` hooks in a Kubernetes cluster, the invocation of the `helm lint`, `helm test`, or `ct lint-and-install` commands is manually executed after a change in code to ensure tests still pass. Once linting and testing continue to pass after a code change, the chart can be packaged by running the `helm package` command. If the chart is served using a GitHub Pages repository (such as the one created in *Chapter 5*, *Building Your First Helm chart*), the `index.yaml` file is created by running `helm repo index`, and the `index.yaml` file, along with the packaged chart, is pushed to the GitHub repository.

While invoking each command manually is certainly feasible, this workflow can become increasingly difficult to sustain as you develop additional Helm charts or add additional contributors. With a manual workflow, it is easy to allow untested changes to be made to your charts and it is difficult to ensure that contributors are adhering to testing and contributing guidelines. Luckily, these issues can be avoided by creating a CI pipeline that automates your release process.

The following steps outline an example CI workflow using the commands and tooling discussed throughout this book so far. It will assume that the resulting charts are saved in a GitHub Pages repository:

1. A chart developer makes a code change to a chart or a set of charts in a `git` monorepo.

2. The developer pushes the change(s) to the remote repository.

3. The charts that have been modified are automatically linted and tested in a Kubernetes namespace by running the `ct lint` and `ct install` commands.

4. If linting and testing is successful, the charts are automatically packaged with the `helm package` command.

5. The `index.yaml` file is automatically generated with the `helm repo index` command.

6. The packaged charts and the updated `index.yaml` file are automatically pushed to the repository. They are pushed to either `stable` or `staging`, depending on the branch that the job was run against.

In the next section, we will perform this process using **Jenkins**. Let's begin by understanding what Jenkins is and how it works.

Understanding Jenkins

Jenkins is an open source server used to perform automated tasks and workflows. It is commonly used to create CI/CD pipelines via Jenkins's **pipeline as code** feature, written in a file called a `Jenkinsfile` that defines a Jenkins pipeline.

A Jenkins pipeline is written using the Groovy **Domain-Specific Language (DSL)**. Groovy is a language similar to Java but, unlike Java, it can be used as an object-oriented scripting language, lending itself to writing easy-to-read automation. Throughout this chapter, we will walk you through two existing `Jenkinsfile` files that have already been prepared for you. You do not need to have any prior experience with writing a `Jenkinsfile` file from scratch, as a deep dive into Jenkins is beyond the scope of this book. With that said, by the end of this chapter, you should be able to take the concepts learned and apply them to an automation tool of your choice. While Jenkins is featured in this chapter, its concepts can be applied to any other automation tool.

When a `Jenkinsfile` file is created, the defined set of steps of the workflow is executed on the Jenkins server itself or in a separate agent delegated to run the job, instead. Additional capabilities can be integrated with Kubernetes by automatically scheduling Jenkins agents as separate Pods whenever a build is kicked off, simplifying the creation and management of agents. After an agent completes, it can be configured to automatically terminate so that the next build can run in a fresh, clean Pod. In this chapter, we will run the example pipelines using Jenkins agents.

Jenkins also lends itself well to the concept of GitOps by providing the ability to scan a source control repository for the presence of a `Jenkinsfile` file. For each branch that contains a `Jenkinsfile` file, a new job is automatically configured that will begin by cloning the repository against the desired branch. This makes it simple to test new features and fixes as new jobs can be automatically created alongside their corresponding branches.

With a basic understanding of Jenkins, let's now install Jenkins on our Minikube environment.

Installing Jenkins

As with many applications that are commonly deployed on Kubernetes, Jenkins can be deployed with one of many different community Helm charts from Helm Hub. In this chapter, we will use the Jenkins Helm chart from the **Codecentric** software development company. Add the `codecentric` chart repository to begin installing the Codecentric Jenkins Helm chart:

```
$ helm repo add codecentric https://codecentric.github.io/
helm-charts
```

Among the expected Kubernetes-related values, such as configuring the resource limits and the service type, the `codecentric` Jenkins Helm chart contains other Jenkins-related values used to automatically configure different Jenkins components.

Since configuring these values requires a deeper understanding of Jenkins that is beyond the scope of this book, a `values` file is provided for you that will automatically prepare the following Jenkins configurations:

- Add relevant Jenkins plugins that are not included in the base image.
- Configure the credentials required to authenticate with GitHub.
- Configure a Jenkins agent specifically designed for testing and installing Helm charts.
- Configure Jenkins to automatically create a new job based on the presence of the `Jenkinsfile` file.
- Skip manual prompts that normally occur on the startup of a new installation.
- Disable authentication to simplify Jenkins access for this chapter.

The `values` file will also configure the following Kubernetes-related details:

- Set resource limits against the Jenkins server.
- Set the Jenkins service type to `NodePort`.
- Create the ServiceAccounts and RBAC rules required for Jenkins and Jenkins agents to run jobs and deploy Helm charts in the Kubernetes environment.
- Set the Jenkins `PersistentVolumeClaim` size to `2Gi`.

This values file is available at `https://github.com/PacktPublishing/-Learn-Helm/blob/master/jenkins/values.yaml`. When browsing the content of these values, you may notice that the configuration defined under `fileContent` contains Go templating. The beginning of this value can be seen here:

```
fileContent: |
  credentials:
    system:
      domainCredentials:
        - credentials:
          - usernamePassword:
              scope: GLOBAL
              id: github-auth
              username: {{ required "value 'githubUsername' is required" .Values.githubUsername }}
              password: {{ required "value 'githubPassword' is required" .Values.githubPassword }}
              description: Password to authenticate with GitHub
```

Figure 7.3 – The `values.yaml` file for the Jenkins Helm chart contains Go templating

While Go templating is not normally valid in a `values.yaml` file, the Codecentric Jenkins Helm chart supplies the `fileContent` configuration to a template function called `tpl`. A simplified view of what this looks like on the template side is as follows:

```
{{- tpl .Values.fileContent }}
```

The `tpl` command will parse the `fileContent` value as a Go template, allowing it to contain Go templating even though it is defined in a `values.yaml` file.

For this chapter, the Go templating defined in the `fileContent` configuration helps ensure that Jenkins is installed in a way that corresponds with this chapter's requirements. Namely, the templating will require the following additional values to be provided during installation:

- `githubUsername`: The GitHub username

- `githubPassword`: The GitHub password

- `githubForkUrl`: The URL of your Packt repository fork, which was taken in the *Technical requirements* section of this chapter

- `githubPagesRepoUrl`: The URL of your GitHub Pages Helm repository, which was created at the end of *Chapter 5, Building Your First Helm Chart*

Note that this is not the URL to your static site, but the URL to the GitHub repository itself—for example, `https://github.com/$GITHUB_USERNAME/Learn-Helm-Chart-Repository.git`.

The four values described in the preceding list can be provided using the `--set` flag, or they can be provided from an additional `values` file using the `--values` flag. If you choose to create a separate `values` file, ensure that you do not commit and push that file to source control as it contains sensitive information. The example in this chapter favors the `--set` flag for these four values. In addition to the values described, the `values.yaml` file included in the Packt repository should also be provided using the `--values` flag.

Install your `Jenkins` instance with the `helm install` command, using the following example as a reference:

```
$ helm install jenkins codecentric/jenkins \
  -n chapter7 --version 1.5.1 \
  --values Learn-Helm/jenkins/values.yaml \
  --set githubUsername=$GITHUB_USERNAME \
  --set githubPassword=$GITHUB_PASSWORD \
  --set githubForkUrl=https://github.com/$GITHUB_USERNAME/-Learn-Helm.git \
  --set githubPagesRepoUrl=https://github.com/$GITHUB_USERNAME/Learn-Helm-Chart-Repository.git
```

You can monitor the installation by running a watch against the Pods in the `chapter7` namespace:

```
$ kubectl get Pods -n chapter7 -w
```

Note that in very rare cases, your Pod may become stuck at the `Init:0/1` stage. This can occur if availability issues to external dependencies, such as if the Jenkins plugin site and its mirrors were experiencing downtime. If this occurs, try deleting your release and reinstalling it after several minutes.

Once your Jenkins Pod reports 1/1 under the READY column, your Jenkins instance is ready to be accessed. Copy and paste the following contents of the displayed post-installation notes to reveal the Jenkins URL:

```
$ export NODE_PORT=$(kubectl get service --namespace chapter7
-o jsonpath='{.spec.ports[0].nodePort}' jenkins-master)
```

```
$ export NODE_IP=$(kubectl get nodes --namespace chapter7 -o
jsonpath='{.items[0].status.addresses[0].address}')
```

```
echo "http://$NODE_IP:$NODE_PORT"
```

When you access Jenkins, your front page should look similar to the following screenshot:

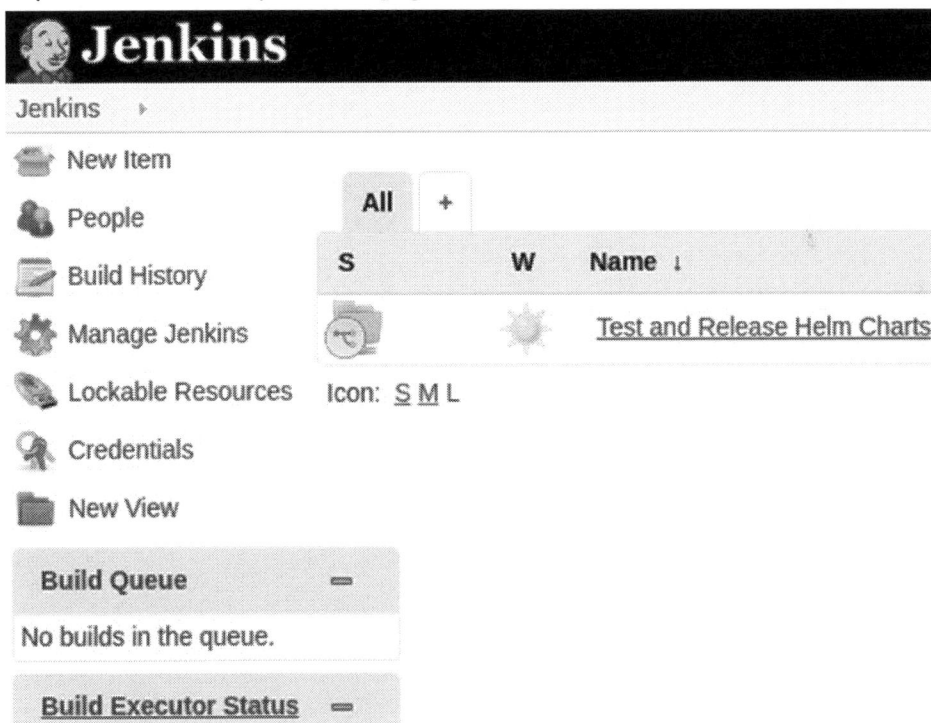

Figure 7.4 – The Jenkins home page after running the Helm installation

If the chart were installed properly, you'll notice that a new job called **Test and Release Helm Charts** is created. At the bottom left-hand corner of the page, you'll notice the **Build Executor Status** panel, which is used to provide an overview of the active jobs that are currently running. A job is automatically triggered for the first time when it is created, which is why you will see it running when you log in to your Jenkins instance.

Now that Jenkins is installed and its frontend has been validated, let's walk through the example `Jenkinsfile` file from the Packt repository to understand how the CI pipeline works. Note that we will not display the full contents of the `Jenkinsfile` file in this chapter as we want to simply highlight the key areas of interest. The full contents of the file can be viewed in the Packt repository at `https://github.com/PacktPublishing/-Learn-Helm/blob/master/helm-charts/Jenkinsfile`.

Understanding the pipeline

The first thing that occurs when the `Test and Deploy Helm Charts` job is triggered is that a new Jenkins agent is created. By leveraging the values provided in `Learn-Helm/jenkins/values.yaml`, the Jenkins chart installation automatically configures a Jenkins agent called `chart-testing-agent`. The following line designates that agent as the agent for this `Jenkinsfile` file:

```
agent { label 'chart-testing-agent' }
```

This agent is configured by the Jenkins chart values to run using the chart testing image provided by the Helm community. The chart testing image, located at `quay.io/helmpack/chart-testing`, contains many of the tools that were discussed in *Chapter 6, Testing Helm Charts*. Specifically, this image contains the following tools:

- `helm`
- `ct`
- `yamllint`
- `yamale`
- `git`
- `Kubectl`

Since this image contains all of the tools required to test the Helm charts, it can be used as the primary image to perform CI for our Helm charts.

When a Jenkins agent is run, it clones your GitHub fork, specified by the `githubForkUrl` value, using `githubUsername` and `githubPassword` for authentication. This is performed implicitly by Jenkins, so no code needs to be specified within the `Jenkinsfile` file to perform this action.

After the Jenkins agent clones your repository, it begins executing the stages defined in the `Jenkinsfile` file. Stages are logical groupings within a pipeline that can help visualize the high-level steps. The first stage that will be performed is the lint stage, which contains the following command:

```
sh 'ct lint'
```

The `sh` portion in the preceding command is a command used to run a bash shell or script and invokes the `lint` subcommand of the `ct` tool. As you will recall, this command lints the `Chart.yaml` and `values.yaml` files on all charts that have been modified against the master branch, which we covered in *Chapter 6, Testing Helm Charts*.

If the linting is successful, the pipeline will continue on to the test stage and will run the following command:

```
sh 'ct install --upgrade'
```

This command should look familiar, also. It installs each modified chart from its version on the master branch and performs the defined test suites. It also ensures any upgrades from the previous version are successful, which aids in helping to prevent regressions.

Note that the two previous stages could have been combined by running a single `ct lint-and-install --upgrade` command. This would still have resulted in a valid pipeline, but this example, which is broken up into separate stages, allows better visualization of the actions that are performed.

If the test stage is successful, the pipeline proceeds to the package charts stage, which executes the following command:

```
sh 'helm package --dependency-update helm-charts/charts/*'
```

The command at this stage will simply package each chart contained under the `helm-charts/charts` folder. It will also update and download each dependency that is declared.

If the packaging is successful, the pipeline proceeds to the final stage, called `push charts to repo`. This is the most complex stage, so we will break it up into smaller steps. The first step can be seen here:

```
// Clone GitHub Pages repository to a folder called 'chart-repo'
sh "git clone ${env.GITHUB_PAGES_REPO_URL} chart-repo"

// Determine if these charts should be pushed to 'stable' or 'staging' based on the branch
def repoType
if (env.BRANCH_NAME == 'master') {
  repoType = 'stable'
} else {
  repoType = 'staging'
}

// Create the corresponding 'stable' or 'staging' folder if it does not exist
def files = sh(script: 'ls chart-repo', returnStdout: true)
if (!files.contains(repoType)) {
  sh "mkdir chart-repo/${repoType}"
}
```

Since the Helm chart repository that we are pushing to is a separate GitHub Pages repository, we must clone the repository so that we can add the new charts and push the changes. Once the GitHub Pages repository is cloned, a variable called `repoType` is set, depending on the branch that the CI/CD pipeline runs against. This variable is used to determine whether the charts packaged in the previous stage should be pushed to the `stable` or `staging` chart repository.

For this pipeline, `stable` implies that the charts have been tested, validated, and merged into the master branch. `staging` implies that the chart is under development and has not yet been merged into the master branch nor been officially released. You can, alternatively, release charts under the stable repository when you cut to a release branch, but for this example, we will take the former approach of assuming every merge into master is a new release.

`stable` and `staging` are served as two separate chart repositories; this can be done by creating two separate directories at the top level of the GitHub Pages repository:

```
Learn-Helm-Repository/
  stable/
  staging/
```

The stable and staging folders then contain their own `index.yaml` files to differentiate them as separate chart repositories.

For convenience, the final snippet of the preceding pipeline excerpt creates the `stable` or `staging` folders automatically if the pipeline execution based on the branch relies on its existence.

Now that the type of repository that the charts should be pushed to has been determined, we proceed to the next stage of the pipeline, as follows:

```
// Move charts from the packaged-charts folder to the
corresponding 'stable' or 'staging' folder
sh "mv packaged-charts/*.tgz chart-repo/${repoType}"

// Generate the updated index.yaml
sh "helm repo index chart-repo/${repoType}"

// Update git config details
sh "git config --global user.email 'chartrepo-robot@example.
com'"
sh "git config --global user.name 'chartrepo-robot'"
```

The first command copies each of the packaged charts from the previous stage to the `stable` or `staging` folders. Next, the `stable` or `staging` `index.yaml` file is updated using the `helm repo index` command to reflect the changed or added charts.

One point to keep in mind is that if we use a different chart repository solution, such as **ChartMuseum** (a chart repository solution maintained by the Helm community), the `helm repo index` command is not needed since the `index.yaml` file is automatically updated when ChartMuseum receives a new packaged Helm chart. For implementations that do not automatically calculate the `index.yaml` file, such as GitHub Pages, the `helm repo index` command is necessary, as we can see in this pipeline.

The final two commands from the preceding snippet set the git username and email, which are required to push contents to a git repository. For this example, we will set the username to chartrepo-robot to indicate that a CI/CD process facilitated the git interactions and we will set the email to chartrepo-robot@example.com as an example value. You probably want the email to represent the organization in charge of maintaining the chart repository.

The final step is to push the changes. This action is captured in the final pipeline snippet, shown here:

```
// Add and commit the changes
sh 'git add --all'
sh "git commit -m 'pushing charts from branch ${env.BRANCH_
NAME}'"
withCredentials([usernameColonPassword(credentialsId: 'github-
auth', variable: 'USERPASS')]) {
    script {

        // Inject GitHub auth and push to the master branch, where
the charts are being served
        def authRepo = env.GITHUB_PAGES_REPO_URL.replace('://',
"://${USERPASS}@")
        sh "git push ${authRepo} master"
    }
}
```

The packaged charts are first added and committed using the git add and git commit commands. Next, a push to the repository is performed with the git push command, using a credential called github-auth. This credential was created during installation from the githubUsername and githubPassword values. The github-auth credential allows you to securely refer to these secrets without printing them in plaintext in your pipeline code.

Note that the Helm community has published a tool called Chart Releaser (https://github.com/helm/chart-releaser) that can be used as an alternative to generating the index.yaml file with the helm repo index command and uploading it to GitHub with git push. The Chart Releaser tool is designed to abstract some of this additional complexity by managing the Helm charts contained in GitHub Pages.

We have decided not to implement the pipeline using this tool in this chapter, however, because `Chart Releaser` does not support Helm 3 (at the time of writing).

Now that we have provided an overview of the CI pipeline, let's run through an example execution.

Running the pipeline

As we discussed earlier, the first run of this pipeline was actually triggered automatically when we installed Jenkins. The job was run against the master branch and can be seen by clicking the **Test and Release Helm Charts** link on the Jenkins landing page. You will observe that one successful job ran against the master branch:

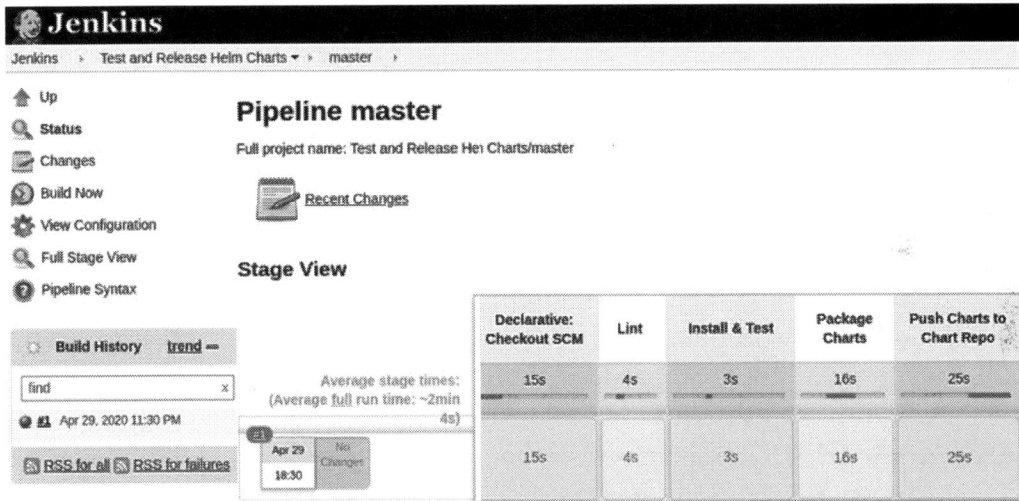

Figure 7.5 – The first runthrough of the pipeline

Every pipeline build in Jenkins has an associated log that contains the output of the execution. You can access the log for this build by selecting the **#1** link next to the blue circle on the left-hand side and then selecting **Console Output** on the next screen. The logs for this build reveal that the first stage, `Lint`, succeeded by displaying this message:

```
All charts linted successfully
----------------------------------
No chart changes detected.
```

This is what we would expect because no charts were changed from the perspective of the master branch. A similar output can be seen under the install stage as well:

```
All charts installed successfully

------------------------------------
No chart changes detected.
```

Because both the Lint and Install stages completed without error, the pipeline continued to the Package Charts stage. Here, you can view the output::

```
+ helm package --dependency-update helm-charts/charts/guestbook
helm-charts/charts/nginx
Successfully packaged chart and saved it to: /home/jenkins/
agent/workspace/t_and_Release_Helm_Charts_master/guestbook-
1.0.0.tgz
Successfully packaged chart and saved it to: /home/jenkins/
agent/workspace/t_and_Release_Helm_Charts_master/nginx-
1.0.0.tgz
```

Finally, the pipeline concludes by cloning your GitHub Pages repository, creating a stable folder within it, copying the packaged charts over to the stable folder, committing the changes to the GitHub Pages repository locally, and pushing the changes to GitHub. We can observe that each file that was added to our repository is outputted in the following lines:

```
+ git commit -m 'pushing charts from branch master'
[master 9769f5a] pushing charts from branch master
 3 files changed, 32 insertions(+)
  create mode 100644 stable/guestbook-1.0.0.tgz
  create mode 100644 stable/index.yaml
  create mode 100644 stable/nginx-1.0.0.tgz
```

You may be curious to know what your GitHub Pages repository looks like after the automatic push. Your repository should look as follows, with a new stable folder containing the Helm charts:

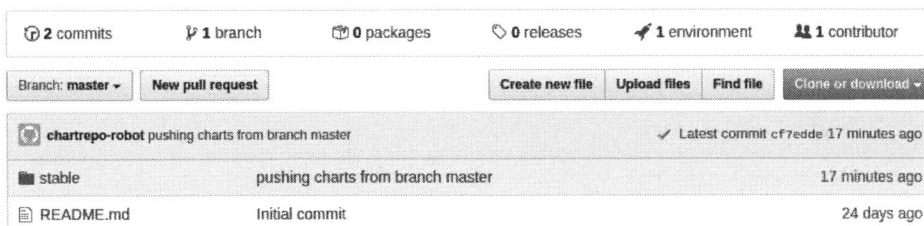

Figure 7.6 – The state of the repository after the CI pipeline completes

In the `stable` folder, you should be able to see three different files, two separate charts, and one `index.yaml` file:

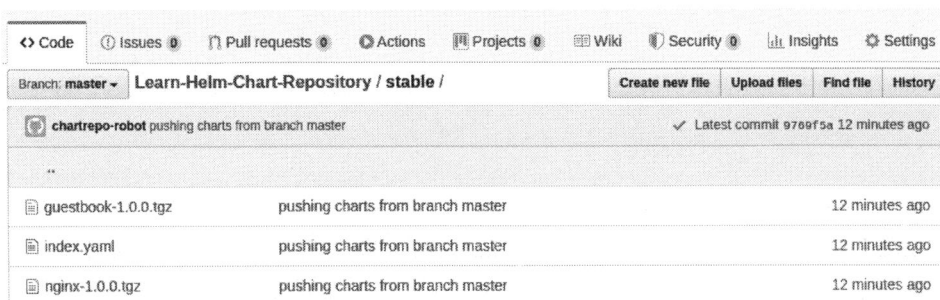

Figure 7.7 – The contents of the `stable` folder

This first pipeline build successfully created the initial set of `stable` charts, but it did not demonstrate how new charts can be linted and tested before being deemed stable and ready for end users to consume. To demonstrate this, we need to cut a feature branch off the master branch to modify one or more charts, push the changes to the feature branch, and then start a new build in Jenkins.

To begin, create a new branch called `chapter7` off of the master branch:

```
$ cd $PACKT_FORK_DIR
$ git checkout master
$ git checkout -b chapter7
```

On this branch, we will simply modify the version of the `ngnix` chart to trigger the chart's linting and testing. NGINX is a web server and a reverse proxy. It is much more lightweight than the Guestbook application we have been working with in this book, so for that reason, we will use the `ngnix` chart from the Packt repository for this example to avoid any resource constraints that might occur with Jenkins also running in your Minikube environment.

In the `helm-charts/charts/nginx/Chart.yaml` file, change the version of the chart from `1.0.0` to `1.0.1`:

```
version: 1.0.1
```

Run `git status` to confirm that a change was detected:

```
$ git status
On branch chapter7
Changes not staged for commit:
  (use 'git add <file>...' to update what will be committed)
  (use 'git checkout -- <file>...' to discard changes in
working directory)

        modified:   helm-charts/charts/nginx/Chart.yaml

no changes added to commit (use 'git add' and/or 'git commit
-a')
```

Notice that the `nginx` `Chart.yaml` file has been modified. Add the file and then commit the changes. Finally, you can proceed with pushing the change to your fork:

```
$ git add helm-charts
$ git commit -m 'bumping NGINX chart version to demonstrate
chart testing pipeline'
$ git push origin chapter7
```

Within Jenkins, we need to trigger a repository scan so that Jenkins can detect and start a new build against this branch. Navigate to the **Test and Release Helm Charts** page. You can easily do so by clicking on the **Test and Release Helm Charts** tab on the top bar:

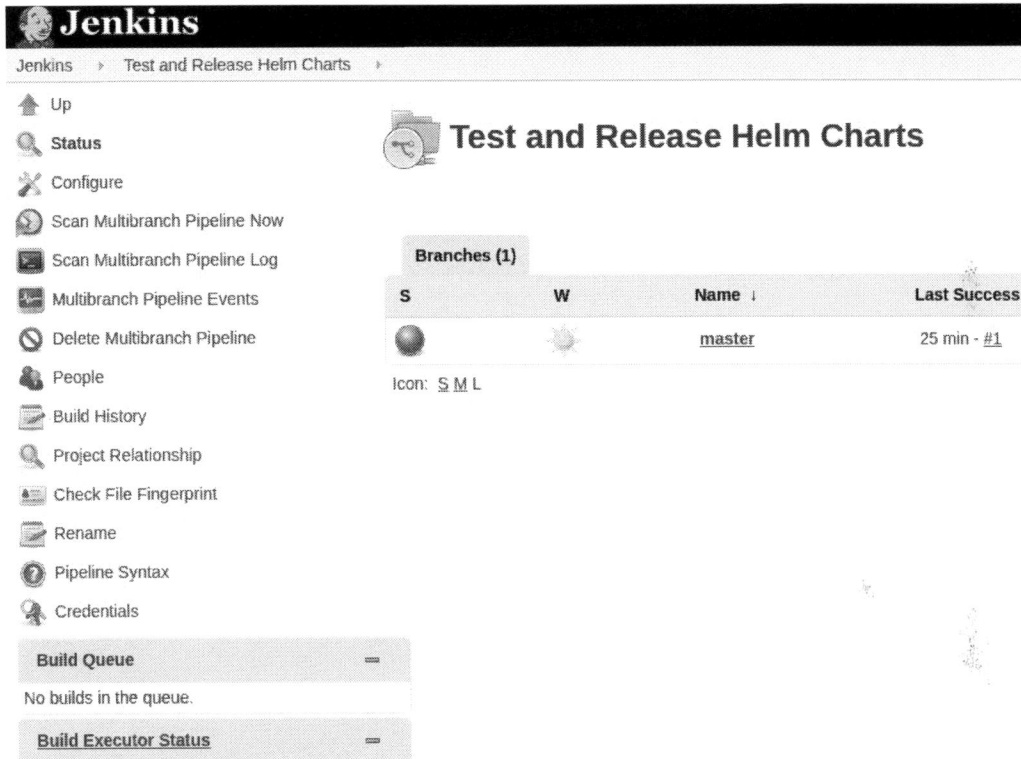

Figure 7.8 – The Test and Release Helm Charts page

Once selected, click the **Scan Multibranch Pipeline Now** button in the left-hand side menu. This allows Jenkins to detect your new branch and to automatically start a new build. The scan should complete within approximately 10 seconds. Refresh the page and the new `chapter7` branch should appear on the page as follows:

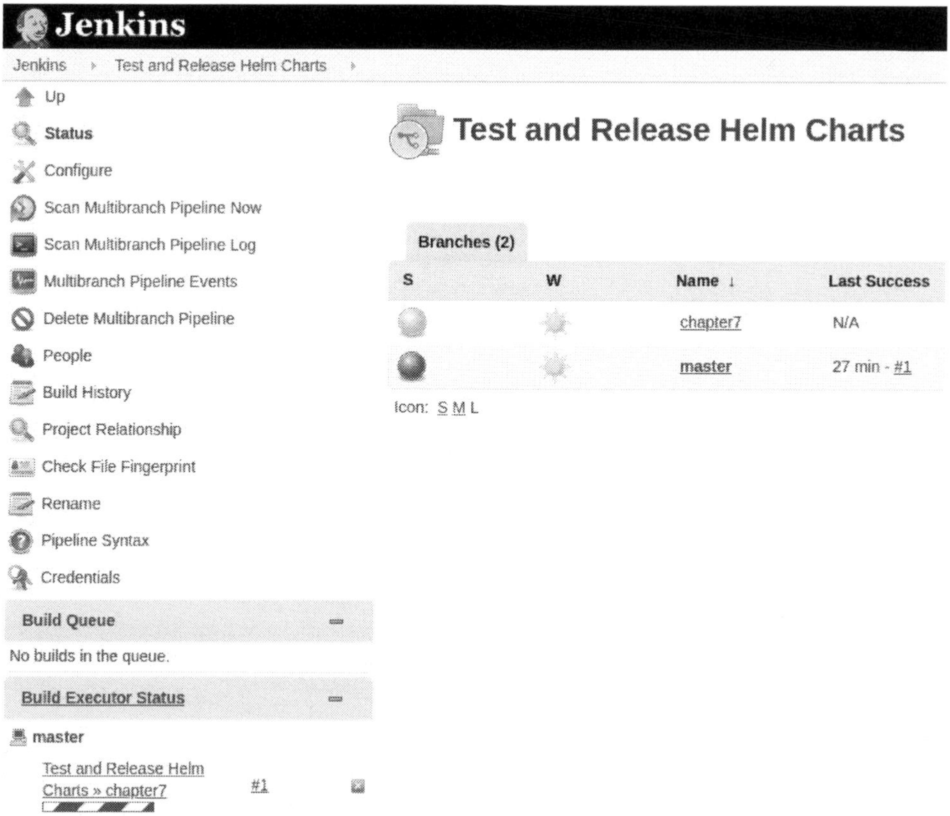

Figure 7.9 – The Test and Deploy Helm Charts page after scanning for the new `chapter7` branch

The `chapter7` job will run for a longer period of time than the master job since the `chapter7` job contains a modified Helm chart that is tested with the chart testing tool. You can observe this pipeline in action by navigating to the console output for `chapter7`. From the **Test and Release Helm Charts** overview page, select the `chapter 7` branch and then the **#1** link at the bottom left-hand side. Finally, select the **Console Output** link. If you navigate to this page while the pipeline is still running, you will receive the log updates as they occur in real time. Wait until the end of the pipeline, where the following message should be displayed:

```
Finished: SUCCESS
```

Toward the beginning of the console output logs, notice how the `ct lint` and `ct install` commands were run against the `ngnix` chart as this was the only chart where a change occurred:

```
Charts to be processed:
------------------------------------------------------------------
  nginx => (version: '1.0.1', path: 'helm-charts/charts/nginx')
```

The additional output for each command should already be familiar as it is the same as the output that was described in *Chapter 6, Testing Helm Charts*.

In your GitHub Pages repository, you should see the new version of the `ngnix` chart in the `staging` folder as it was not built against the master branch:

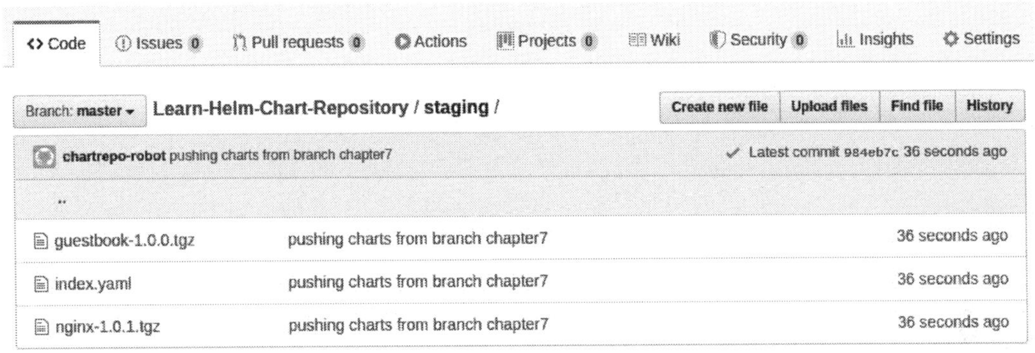

Figure 7.10 – The contents of the `staging` folder

To release the `nginx-1.0.1.tgz` chart, you need to merge the `chapter7` branch into the master branch, which will cause this chart to be pushed to the stable repository. On the command line, merge your `chapter7` branch into the master branch and push it to the `remote` repository:

```
$ git checkout master
$ git merge chapter7
$ git push origin master
```

Within Jenkins, navigate to the master pipeline job by returning to the **Test and Release Helm Charts** page and clicking on the **master** job. Your screen should appear as follows:

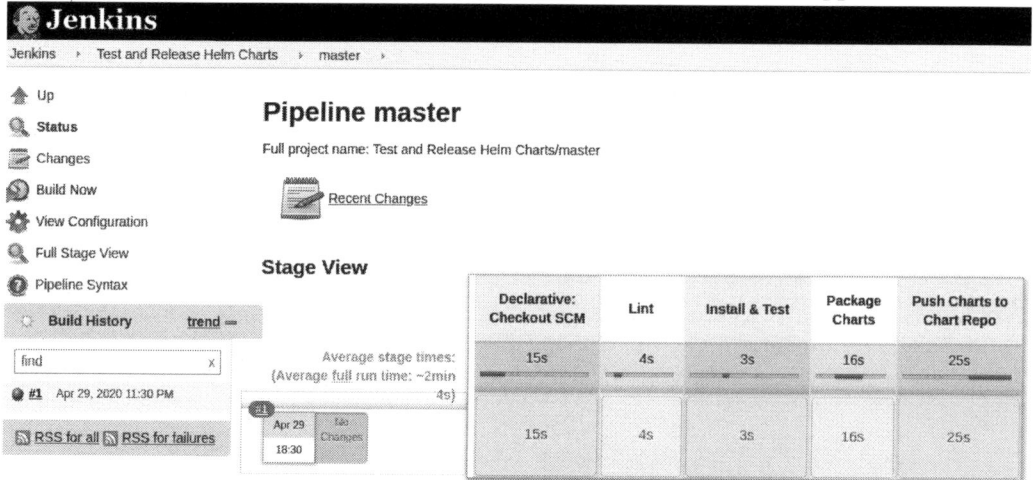

Figure 7.11 – The master job for the Test and Release Helm charts project

Once on this page, click on the **Build Now** link on the left-hand side. Once again, notice in the logs that chart tests were skipped because the chart testing tool compared the clone against the master branch. Since the content is the same, the tool determines that there is no testing to be done. When the build finishes, navigate to your GitHub Pages repository to confirm the new `nginx-1.0.1.tgz` chart is under the `stable` repository:

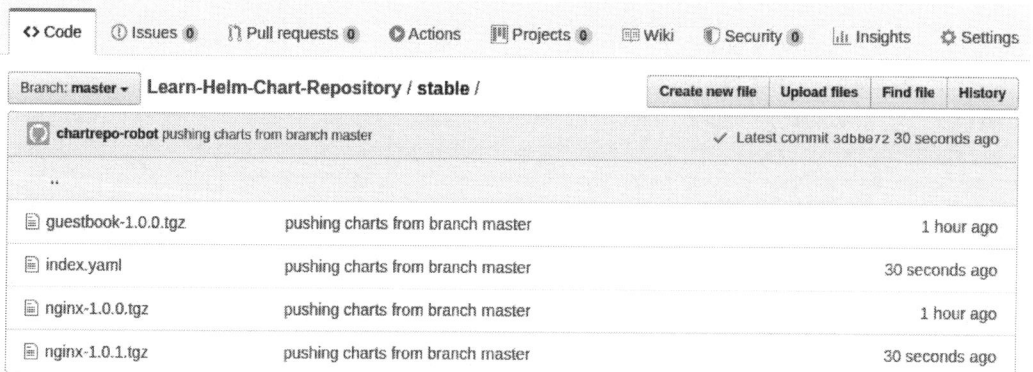

Figure 7.12 – The state of the repository after the new `nginx` chart has been added

You can verify that these charts are deployed properly to the GitHub Pages `stable` repository by adding the repository locally using `helm repo add`. In *Chapter 5, Building Your First Helm Chart*, you added the root location of the GitHub Pages repository. However, we modified the file structure to contain the `stable` and `staging` folders. If it is still configured, you can remove this repository by running the following command:

```
$ helm repo remove learnhelm
```

The repository can be added again with the updated location of the `stable` repository:

```
$ helm repo add learnhelm $GITHUB_PAGES_SITE_URL/stable
```

Note that the value of `$GITHUB_PAGES_SITE_URL` references the static site that GitHub serves and not your actual `git` repository. Your GitHub Pages site URL should have a format similar to `https://$GITHUB_USERNAME.github.io/Learn-Helm-Repository/stable`. The exact link can be found in the **Settings** tab of your GitHub Pages repository.

After adding the `stable` repository, run the following command to view each of the charts that have been built and pushed over the course of the two master builds:

```
$ helm search repo learnhelm --versions
```

You should see three results, two of which contain both versions of the `nginx` chart that was built and pushed:

```
NAME                      CHART VERSION    APP VERSION      DESCRIPTION
learnhelm/guestbook       1.0.0            v4               A Helm chart for Kubernetes
learnhelm/nginx           1.0.1            1.16.0           A Helm chart for Kubernetes
learnhelm/nginx           1.0.0            1.16.0           A Helm chart for Kubernetes
```

Figure 7.13 – Results from the `helm search repo` command

In this section, we discussed how the life cycle of Helm charts can be managed through a CI pipeline. By following an automated workflow using the example provided, you can easily perform routine linting and testing before releasing charts to end users.

While this section focused primarily on the CI of Helm charts, CD and GitOps can also be implemented to deploy Helm charts to different environments. We will explore how a CD pipeline can be built in the next section.

Creating a CD pipeline to deploy applications with Helm

A CD pipeline is a set of repeatable steps that can deploy to one or more different environments in an automated fashion. In this section, we will create a CD pipeline to deploy the `nginx` chart that we tested and pushed to our GitHub Pages repository in the previous section. GitOps will also be leveraged by referencing the `values` files saved to a `git` repository.

Let's design the high-level steps that need to be included in this pipeline.

Designing the pipeline

In previous chapters, deploying to a Kubernetes environment with Helm was a manual process. This CD pipeline, however, is designed to deploy to multiple different environments while abstracting the use of Helm.

The following steps describe the CD workflow that we will cover in this section:

1. Add the stable GitHub Pages repository containing the `nginx` chart release.
2. Deploy the `nginx` chart to the development environment.
3. Deploy the `nginx` chart to the **Quality Assurance** (**QA**) environment.
4. Wait for the user to approve the pipeline to proceed to the production deployment.
5. Deploy the `nginx` chart to the production environment.

The CD workflow is contained in a separate `Jenkinsfile` file to the file created previously for the CI pipeline. Before we create the `Jenkinsfilc` file, let's update the Minikube and Jenkins environments so that we can perform the CD process.

Updating the environments

The development, QA, and production environments will be modeled by different namespaces within your local Minikube cluster. While we would usually discourage you from allowing non-production (development and QA) and production environments to coexist within the same cluster, we will co-locate these three environments just to demonstrate our example CD process.

Create the dev, qa, and prod namespaces to represent each of these environments:

```
$ kubectl create ns dev
$ kubectl create ns qa
$ kubectl create ns prod
```

You should also delete the chapter7 branch that you created in the previous section. This branch should be deleted because when the new CD pipeline is created, Jenkins will attempt to run it against each of your repository's branches. For simplicity and to avoid resource constraints, we recommend advancing with only the master branch.

Remove the chapter7 branch from your repository with the following commands:

```
$ git push -d origin chapter7
$ git branch -D chapter7
```

Finally, you will need to upgrade your Jenkins instance to set an environment variable called GITHUB_PAGES_SITE_URL. This is the location of your chart repository in GitHub Pages that has a https://$GITHUB_USERNAME.github.io/Learn-Helm-Chart-Repository/stable format. The environment variable is referenced in the CD pipeline to add the stable GitHub Pages chart repository with helm repo add. To add this variable, you can reuse the values that were previously applied by using the --reuse-values flag, while also specifying an additional value called githubPagesSiteUrl by using --set.

Execute the following command to upgrade your Jenkins instance:

```
$ helm upgrade jenkins codecentric/jenkins \
  -n chapter7 --version 1.5.1 \
  --reuse-values --set githubPagesSiteUrl=$GITHUB_PAGES_SITE_
URL
```

This upgrade will cause your Jenkins instance to restart. You can wait for the Jenkins Pod to be ready by running a watch against the chapter7 namespace's Pods:

```
$ kubectl get Pods -n chapter7 -w
```

The Jenkins Pod is available when it indicates that 1/1 containers are ready.

Once Jenkins is ready, access the Jenkins instance by using the same URL from the previous section. You should find another job, called `Deploy NGINX Chart`, which represents the CD pipeline:

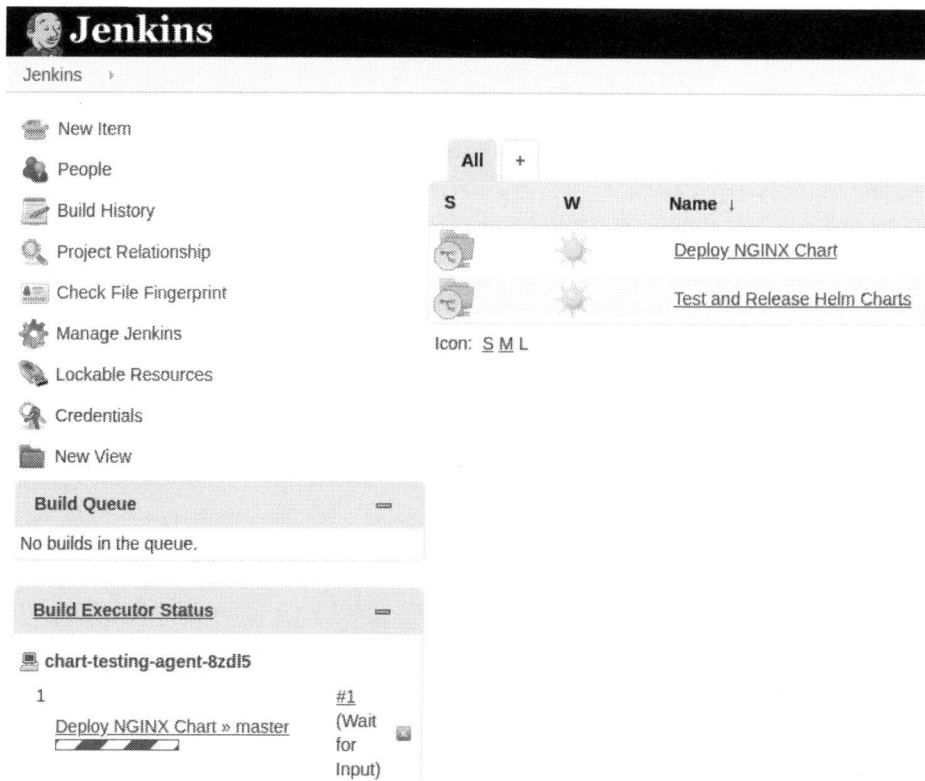

Figure 7.14 – The Jenkins front page after upgrading the Jenkins release

This job is configured in the `values.yaml` file to be created when `GITHUB_PAGES_SITE_URL` is set (to help improve the flow of this chapter).

Note that as with the CI pipeline, the CD pipeline also starts automatically since it is detected for the first time. Before we review this pipeline's logs, let's examine the process that makes up the CD pipeline.

Understanding the pipeline

In this section, we will just review the key areas of the pipeline, but the full CD pipeline has been written up and is located at `https://github.com/PacktPublishing/-Learn-Helm/blob/master/nginx-cd/Jenkinsfile`.

As with the previous CI pipeline, to test and release Helm charts, the CD pipeline begins by dynamically creating a new Jenkins agent as a Kubernetes Pod running the chart testing image:

```
agent { label 'chart-testing-agent' }
```

Although we are not using the `ct` tool in this pipeline, the chart testing image contains the Helm CLI that is required to perform the `nginx` deployments, so the image suffices for this example CD pipeline. However, it would also be acceptable to create a smaller image that removes the tools that are not utilized.

Once an agent is created, Jenkins implicitly clones your fork, as it did previously in the CI pipeline.

The first explicitly defined stage of the pipeline is called `Setup`, which adds your `stable` chart repository hosted in GitHub Pages to the local Helm client on the Jenkins agent:

```
sh "helm repo add learnhelm ${env.GITHUB_PAGES_SITE_URL}"
```

Once the repository is added, the pipeline can begin deploying NGINX to the different environments. The next stage, called `Deploy to Dev`, deploys the NGINX chart to your dev namespace:

```
dir('nginx-cd') {
    sh "helm upgrade --install nginx-${env.BRANCH_NAME}
learnhelm/nginx --values common-values.yaml --values dev/
values.yaml -n dev --wait"
}
```

The first detail you might notice about this stage is the `dir('nginx-cd')` closure. This is the `Jenkinsfile` syntax to set the working directory of the commands contained within it. We will explain the `nginx-cd` folder in greater detail soon.

You can also see that this stage runs the `helm upgrade` command with the provided `--install` flag. `helm upgrade` is normally performed against an already-existing release and fails if attempted against a release that doesn't exist. The `--install` flag, however, installs the chart if a release does not already exist. If a release does already exist, the `helm upgrade` command upgrades the release. The `--install` flag is convenient for use for automated processes, such as the CD pipeline described in this section, because it prevents you from needing to perform a check to determine the existence of a release.

Another interesting detail about this `helm upgrade` command is that it uses the `--values` flag twice—once against a file called `common-values.yaml` and once against a file called `dev/values.yaml`. Both of these files are located in the `nginx-cd` folder. The following contents are found in the `nginx-cd` folder:

```
nginx-cd/
  dev/
    values.yaml
  qa/
    values.yaml
  prod/
    values.yaml
  common-values.yaml
  Jenkinsfile
```

When deploying an application to different environments, you may need to slightly modify the application's configuration to allow it to integrate with other services in the environment. Each of the `values` files under the `dev`, `qa`, and `prod` folders contain an environment variable that is set on the NGINX deployment, depending on the environment that it is deployed to. For example, the `dev/values.yaml` file contents are shown here:

```
env:
  - name: ENVIRONMENT
    value: dev
```

Similarly, the `qa/values.yaml` file contents are shown here:

```
env:
  - name: ENVIRONMENT
    value: qa
```

The `prod/values.yaml` file contents are as follows:

```
env:
  - name: ENVIRONMENT
    value: prod
```

While the NGINX chart that is deployed in this example is straightforward and does not strictly require these values to be specified, you will find it helpful to separate environment-specific configurations in separate `values` files using the method shown here for complex and real-world use cases. The corresponding values file can then be applied to the installation by passing it to the `helm upgrade --install` command with `--values ${env}/values.yaml`, where `${env}` represents either `dev`, `qa`, or `prod`.

The `common-values.yaml` file, as its name implies, is used for values that are common across all the deployment environments. The `common-values.yaml` file for this example is written as follows:

```
service:
  type: NodePort
```

This file indicates that each NGINX service created during the installation of the chart should have a `NodePort` type. All the other default values set in the NGINX chart's `values.yaml` file are also applied to each environment since they have not been overridden in the `common-values.yaml` file or the individual `values.yaml` environment files.

One important point to note is that your application should be deployed as identically as possible across each of your deployment environments. Any value that changes the physical properties of your running Pods or containers should be specified in the `common-values.yaml` file. These configurations include, but are not limited to, the following:

- The replica count
- The resource requests and limits
- The service type
- The image name
- The image tag
- `ImagePullPolicy`
- The volume mounts

Values that change the configuration to integrate with environment-specific services can be modified in the individual environment `values` files. These configurations may include the following:

- The location of metrics or monitoring services
- The location of a database or backend service
- The application/ingress URL
- The notification services

Circling back to the Helm command used in the `Deploy to Dev` stage of the CD pipeline, a combination of the `--values common-values.yaml` and `--values dev/values.yaml` flags merges both of these `values` files to install the `nginx` chart in `dev`. This command also uses the `-n dev` flag to indicate that the deployment should be performed in the `dev` namespace. In addition, the `--wait` flag is used to pause the `nginx` Pod until it is reported as `ready`.

Continuing with the pipeline, the next stage after deploying to `dev` is a smoke test. This stage runs the following command:

```
sh 'helm test nginx -n dev'
```

The NGINX chart contains a test hook that checks the connection of the NGINX Pod. If the `test` hook is able to verify that a connection to the Pod can be made, the test is returned as successful. While the `helm test` command is often reserved for chart testing, it can also be used as a good way of performing a basic smoke test during the CD process. A smoke test is a test performed to ensure that the critical functions of an application work as designed after a deployment. Since the NGINX chart test does not interfere in any way with the running application or the rest of the deployment environment, the `helm test` command is an appropriate method of making sure that the NGINX chart is deployed successfully.

After the smoke test, the example CD pipeline runs the next stage, called `Deploy to` QA. This stage contains a conditional that assesses whether the current branch the pipeline is executing against is the master branch, as shown:

```
when {
    expression {
        return env.BRANCH_NAME == 'master'
    }
}
```

This conditional allows you to use feature branches to test the deployment code contained in the `values.yaml` files without promoting it to higher environments. It implies that only Helm values contained in the master branch should be production-ready, although this is not the only strategy you can take when you release an application in a CD pipeline. Another common strategy is to allow higher-level promotions to take place on release branches that begin with the `release/` prefix.

The Helm command used in the `Deploy to QA` stage is displayed as follows:

```
dir('nginx-cd') {
    sh "helm upgrade --install nginx-${env.BRANCH_NAME}
learnhelm/nginx --values common-values.yaml --values qa/values.
yaml -n qa --wait"
}
```

Given your knowledge of the `Deploy to Dev` stage and the separation of common and environment-specific values, the code for `Deploy to QA` is predictable. It references the `qa/values.yaml` file for QA-specific values and passes the `-n qa` flag to deploy to the qa namespace.

After deploying to qa, or a similar testing environment, you can run the smoke test described earlier again to ensure that the basic functions of the qa deployment work properly. You can also include any other automated tests, at this stage, that would be necessary to verify the function of your application before their deployment to `prod`. These details have been omitted from this example pipeline.

The next stage of the pipeline is called `Wait for Input`:

```
stage('Wait for Input') {
    when {
        expression {
            return env.BRANCH_NAME == 'master'
        }
    }
    steps {
        container('chart-testing') {
            input 'Deploy to Prod?'
        }
    }
}
```

This input step pauses the Jenkins pipeline and prompts the user with a `Deploy to Prod?` question. The user is given two choices—`Proceed` and `Abort`—in the console log of the running job. While the production deployment can be executed automatically without this manual step, many developers and companies prefer to have a human gate between the `non-prod` and `prod` deployments. This `input` command provides an opportunity for the user to make a decision about whether to continue the deployment or to abort the pipeline after the qa stage.

If the user decides to proceed, the final stage is executed, called `Deploy to Prod`:

```
dir('nginx-cd') {
    sh "helm upgrade --install nginx-${env.BRANCH_NAME}
learnhelm/nginx --values common-values.yaml --values prod/
values.yaml -n prod --wait"
}
```

This stage is almost identical to the `Deploy to Dev` and `Deploy to QA` stages, with the exception of the production-specific `values` file and the `prod` namespace defined as part of the `helm upgrade --install` command.

Now that the example CD pipeline has been outlined, let's observe the pipeline run that started when you upgraded your Jenkins instance.

Running the pipeline

To see this CD pipeline in action, navigate to the master branch of the `Deploy NGINX Chart` job. On the Jenkins front page, click on **Deploy NGINX Chart** and **master**. Your screen should appear as follows:

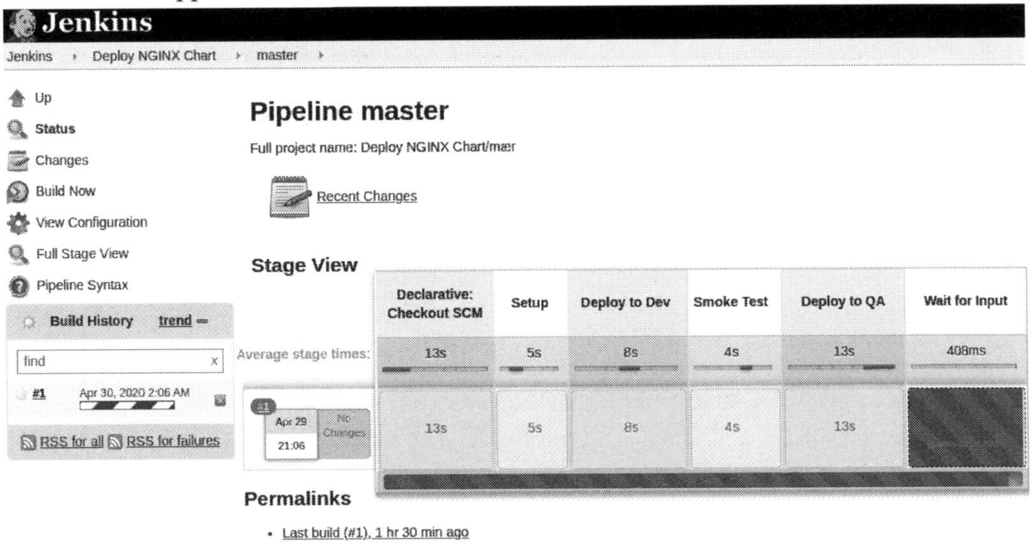

Figure 7.15 – The master branch of the Deploy NGINX Chart CD pipeline

Once you have navigated to this page, click on the **#1** link and navigate to the console logs:

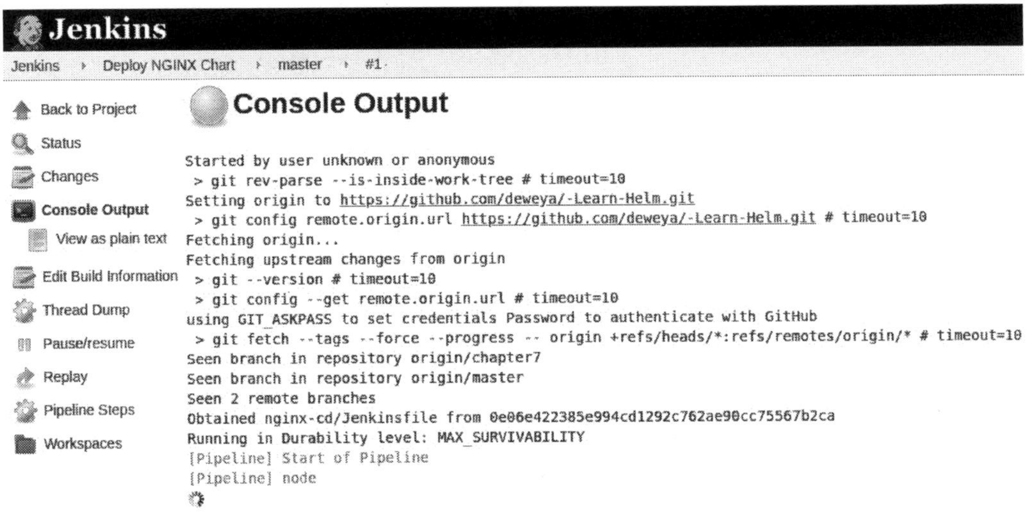

Figure 7.16 – The Console Output page for the Deploy NGINX Chart CD pipeline

When you navigate to the logs, you should see a prompt that says `Deploy to Prod?`. We will address this soon. First, let's look back at the beginning of the log to review the pipeline's execution up to this point.

The first deployment you can see is the `dev` deployment:

```
+ helm upgrade --install nginx-master learnhelm/nginx --values
common-values.yaml --values dev/values.yaml -n dev --wait
Release 'nginx-master' does not exist. Installing it now.
NAME: nginx-master
LAST DEPLOYED: Thu Apr 30 02:07:55 2020
NAMESPACE: dev
STATUS: deployed
REVISION: 1
NOTES:
1. Get the application URL by running these commands:
   export NODE_PORT=$(kubectl get --namespace dev -o
jsonpath='{.spec.ports[0].nodePort}' services nginx-master)
   export NODE_IP=$(kubectl get nodes --namespace dev -o
jsonpath='{.items[0].status.addresses[0].address}')
   echo http://$NODE_IP:$NODE_PORT
```

Then, you should see the smoke test, which was run by the `helm test` command:

```
+ helm test nginx-master -n dev
Pod nginx-master-test-connection pending
Pod nginx-master-test-connection pending
Pod nginx-master-test-connection succeeded
NAME: nginx-master
LAST DEPLOYED: Thu Apr 30 02:07:55 2020
NAMESPACE: dev
STATUS: deployed
REVISION: 1
TEST SUITE:     nginx-master-test-connection
Last Started:   Thu Apr 30 02:08:03 2020
Last Completed: Thu Apr 30 02:08:05 2020
Phase:          Succeeded
```

After the smoke test came the qa deployment:

```
+ helm upgrade --install nginx-master learnhelm/nginx --values
common-values.yaml --values qa/values.yaml -n qa --wait
Release 'nginx-master' does not exist. Installing it now.
NAME: nginx-master
LAST DEPLOYED: Thu Apr 30 02:08:09 2020
NAMESPACE: qa
STATUS: deployed
REVISION: 1
```

This brings us to the input stage, which we saw when we first opened the logs:

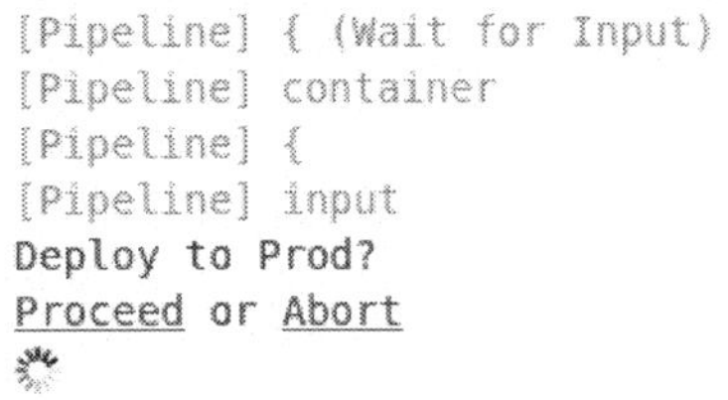

```
[Pipeline] { (Wait for Input)
[Pipeline] container
[Pipeline] {
[Pipeline] input
Deploy to Prod?
Proceed or Abort
```

Figure 7.17 – The input step before deploying to prod

Click the **Proceed** link to continue the pipeline execution, as clicking **Abort** will fail the pipeline and prevent the production deployment from occurring. You will then see the prod deployment occur:

```
+ helm upgrade --install nginx-master learnhelm/nginx --values
common-values.yaml --values prod/values.yaml -n prod --wait

Release 'nginx-master' does not exist. Installing it now.

NAME: nginx-master
LAST DEPLOYED: Thu Apr 30 03:46:22 2020
NAMESPACE: prod
STATUS: deployed
REVISION: 1
```

Finally, if the production deployment is successful, you will see the following message at the end of the pipeline:

```
[Pipeline] End of Pipeline
Finished: SUCCESS
```

You can manually verify that the deployments were successful from your command line. Run the `helm list` command to find the `nginx-master` releases:

```
$ helm list -n dev
$ helm list -n qa
$ helm list -n prod
```

Each command should list the `nginx` release in each namespace:

```
NAME                    NAMESPACE          REVISION
nginx-master            dev                1
```

You can also use `kubectl` to list the Pods in each namespace and verify that NGINX was deployed:

```
$ kubectl get Pods -n dev
$ kubectl get Pods -n qa
$ kubectl get Pods -n prod
```

The result for each namespace will be similar to the following (`dev` will also have a completed test Pod that was performed in the smoke test stage):

```
NAME                      READY   STATUS    RESTARTS   AGE
nginx-fcb5d6b64-rmc2j     1/1     Running   0          46m
```

In this section, we discussed how Helm can be used in a CD pipeline to deploy an application across multiple environments in Kubernetes. The pipeline relied on the GitOps practice of storing configuration (the `values.yaml` files) in source control and referenced these files to properly configure NGINX. With an understanding of how Helm can be used in a CD environment, you can now clean up your Minikube cluster.

Cleaning up

To clean up your Minikube cluster of this chapter's exercises, delete the `chapter7`, `dev`, `qa`, and `prod` namespaces:

```
$ kubectl delete ns chapter7
$ kubectl delete ns dev
$ kubectl delete ns qa
$ kubectl delete ns prod
```

You can also shut down your Minikube VM:

```
$ minikube stop
```

Summary

Invoking the Helm CLI in CI and CD pipelines is an efficient way of further abstracting the capabilities that Helm provides. Chart developers can automate the end-to-end chart development process by writing a CI pipeline that lints, tests, packages, and releases charts to a chart repository. End users can write a CD pipeline that uses Helm to deploy a chart across multiple different environments, leveraging GitOps to ensure applications can be deployed and configured as code. Writing pipelines helps developers and companies scale applications faster and more easily by abstracting and automating processes that could otherwise become tedious and introduce human error.

In the next chapter, we will introduce another option for abstracting the Helm CLI— writing a Helm operator.

Further reading

To learn more about the chart testing container image, go to `https://helm.sh/blog/chart-testing-intro/`.

To learn more about Jenkins and Jenkins pipelines, check out the Jenkins project documentation (`https://jenkins.io/doc/`), the Jenkins pipeline documentation (`https://jenkins.io/doc/book/pipeline/`) and the Multibranch Pipeline plugin documentation (`https://plugins.jenkins.io/workflow-multibranch/`).

Questions

1. What is the difference between CI and CD?

2. What is the difference between CI/CD and GitOps?

3. What high-level steps are included in a CI/CD pipeline for creating and releasing Helm charts?

4. What advantages does CI bring to chart developers?

5. What high-level steps are included in a CD pipeline for deploying Helm charts?

6. What advantages does a CD pipeline bring to a chart's end users?

7. How can you maintain an application's configuration as code for multiple environments? What can you do to reduce boilerplate across the `values` files?

8
Using Helm with the Operator Framework

One of the advantages of using Helm is the ability to synchronize the local and the live states. With Helm, the local state is managed with values files that, when provided using the `install` or `upgrade` command, apply the values to synchronize the live state in a Kubernetes cluster. In previous chapters, this was performed by invoking these commands when a change to the application was desired.

Another way these changes can be synchronized is to create an application inside the cluster that checks periodically that the desired state matches the current configurations within an environment. If the state does not match, the application can automatically modify the environment to match the desired state. This application is referred to as a Kubernetes operator. In this chapter, we will create a Helm-based operator that helps ensure the locally defined state always matches the live state of the cluster. If it does not, the operator will execute the appropriate Helm commands to update the environment.

We will cover the following topics in this chapter:

- Understanding Kubernetes Operators
- Creating a Helm Operator
- Using Helm to manage Operators and **Custom Resources (CRs)**
- Cleaning up your Kubernetes environment

Technical requirements

For this chapter, you will need to have the following technologies installed on your local machine:

- `minikube`
- `helm`
- `kubectl`

In addition to these tools, you should find the Packt repository containing resources associated with the examples on GitHub at `https://github.com/PacktPublishing/-Learn-Helm`. This repository will be referenced throughout this chapter.

Understanding Kubernetes Operators

Automation is at the core of the Kubernetes platform. As covered in *Chapter 1, Understanding Kubernetes and Helm*, Kubernetes resources can be managed either implicitly by running `kubectl` commands or declaratively by applying **YAML**-formatted representations. Once the resources are applied using the Kubernetes **Command-Line Interface (CLI)**, one of the fundamental principles of Kubernetes is to match the current state of resources within the cluster to the desired state, a process known as **the control loop**. This ongoing, non-terminating pattern of monitoring the state of the cluster is implemented through the use of controllers. Kubernetes includes numerous controllers that are native to the platform, with examples ranging from admission controllers that intercept requests to the Kubernetes **Application Programming Interface (API)** to replication controllers that manage the number of Pod replicas that are running.

As interest in Kubernetes began to grow, the combination of providing users the ability to extend the capabilities of the base platform, as well as a way to provide more intelligence around managing the life cycle of applications, led to the creation of several important concepts that have defined the second wave of Kubernetes development. First, the introduction of the **Custom Resource Definitions (CRDs)** enabled users the ability to extend the default Kubernetes API, the mechanism for interacting with the Kubernetes platform, in order to create and register new types of resources. Registering a new CRD creates a new **Representational State Transfer (RESTful)** resource path on the Kubernetes API server. So, similar to how you can use the Kubernetes CLI to execute `kubectl get pods` to retrieve all Pod objects, registering a new CRD for an object type called **Guestbook**, for example, allows for the capability of invoking `kubectl get guestbook` to view all Guestbook objects that have been previously created. With this new capability realized, developers could now create controllers of their own to monitor these types of CRs to manage the lifecycle of applications that can be described through the use of CRDs.

The second major trend was the advances in the types of applications that were being deployed onto Kubernetes. Instead of small and simple applications, more complex and stateful applications were being deployed more frequently. These types of advanced applications typically require a higher level of management and maintenance, such as handling the deployment of multiple components, as well as considerations around 'day 2' activities, such as backup and restorations. These tasks extend beyond the typical types of controllers found in Kubernetes, as deep knowledge related to the application they are managing must be embedded within. This pattern of using a CR to manage applications and their components is known as an **Operator** pattern. First coined by the software company CoreOS in 2016, Operators aim to capture the knowledge that a human operator would have for managing the lifecycle of an application. Operators are packaged as normal containerized applications—deployed within pods—that react on changes to the API against CRs.

Operators are commonly written using a toolkit called the Operator Framework, and are based on one of the following three different technologies:

- Go
- Ansible
- Helm

Go-based Operators leverage the Go programming language to implement control loop logic. Ansible-based Operators leverage the Ansible CLI tool and Ansible playbooks. Ansible is an automation tool whose logic is written in YAML files called playbooks.

In this chapter, we will focus on Helm-based Operators. Helm Operators base their control loop logic on Helm charts and a subset of the features provided by the Helm CLI. As a result, they represent an easy way for Helm users to implement their Operators.

With an understanding of Operators, let's create an operator of our own, using Helm.

Creating a Helm operator

In this section, we will write a Helm-based operator that will be used to install the Guestbook Helm chart created in *Chapter 5, Building Your First Helm Chart*. This chart can be seen under the `guestbook/` folder of the Packt repository (`https://github.com/PacktPublishing/-Learn-Helm/tree/master/helm-charts/charts/guestbook`).

An operator is built as a container image that contains the control loop logic to maintain an application. The following diagram demonstrates how the Guestbook Operator will function once it is deployed:

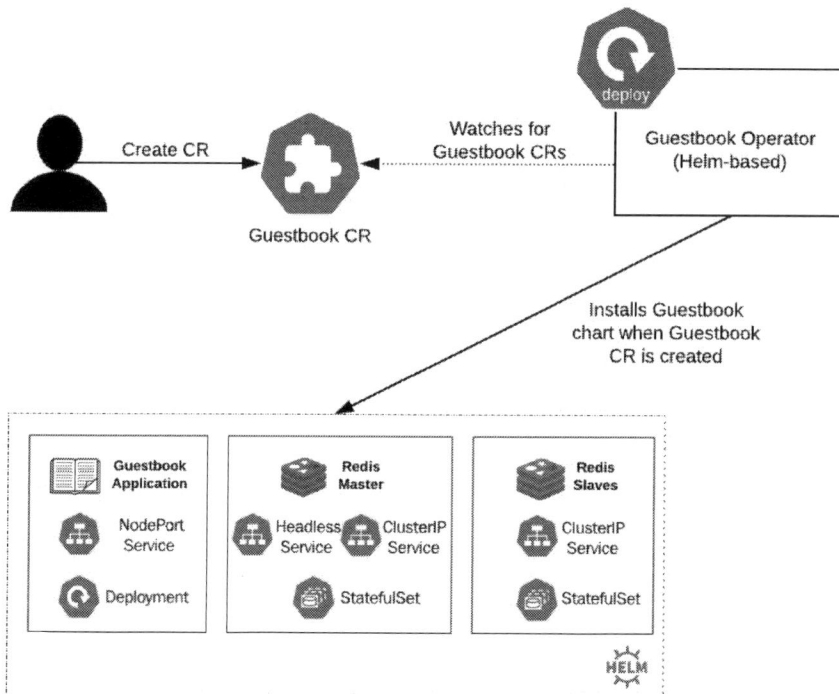

Figure 8.1 – Guestbook Operator workflow

The Guestbook Operator will constantly watch for changes to Guestbook CRs. When a Guestbook CR is created, the Guestbook Operator will install the Guestbook chart you created in *Chapter 5, Building Your First Helm Chart*. Conversely, if the Guestbook CR is deleted, the Guestbook Operator will remove the Guestbook Helm chart.

With an understanding of how the Guestbook Operator will function, let's set up an environment in which the operator can be built and deployed.

Setting up the environment

First, since the operator will be deployed to Kubernetes, you should start your Minikube environment by running the following command:

```
$ minikube start
```

After starting Minikube, create a namespace called `chapter8`, as follows:

```
$ kubectl create ns chapter8
```

Since the Guestbook Operator is built as a container image, you will need to create an image repository that can store it so it can later be referenced. To store this image, we will create a new repository in Quay (`quay.io`), a public container registry (though if you have an account elsewhere, that will suffice as well). We will also prepare a local development environment with the necessary tooling required to build the operator image.

Let's begin by creating a new image repository in Quay.

Creating a Quay repository

Creating a new repository in Quay requires you to have a Quay account. Follow these steps to create a Quay account:

1. Navigate to `https://quay.io/signin/` in your browser. You will be prompted by a screen to enter your Quay credentials, as illustrated in the following screenshot:

Figure 8.2 – Red Hat Quay sign-in page

2. At the bottom of the page, click the **Create Account** link. You will be prompted with a set of dialog boxes to create a new Quay account, as illustrated in the following screenshot:

RED HAT® Quay.io

Create new account

Username:

Requested username

E-mail address:

Your email address

Password:

Create a password

Verify your password

Create Free Account

Sign In • Forgot Password?

Figure 8.3 – Red Hat Quay **Create new account** page

3. Enter your desired credentials, and then select **Create Free Account**.

4. You will soon be sent an email confirmation. Click the link on the confirmation email to verify your account and continue using Quay with your new account.

    Once you have created a new Quay account, you can continue to create a new image repository for the operator image.

To create a new image repository, select the + plus icon at the top-right corner of the Quay page and select **New Repository**, as illustrated in the following screenshot:

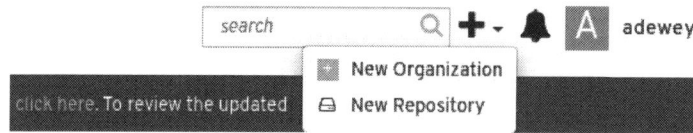

Figure 8.4 – Selecting 'New Repository' to create a new image repository

5. You will then be taken to the **Create New Repository** page, where you should enter the following details:

For **Repository Name**, enter `guestbook-operator`.

Select the **Public** radio button, indicating unauthenticated access to the repository. This change will simplify how Kubernetes will be able to access the image.

The remainder of the options can be kept at the default values. Once complete, the **Create New Repository** page should appear, as illustrated in the following screenshot:

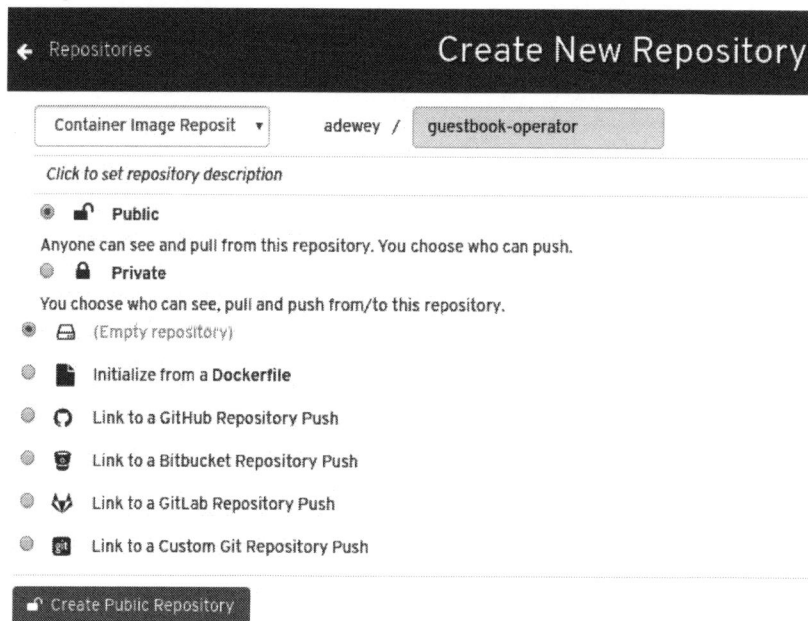

Figure 8.5 – The 'Create New Repository' page in Quay

6. Select the **Create Public Repository** button to create the Quay repository.

Now that a repository has been created to store the Guestbook Operator image, let's prepare an environment with the tooling required to build a Helm operator.

Preparing a local development environment

In order to create a Helm operator, you will need the following CLI tools at a minimum:

- `operator-sdk`

- `docker`, `podman`, or `buildah`

The `operator-sdk` CLI is a toolkit used to help develop Kubernetes Operators. It contains inherent logic to simplify the operator development process. Under the hood, `operator-sdk` requires a container management tool that it can use to build the operator image. The `operator-sdk` CLI supports `docker`, `podman`, and `buildah` as the underlying container management tools.

To install the `operator-sdk` CLI, you can simply download a release from their GitHub repository at `https://github.com/operator-framework/operator-sdk/releases`. However, the process used to install `docker`, `podman`, or `buildah` may vary greatly, depending on your operating system; not to mention, that Windows users will not be able to use the `operator-sdk` toolkit natively.

Fortunately, the Minikube **Virtual Machine (VM)** can be leveraged as a working environment for developers of many different operating systems since it is a Linux VM and also contains the Docker CLI. In this section, we will install `operator-sdk` to the Minikube VM and will use this environment to create the operator. Note that while the steps provided are designed to run in the VM, most of these steps will also apply to all Linux and Mac machines.

Follow these steps to install `operator-sdk` on the Minikube VM:

1. Gain access to the VM by running the `minikube ssh` command, as follows:

```
$ minikube ssh
```

2. Once inside the VM, you need to download the `operator-sdk` CLI. This can be accomplished using the `curl` command. Note that the `operator-sdk` version used at the time of writing was version `0.15.2`.

To download this version of the `operator-sdk` CLI, run the following command:

```
$ curl -o operator-sdk -L https://github.com/operator-
framework/operator-sdk/releases/download/v0.15.2/
operator-sdk-v0.15.2-x86_64-linux-gnu
```

3. Once downloaded, you will need to change the permission of the `operator-sdk` binary to be user-executable. Run the `chmod` command to make this modification, as follows:

```
$ chmod u+x operator-sdk
```

4. Next, move the `operator-sdk` binary to a location managed by the VM's PATH variable, such as `/usr/bin`. Because this operation requires a root privilege, you will need to run the `mv` command using `sudo`, as follows:

```
$ sudo mv operator-sdk /usr/bin
```

5. Finally, verify your `operator-sdk` installation by running the `operator-sdk version` command, like this:

```
$ operator-sdk version
operator-sdk version: 'v0.15.2', commit:
'ffaf278993c8fcb00c6f527c9f20091eb8dd3352', go version:
'go1.13.3 linux/amd64'
```

If this command executes without error, you have successfully installed the `operator-sdk` CLI.

6. As an additional step, you should also clone the Packt repository in your Minikube VM since we will later leverage the guestbook Helm chart to build a Helm operator. Run the following command in your VM to clone the repository:

```
$ git clone https://github.com/PacktPublishing/-Learn-
Helm.git Learn-Helm
```

Now that you have a Quay image repository and a local development environment created from the Minikube VM, let's begin writing the Guestbook Operator. Note that an example of the operator code is located in the Packt repository at `https://github.com/PacktPublishing/-Learn-Helm/tree/master/guestbook-operator`.

Scaffolding the operator file structure

Similar to Helm charts themselves, Helm Operators built by the `operator-sdk` CLI
have a specific file structure that must be adhered to. The file structure is explained in the
following table:

File or Folder	Definition
build/	Folder containing a Dockerfile to build the operator image
deploy/	Folder containing files to deploy the operator to Kubernetes
helm-charts/	Folder containing Helm charts that the operator is in charge of installing
watches.yaml	File that defines the custom resources that the operator is in charge of watching.

Figure 8.6 – The file structures explained

The operator file structure can be easily created using the `operator-sdk new`
command. In your Minikube VM, execute the following command to scaffold the
Guestbook Operator:

```
$ operator-sdk new guestbook-operator --type helm --kind
Guestbook --helm-chart Learn-Helm/helm-charts/charts/guestbook
INFO[0000] Creating new Helm operator 'guestbook-operator'.
INFO[0003] Created helm-charts/guestbook
WARN[0003] Using default RBAC rules: failed to get Kubernetes
config: could not locate a kubeconfig
INFO[0003] Created build/Dockerfile
INFO[0003] Created watches.yaml
INFO[0003] Created deploy/service_account.yaml
INFO[0003] Created deploy/role.yaml
INFO[0003] Created deploy/role_binding.yaml
INFO[0003] Created deploy/operator.yaml
INFO[0003] Created deploy/crds/charts.helm.k8s.io_v1alpha1_
guestbook_cr.yaml
INFO[0003] Generated CustomResourceDefinition manifests.
INFO[0003] Project creation complete.
```

The `operator-sdk new` command created a local directory called `guestbook-operator`, which contains the operator contents. It is specified that a Helm operator should be created using the `--type` flag, along with `Guestbook` as the name of the CR.

Finally, the `--helm-chart` flag instructed the `operator-sdk` CLI to copy the source Guestbook chart to the operator directory.

With the Guestbook operator successfully scaffolded, let's build the operator and push it to your Quay registry.

Building the operator and pushing it to Quay

The `operator-sdk` CLI provides an `operator-sdk build` command that makes it straightforward to build an operator image. This command is designed to be run against the top-level directory of an operator, and will build the image by referencing the Dockerfile located under the operator's `build/` folder.

In your Minikube VM, run the `operator-sdk build` command, substituting your Quay username where directed, as follows:

```
$ cd guestbook-operator
$ operator-sdk build quay.io/$QUAY_USERNAME/guestbook-operator
```

If the build is successful, you will receive the following message:

```
INFO[0092] Operator build complete.
```

Since the Minikube VM has Docker installed, the `operator-sdk` CLI used Docker in the background to build the image. You can run the `docker images` command to verify that the image has been built, as follows:

```
$ docker images
```

With the operator image built locally, it must be pushed to an image registry so that it can be pulled from Kubernetes. In order to push an image to a registry using Docker, you must first authenticate with the target registry. Use the `docker login` command to log in to Quay, as shown in the following code snippet:

```
$ docker login quay.io --username $QUAY_USERNAME --password
$QUAY_PASSWORD
```

Once logged in to Quay, use the `docker push` command to push your operator image to your Quay registry, like this:

```
$ docker push quay.io/$QUAY_USERNAME/guestbook-operator
```

When the push is finished, return to the `guestbook-operator` repository that you created in the *Creating a Quay repository* section. You should be able to see a new tag published under the **Repository tags** section, as illustrated in the following screenshot:

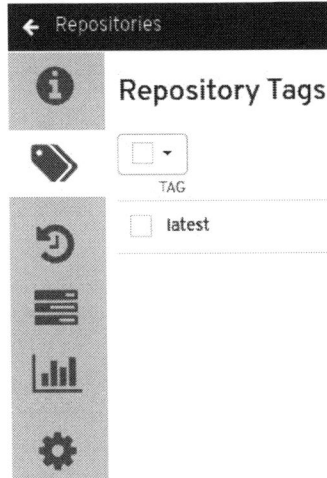

Figure 8.7 – A new tag should be pushed to your Quay registry

Now that your operator has been pushed to a container registry, let's continue by deploying the operator to your Kubernetes environment.

Deploying the Guestbook Operator

When scaffolding the Guestbook Operator, the `operator-sdk` CLI also created a folder called `deploy` and generated the files required to deploy the operator within.

The following file structure depicts the contents of the `deploy` folder:

```
deploy/
  crds/
    charts.helm.k8s.io_guestbooks_crd.yaml
    charts.helm.k8s.io_v1alpha1_guestbook_cr.yaml
  operator.yaml
  role_binding.yaml
```

```
role.yaml
```

```
service_account.yaml
```

The `crds/` folder contains the YAML resource required to create the Guestbook CRD (`charts.helm.k8s.io_guestbooks_crd.yaml`). This file is required to register the new Guestbook API endpoint with Kubernetes. In addition, the `crds/` folder contains an example Guestbook CR application (`charts.helm.k8s.io_v1alpha1_guestbook_cr.yaml`). Creating this file will trigger the operator to install the Guestbook Helm chart.

Review the contents of the CR in order to become familiar with the types of properties defined, as follows:

```
$ cat guestbook-operator/deploy/crds/charts.helm.k8s.io_
v1alpha1_guestbook_cr.yaml
```

A snippet of the output is provided in the following code block:

```
apiVersion: charts.helm.k8s.io/v1alpha1
kind: Guestbook
metadata:
  name: example-guestbook
spec:
  # Default values copied from <project_dir>/helm-charts/guestbook/values.yaml

  affinity: {}
  fullnameOverride: ""
  image:
    pullPolicy: IfNotPresent
    repository: gcr.io/google-samples/gb-frontend
  imagePullSecrets: []
  ingress:
    annotations: {}
    enabled: false
```

Figure 8.8 – Snippet of the Guestbook CR

Each of the entries under the `spec` stanza refer to the Guestbook chart's `values.yaml` file. The `operator-sdk` tool automatically created this example CR with each of the default values that were included from this file. Additional entries can be added or modified before applying this CR, to override other values of the Guestbook chart. These values are consumed by the operator at runtime to deploy the Guestbook application accordingly.

The `deploy/operator.yaml` file defines the actual operator itself and contains a simple deployment resource. We will return soon to this file's contents.

The `role_binding.yaml`, `role.yaml` and `service_account.yaml` files were created in order to provide the operator with the permissions necessary to watch for Guestbook CRs and install the Guestbook Helm chart to Kubernetes. It performs these actions by authenticating with the Kubernetes API using the service account defined in the `service_account.yaml` file. Once authenticated, the operator will be provided authorization based on the `role.yaml` and `role_binding.yaml` resources. The `role.yaml` file lists the finely grained permissions that describe the exact resources and actions that the operator is allowed to perform. The `role_binding.yaml` file binds the role to the operator's service account.

With an understanding of each resource created under the operator's `deploy/` folder, follow these steps to deploy your Guestbook operator:

1. Unfortunately, the Minikube VM does not contain `Kubectl`, so you must first exit to your local system if you are still connected to the VM from the command line, by running the following command:

    ```
    $ exit
    ```

2. The resources that were created with `operator-sdk` earlier are also located in the Packt repository under the `guestbook-operator/` folder. If you have not cloned this repository in previous chapters, clone it now using the following command:

    ```
    $ git clone https://github.com/PacktPublishing/-Learn-Helm.git Learn-Helm
    ```

    As a quick aside, note that the only resource in the Packt repository that is modified from the resources you created in your Minikube VM is the `role.yaml` file. The `operator-sdk` CLI generated a simple `role.yaml` file based on the template files that were included in the guestbook Helm chart. However, if you can recall, the guestbook chart contained a couple of resources that would only be included based on a conditional value. These resources were the `Job` and `PersistentVolumeClaim` hook resources that were only included if persistent storage was enabled. One example of this is shown in the `PersistentVolumeClaim` template, in the following code snippet:

    ```
    {{- if .Values.redis.master.persistence.enabled }}
    apiVersion: v1
    kind: PersistentVolumeClaim
    ```

The `operator-sdk` CLI did not automatically create the **Role-Based Access Control** (**RBAC**) rules for `Jobs` and `PersistentVolumeClaims` since it did not know whether this template would be included.

As a result, the authors have added these rules to the `role.yaml` file, located at `https://github.com/PacktPublishing/-Learn-Helm/blob/master/guestbook-operator/deploy/role.yaml#L81-L104`.

3. The Guestbook operator will be dependent on a new API endpoint. Create this endpoint by applying the CRD under the `guestbook-operator/deploy/crds` folder, as follows:

```
$ kubectl apply -f guestbook-operator/deploy/crds/charts.
helm.k8s.io_guestbooks_crd.yaml
```

We will use the second file under that folder (the CR) later to deploy the Guestbook application.

4. Next, you will need to modify the `guestbook-operator/deploy/operator.yaml` file to specify the operator image that you built earlier. You will notice the following lines of code within this file:

```
# Replace this with the built image name
image: REPLACE_IMAGE
```

Replace the `REPLACE_IMAGE` text with the location of your operator image. This value should be similar to `quay.io/$QUAY_USERNAME/guestbook-operator`.

5. Once you have applied the CRD and updated your `operator.yaml` file, you can proceed to apply each of the resources under the `guestbook-operator/deploy/` folder by running the following command:

```
$ kubectl apply -f guestbook-operator/deploy -n chapter8
```

6. Wait for the operator to report the `1/1` ready state by running a watch against the Pods in the `chapter8` namespace, like this:

```
$ kubectl get pods -n chapter8 -w
```

Now that the Guestbook operator has been deployed, let's use it to install the Guestbook Helm chart.

Deploying the Guestbook application

When using Helm normally as a standalone CLI tool, you would install a Helm chart by running the `helm install` command. With a Helm operator, you install a Helm chart by creating a CR. Install the Guestbook Helm chart by creating the provided CR located under the `guestbook-operator/deploy/crds/` folder, as shown in the following code snippet:

```
$ kubectl apply -f guestbook-operator/deploy/crds/charts.helm.
k8s.io_v1alpha1_guestbook_cr.yaml -n chapter8
```

Run another `watch` command against the Pods in the `chapter8` namespace, as shown in the following code snippet, and you should be able to see the Guestbook and Redis Pods spin up as a result of the Helm chart installation:

```
$ kubectl get pods -n chapter8 -w
```

The following code block depicts each Pod in its READY state:

```
NAME                                   READY
STATUS       RESTARTS
example-guestbook-65bc5fdc55-jvkdz     1/1     Running   0
guestbook-operator-6fddc8d7cb-94mzp    1/1     Running   0
redis-master-0                         1/1     Running   0
redis-slave-0                          1/1     Running   0
redis-slave-1                          1/1     Running   0
```

When you created the Guestbook CR, a `helm install` command was executed by the operator to install the Guestbook chart. You can confirm the release that was created by running `helm list`, like this:

```
$ helm list -n chapter8
NAME                 NAMESPACE   REVISION   UPDATED
example-guestbook    chapter8    1          2020-02-24
```

An upgrade of the release can be performed by modifying the `example-guestbook` CR. Modify your `guestbook-operator/deploy/crds/charts.helm.k8s.io_v1alpha1_guestbook_cr.yaml` file to change the number of replicas from 1 to 2, like this:

```
replicaCount: 2
```

Apply the change once you have updated the `replicaCount` value, as follows:

```
$ kubectl apply -f guestbook-operator/deploy/crds/charts.helm.
k8s.io_v1alpha1_guestbook_cr.yaml -n chapter8
```

The modification to the Guestbook CR will trigger a `helm upgrade` command against the `example-guestbook` release. As you may recall from *Chapter 5, Building Your First Helm Chart*, the upgrade hook for the Guestbook Helm chart will initiate a backup of the Redis database. If you run a watch against the Pods in the `chapter8` namespace after modifying the CR, you will notice a backup `Job` begin and will see one of the two Guestbook Pods terminate once the backup is finished. You will also notice from the `helm list` command in the following code snippet that the revision number of the `example-guestbook` release was increased to 2:

```
$ helm list -n chapter8
```

NAME	NAMESPACE	REVISION	UPDATED
example-guestbook	chapter8	2	2020-02-24

Although the revision number was increased to 2, one limitation of Helm-based Operators as of writing is that you cannot initiate a rollback to a previous revision as you can by using the CLI. If you attempt to run `helm history` against the `example-guestbook` release, you will also notice that only the second revision is in the release history, as illustrated in the following code snippet:

```
$ helm history example-guestbook -n chapter8
```

REVISION	UPDATED	STATUS
2	Tue Feb 25 04:36:10 2020	deployed

This is an important difference between using Helm regularly with the CLI and using Helm via a Helm-based operator. Because the release history is not retained, the Helm-based operator does not allow you to perform an explicit rollback. However, a `helm rollback` command will be run in cases where upgrades fail. In this case, the rollback hook will be executed in an attempt to roll back to the attempted upgrade.

Although the Helm-based operator does not retain release history, one area in which it excels is synchronizing the desired and live states of an application. This is because the operator constantly watches the state of the Kubernetes environment and ensures that the application is always configured to match the configuration specified on the CR. In other words, if one of the Guestbook application's resources is modified, the operator will immediately revert the change to make it match the specification as defined on the CR. You can see this in action by modifying a field on one of the Guestbook resources.

As an example, we will change the Guestbook deployment's replica count directly from 2 to 3 and watch the operator revert this back to 2 replicas automatically to re-synchronize the desired state defined in the CR.

Execute the following `kubectl patch` command to change the replica count of the Guestbook deployment from 2 to 3:

```
$ kubectl patch deployment example-guestbook -p
'{'spec':{'replicas':3}}' -n chapter8
```

Normally, this would simply add an additional replica of your Guestbook application. However, because the Guestbook CR currently defines only 2 replicas, the operator quickly changes the replica count back to 2 and terminates the additional Pod that was created. If you actually wanted to increase the replica count to 3, you would have to update the `replicaCount` value on the Guestbook CR. This process provides the advantage of ensuring that the desired state matches the live state of the cluster.

Uninstalling the Guestbook application with a Helm-based operator is as simple as removing the CR. Delete the `example-guestbook` CR to uninstall the release, like this:

```
$ kubectl delete -f guestbook-operator/deploy/crds/charts.helm.
k8s.io_v1alpha1_guestbook_cr.yaml -n chapter8
```

This will remove the `example-guestbook` release and all of the dependent resources.

You can also remove the Guestbook Operator and its resources as well, since we will not need them in the next section. You can do this by running the following command:

```
$ kubectl delete -f guestbook-operator/deploy/ -n chapter8
```

In general, you should always make sure that you delete the CR first before deleting the operator. The operator is programmed to perform a `helm uninstall` command on your release when you delete the CR. If you accidentally delete the operator first, you will have to manually run `helm uninstall` from the command line.

In this section, you created a Helm operator and learned how to deploy an application using an operator-based approach. In the next section, we will continue the discussion on Operators by investigating how they can be managed using Helm.

Using Helm to manage Operators and CRs

In the previous section, you installed the Guestbook Operator by first creating the CRD that is found underneath the `guestbook-operator/deploy/crds/` folder. Next, you created the operator resources contained underneath the `guestbook-operator/deploy/` folder. Finally, you created the CR to deploy the Guestbook application. Each of these tasks was performed by using the Kubectl CLI, but this instead can also be accomplished using Helm charts to provide a more flexible and repeatable solution toward installing and managing an operator.

Helm allows you to provide a special directory called `crds/` inside your Helm chart, which is used to create CRDs whenever the chart is installed. Helm creates CRDs before any of the other resources defined under the `templates/` folder, making it simpler to install applications such as Operators that depend on the presence of CRDs.

The following file structure depicts a Helm chart that could be used to install the Guestbook Operator:

```
guestbook-operator/
  Chart.yaml
  crds/
    charts.helm.k8s.io_guestbooks_crd.yaml
  templates/
    operator.yaml
    role_binding.yaml
    role.yaml
    Service_account.yaml
  values.yaml
```

This Helm chart, upon installation, would first install the Guestbook CRD. If the CRD is already present in the cluster, it would skip CRD creation and would simply create the template resources instead. Note that while CRDs can be convenient to include in a Helm chart, there are several limitations. First, CRDs in a Helm chart cannot contain any Go templating, so CRDs cannot benefit from parameterization as in typical resources. CRDs can also never be upgraded, rolled back, or deleted. As a result, users must take care to modify or remove the CRDs manually if these actions are desired. Finally, installing such a chart as previously described would require a cluster-admin privilege, the highest privilege permitted in Kubernetes, because the chart contains at least one CRD resource.

The Helm chart described previously can be used by cluster administrators to easily install the Guestbook operator. This, however, is only half of the equation, as end users must still create CRs to deploy the Guestbook application. Luckily, end users of the operator can also leverage Helm by creating a Helm chart that wraps the Guestbook CR.

An example layout for such a Helm chart is shown in the following file structure:

```
guestbook-cr
  Chart.yaml
  templates/
    guestbook.yaml
  values.yaml
```

The preceding example includes a template called `guestbook.yaml`. This template could contain the Guestbook CR originally generated by the `operator-sdk` CLI, with the name `charts.helm.k8s.io_v1alpha1_guestbook_cr.yaml`. Unlike CRDs, CRs underneath the `templates/` folder benefit from Go templating and lifecycle management, as do all other resources. This methodology provides the most value when the CR contains complex fields that may be conditionally included based on the user-provided values or when multiple different CRs must be included in the same release. With this method, you would also be able to manage the lifecycle of your CRs and maintain a history of revisions.

Now that you have an understanding of how a Helm operator can be created and how Helm can be used to help manage Operators, feel free to clean up your Kubernetes environment in the next section.

Cleaning up your Kubernetes environment

First, run the following command to remove your Guestbook CRD:

```
$ kubectl delete crd guestbooks.charts.helm.k8s.io
```

Before you proceed with the next clean-up steps, note that one of the questions posed later under the *Questions* section will challenge you with writing your own Helm charts to implement the chart designs discussed under the *Using Helm to manage Operators and CRs* section. You may want to postpone these steps to test your implementation.

To continue the clean-up, run the following command to delete your `chapter8` namespace:

```
$ kubectl delete ns chapter8
```

Finally, run the `minikube stop` command to stop your Minikube VM.

Summary

Operators are important to help ensure that the desired state always matches the live state. Such a feat allows users to more easily maintain a source of truth for resource configuration. Users can leverage the Helm-based operator to provide this type of resource reconciliation, and it is easy to get started because this uses Helm charts as its deployment mechanism. When a CR is created, the Helm operator will install the associated Helm chart to create a new release. Subsequent upgrades will be performed when the CR is modified, and the release will be uninstalled when the CR is deleted.

To manage the operator, cluster administrators can create a separate Helm chart used for creating the operator's resources and CRDs. End users can also create a separate Helm chart that can be used for creating the operator's CRs, along with any other resources that may be relevant.

In the next chapter, we will discuss best practices and topics around security within the Helm ecosystem.

Further reading

For more information about the Kubernetes resources, you can check the following links:

- To discover more Operators that have been developed by the community, consult this repository: `https://github.com/operator-framework/awesome-Operators`.
- You can learn more about Operators along with their origins from the Kubernetes documentation at `https://kubernetes.io/docs/concepts/extend-kubernetes/operator/`.

Questions

1. How does a Kubernetes operator work?

2. What are the differences between using the Helm CLI and using a Helm-based operator?

3. Imagine you are tasked with creating a Helm operator out of an existing Helm chart. What steps would you take to complete this task?

4. How do the install, upgrade, rollback, and uninstall lifecycle hooks function in a Helm operator?

5. What is the purpose of the `crds/` folder in a Helm chart?

6. In the *Using Helm to manage Operators and CRs* section, we introduced two different Helm charts that can be used to help manage Operators and CRs. Implement the Helm charts by using the chart layouts provided within that section. The charts should be used to install the Guestbook operator and to install the Guestbook CR. Refer to *Chapter 5, Building Your First Helm Chart* for assistance on creating a Helm chart.

9
Helm Security Considerations

As you have likely come to realize throughout this book, Helm is a powerful tool that presents many deployment possibilities to users. This power can, however, get out of hand if certain security paradigms are not recognized and followed. Luckily, Helm provides many ways to incorporate security into everyday usage in ways that are simple to achieve, from the moment the Helm CLI is downloaded to the moment a Helm chart is installed on a Kubernetes cluster.

In this chapter, we will cover the following topics:

- Data provenance and integrity
- Helm chart security
- Additional considerations around RBAC, values, and chart repositories

Technical requirements

This chapter will make use of the following technologies:

- `minikube`

- `kubectl`

- Helm

- **GNU Privacy Guard** (**GPG**)

The installation and configuration of Minikube, Kubectl, and Helm was covered in *Chapter 2, Preparing a Kubernetes and Helm Environment.*

We will also leverage the `guestbook` chart from the Packt repository, located at `https://github.com/PacktPublishing/-Learn-Helm`, for a later example in this chapter. If you have not already cloned this repository, be sure to do so with the following command:

```
$ git clone https://github.com/PacktPublishing/-Learn-Helm.
git Learn-Helm
```

Data provenance and integrity

When working with any kind of data, there are two often-overlooked questions that should be considered:

- Does the data come from a reliable source or from the source that you expected it to?

- Does the data contain all of the contents that you expected it to?

The first question refers to the topic of **data provenance**. Data provenance is about determining where data originated from.

The second question refers to the topic of **data integrity**. Data integrity is about determining whether the contents you received from a remote location represent what you expected to receive and can help determine whether the data was tampered with as it was sent through the wire. Both data provenance and data integrity can be verified using a concept called **digital signatures**. An author can create a unique signature based on cryptography to sign data and the consumer of that data can use cryptographic tools to verify the authenticity of that signature.

If the authenticity is verified, then the consumer knows that the data originates from the expected source and was not tampered with as it was transferred.

Authors can create a digital signature by first creating a **Pretty Good Privacy (PGP)** keypair. PGP, in this context, refers to OpenPGP, which is a set of standards based on encryption. PGP focuses on establishing asymmetric encryption, which is based on the use of two different keys—private and public.

Private keys are meant to be kept secret, while public keys are designed to be shared. For digital signatures, the private key is used to encrypt data, while a public key is used by consumers to decrypt that data. The PGP keypair is often created using a tool called GPG, which is an open source tool that implements the OpenPGP standard.

Once the PGP keypair is created, the author can use GPG to sign the data. When the data is signed, GPG performs the following steps in the background:

1. A hash is calculated based on the contents of the data. The output is a fixed-length string called the **message digest**.

2. The message digest is encrypted using the author's private key. The output is the digital signature.

To verify the signature, consumers must use the author's public key to decrypt it. This verification can also be performed using GPG.

Digital signatures play a role in Helm in two ways:

*   First, each Helm download has an accompanying digital signature from one of the maintainers that can be used to verify the authenticity of the binary. The signature can be used to verify the origin of the download, as well as its integrity.

*   Second, Helm charts can also be digitally signed to benefit from the same verifications. Authors of a chart sign the chart during packaging and the chart users verify the validity of the chart by using the author's public key.

With an understanding of how data provenance and integrity come into play as they relate to digital signatures, let's create a GPG keypair on your local work station, if you do not already have one, that will be used to elaborate on many of the previously described concepts.

Creating a GPG keypair

In order to create a keypair, you must first have GPG installed on your local machine. Use the following instructions as a guide to install GPG on your local machine. Note that on Linux systems, you probably already have GPG installed:

- For Windows, you can use the Chocolatey package manager, as in the following command:

```
> choco install gnupg
```

  You can also download the installer for Windows from `https://gpg4win.org/download.html`.

- For macOS, you can use the Homebrew package manager using the following command:

```
$ brew install gpg
```

  You can also download the macOS-based installed from `https://sourceforge.net/p/gpgosx/docu/Download/`.

- For Debian-based Linux distributions, you can use the apt package manager, as shown:

```
$ sudo apt install gnupg
```

- For RPM-based Linux distributions, you can use the dnf package manager, as shown:

```
$ sudo dnf install gnupg
```

Once you have installed GPG, you can create your own GPG keypair, which we will use throughout our discussion on data provenance and integrity.

The steps to configure this keypair are as follows:

1. Run the following command to create a new keypair. This command can be run from any directory:

```
$ gpg --generate-key
```

2. Follow the prompts to enter your name and email address. These will be used to identify you as the owner of the keypair and will be the name and email address seen by people who receive your public key.

3. Press the *O* key to continue.

4. You will then be prompted to enter your private key password. Enter and confirm the desired passphrase that will be used for encryption and decryption operations..

You will see an output similar to the following once your GPG keypair has been created:

```
pub   rsa2048 2020-03-11 [SC] [expires: 2022-03-11]
      0486878E76CB5C3D8A915A25B92073C70B46DDF6
uid                      John Doe <jdoe@example.com>
sub   rsa2048 2020-03-11 [E] [expires: 2022-03-11]
```

Figure 9.1: The output following successful creation of the GPG keypair

The output displays information about the public (`pub`) and private (`sub`) keys, as well as the fingerprint of the public key (the second line of the output). The fingerprint is a unique identifier used to identify you as the owner of that key. The third line, beginning with `uid`, displays the name and email address that you entered as you generated your GPG keypair.

With your `gpg` keypair now created, continue to the next section to learn how a Helm download can be verified.

Verifying Helm downloads

As discussed in *Chapter 2, Preparing a Kubernetes and Helm Environment*, one of the ways Helm can be installed is by downloading an archive from GitHub. These archives can be installed from Helm's GitHub releases page (`https://github.com/helm/helm/releases`) by selecting one of the links shown in the following screenshot:

Installation

Download Helm 3.0.0. The common platform binaries are here:

- MacOS amd64 (checksum)
- Linux amd64 (checksum)
- Linux arm (checksum)
- Linux arm64 (checksum)
- Linux i386 (checksum)
- Linux ppc64le (checksum)
- Windows amd64 (checksum)

The Quickstart Guide will get you going from there.

This release was signed with `92AA 783C BAAE 8E3B` and can be found at **@bacongobbler**'s keybase account. Please use the attached signatures for verifying this release using `gpg` .

Figure 9.2: The Installation section from Helm's GitHub releases page

At the bottom of the **Installation** section, you'll notice a paragraph explaining that the release was signed. Each Helm release is signed by a Helm maintainer and can be verified against the digital signature that corresponds to the downloaded Helm release. Each of the digital signatures are located under the **Assets** section.

The following screenshot shows how these are represented:

▼ Assets **18**	
🗇 helm-v3.0.0-darwin-amd64.tar.gz.asc	833 Bytes
🗇 helm-v3.0.0-darwin-amd64.tar.gz.sha256.asc	833 Bytes
🗇 helm-v3.0.0-linux-386.tar.gz.asc	833 Bytes
🗇 helm-v3.0.0-linux-386.tar.gz.sha256.asc	833 Bytes
🗇 helm-v3.0.0-linux-amd64.tar.gz.asc	833 Bytes
🗇 helm-v3.0.0-linux-amd64.tar.gz.sha256.asc	833 Bytes

Figure 9.3: The Assets section from Helm's GitHub releases page

To verify the provenance and integrity of your Helm download, you should also download the corresponding `.asc` file. Note that `.sha256.asc` files are used to verify the integrity only. In this example, we will download the corresponding `.asc` file, which will verify both the provenance and integrity.

Begin verifying a Helm release by following these steps:

1. Download the Helm archive under the installation that corresponds with your operating system. Although the Helm binary is likely already installed, you can still download an archive to follow along with the example. Once you have finished with the example, you can remove the archive from your workstation.

2. Download the `.asc` file that corresponds with your operating system. For example, if you are running an AMD64-based Linux system, you would download the `helm-v3.0.0-linux-amd64.tar.gz.asc` file.

> **Important note**
> The version contained in the filename corresponds to the actual Helm version you are downloading.

Once both files are downloaded, you should see two similar files in the same directory on the command line:

```
helm-v3.0.0-linux-amd64.tar.gz
helm-v3.0.0-linux-amd64.tar.gz.asc
```

The next step involves importing the Helm maintainer's public key to your local gpg keyring. This allows you to decrypt the digital signature contained in the .asc file to verify the provenance and integrity of your download. The maintainer's public key can be retrieved by following the link to their keybase account. The link can be found by hovering your cursor over the keybase account words. In the example from *Figure 9.2*, this location resolves to https://keybase.io/bacongobbler. The public key can then be downloaded by adding /pgp_keys.asc to the end, making the resulting link https://keybase.io/bacongobbler/pgp_keys.asc.

Note that there are multiple Helm maintainers, so your link may differ if you are performing verification on a different release. Be sure that you are downloading the correct public key that corresponds to the key that signed the release.

Let's continue with the verification process:

1. Using the command line, download the public key corresponding to the Helm release signature:

```
$ curl -o release_key.asc https://keybase.io/
bacongobbler/pgp_keys.asc
```

2. Once downloaded, you need to import the public key to your gpg keyring. This is done by running the following command:

```
$ gpg --import release_key.asc
```

If the import is successful, you will see the following message:

```
gpg: key 92AA783CBAAE8E3B: public key 'Matthew Fisher
<matt.fisher@microsoft.com>' imported
gpg: Total number processed: 1
gpg:               imported: 1
```

3. Now that the public key of the digital signature has been imported, you can verify the Helm installation's release by leveraging the --verify subcommand of GPG. This should be run against the helm*.asc file:

```
$ gpg --verify helm-v3.0.0-linux-amd64.tar.gz.asc
```

This command will attempt to decrypt the digital signature contained in the `.asc` file. If it is successful, it means that the Helm download (the file ending in `.tar.gz`) was signed by the person you expect (`Matthew Fisher` for this release) and the download was not modified or altered in any way. A successful output is as follows:

```
gpg: assuming signed data in 'helm-v3.0.0-linux-amd64.
tar.gz'
gpg: Signature made Wed 13 Nov 2019 08:05:01 AM CST
gpg:                      using RSA key
967F8AC5E2216F9F4FD270AD92AA783CBAAE8E3B
gpg: Good signature from 'Matthew Fisher <matt.fisher@
microsoft.com>' [unknown]
gpg: WARNING: This key is not certified with a trusted
signature!
gpg:                   There is no indication that the signature
belongs to the owner.
Primary key fingerprint: 967F 8AC5 E221 6F9F 4FD2  70AD
92AA 783C BAAE 8E3B
```

Upon further inspection of this output, you may notice the `WARNING` message indicating that the key was not certified, which may lead you to question the validity of whether this was actually successful. The verification was successful, but you have not instructed gpg that the maintainer's public key is certified to belong to the person they say it belongs to.

You can perform this certification by following these steps:

1. Check that the last 64 bits (8 characters) of the primary key fingerprint displayed at the end of the output match the 64-bit fingerprint displayed in the Helm releases page. As you will recall from *Figure 9.2*, the fingerprint was displayed, as shown:

```
This release was signed with 92AA 783C BAAE 8E3B and can
be found at @bacongobbler's keybase account.
```

2. As you can see from the preceding code, the last 64 bits of the **primary key fingerprint** is displayed on the Helm releases page, so we know that this public key does belong to who we expect it to. As a result, we can safely certify the maintainer's public key. This can be done by signing the public key using your own `gpg` keypair. Perform this step by using the following command:

```
$ gpg --sign-key 92AA783CBAAE8E3B # Last 64 bits of
```

```
fingerprint
```

3. In the `Really sign?` prompt, enter `y`.

    Now that you have signed the maintainer's public key, the key is now certified. The verification can now be run without displaying a `WARNING` message in the output:

    ```
    $ gpg --verify helm-v3.0.0-linux-amd64.tar.gz.asc
    gpg: assuming signed data in 'helm-v3.0.0-linux-amd64.
    tar.gz'
    gpg: Signature made Wed 13 Nov 2019 08:05:01 AM CST
    gpg:                          using RSA key
    967F8AC5E2216F9F4FD270AD92AA783CBAAE8E3B
    gpg: checking the trustdb
    gpg: marginals needed: 3   completes needed: 1   trust
    model: pgp
    gpg: depth: 0  valid:   2  signed:   1  trust: 0-, 0q,
    0n, 0m, 0f, 2u
    gpg: depth: 1  valid:   1  signed:   0  trust: 1-, 0q,
    0n, 0m, 0f, 0u
    gpg: next trustdb check due at 2022-03-11
    gpg: Good signature from 'Matthew Fisher <matt.fisher@
    microsoft.com>' [full]
    ```

Digital signatures also play a role in verifying the provenance and integrity of Helm charts. We will continue this discussion in the next section.

Signing and verifying Helm charts

Similar to how the Helm maintainers sign releases, you can sign your own Helm charts so that users can verify that the chart they install actually came from you and contains the expected contents. To sign a chart, you must first have a `gpg` keypair present on your local workstation.

Next, you can leverage certain flags from the `helm package` command to sign your chart with a specified key.

Let's demonstrate how this can be accomplished by leveraging the `guestbook` chart from the Packt repository. This chart is located in the `Learn-Helm/helm-charts/charts/guestbook` folder. We will assume that you already have a gpg keypair on your local workstation, but if you do not, you can follow the instructions from the *Setup* section of the *Data provenance and integrity* section of this chapter to configure your keypair.

One important point to note before signing the `guestbook` chart is that you must export your public and secret keyrings to a legacy format if you are using GPG version 2 or greater. Previous versions of GPG stored keyrings in a `.gpg` file format, which is the format that Helm expects your keyring to be in (at the time of writing). Newer versions of GPG store keyrings in the `.kbx` file format, which is not currently supported.

Begin the signing process by converting your GPG public and secret keyrings into the `.gpg` file format:

1. Find your gpg version by running the following command:

```
$ gpg --version
gpg (GnuPG) 2.2.9
libgcrypt 1.8.3
Copyright (C) 2018 Free Software Foundation, Inc.
```

2. If your gpg version is 2 or greater, export your public and secret keyring using the following command:

```
$ gpg --export > ~/.gnupg/pubring.gpg
$ gpg --export-secret-keys > ~/.gnupg/secring.gpg
```

Once your keyrings have been exported, you will be able to sign and package your Helm charts. The `helm package` command provides three key (pun intended) flags that allow you to sign and package a chart:

`--sign`: Allows you to sign a chart using a PGP private key

`--key`: The name of the key to use when signing

`--keyring`: The location of the keyring containing the PGP private key

In the next step, these flags will be used with the `helm package` command to sign and package the guestbook Helm chart.

3. Run the following `helm package` command:

```
$ helm package --sign --key '$KEY_NAME' --keyring
~/.gnupg/secring.gpg guestbook
```

The `$KEY_NAME` variable can refer to either the email, name, or fingerprint associated with the desired key. These details can be discovered by leveraging the `gpg --list-keys` command.

When using the `helm package` command without signing, you would expect to see one file produced as output—the `tgz` archive containing the Helm chart. In this case, when signing and packaging the `guestbook` Helm chart, you will see that the following two files are created:

```
guestbook-1.0.0.tgz
guestbook-1.0.0.tgz.prov
```

The `guestbook-1.0.0.tgz.prov` file is called a **provenance** file. The provenance file contains a provenance record, which displays the following:

- The chart metadata from the `Chart.yaml` file
- The sha256 hash of the Helm `guestbook-1.0.0.tgz` file
- The PGP digital signature of the `guestbook-1.0.0.tgz` file

Users of a Helm chart will leverage the provenance file to verify the data provenance and integrity of the chart. When pushing a chart to a chart repository, developers should be sure to upload both the `.tgz` archive of the Helm chart and the `.tgz.prov` provenance file.

Once you have packaged and signed your Helm chart, you will need to export the public key that corresponds to the private key used to encrypt your digital signature. This will allow users to download your public key and use it during the verification process.

4. Export your public key to the `ascii-armor` format by using the following command:

```
$ gpg --armor --export $KEY_NAME > pubkey.asc
```

If you are releasing the `guestbook` chart publicly, this key can then be saved to a downloadable location by your chart users, such as Keybase. Users could then import this public key by leveraging the `gpg --import` command described in the *Verifying Helm releases* section of this chapter.

Chart users can leverage the `helm verify` command to verify a chart's data provenance and integrity before installation. This command is designed to be run against a locally downloaded `.tgz` chart archive and `.tgz.prov` provenance file.

5. The following command provides an example of running this process against the `guestbook` Helm chart and assumes that your public key has been imported to a keyring called `~/.gnupg/pubring.gpg`:

```
$ helm verify --keyring ~/.gnupg/pubring.gpg guestbook-
  1.0.0.tgz
```

If the verification is successful, no output will be displayed. Otherwise, an error message will be returned. The verification could fail for a variety of reasons, including the following:

The .tgz and .tgz.prov files are not in the same directory.

The .tgz.prov file is corrupt.

The file hashes do not match, indicating a loss of integrity.

The public key used to decrypt the signature does not match the private key used to originally encrypt it.

The `helm verify` command is designed to be run on locally downloaded charts, so users may find it better to instead leverage the `helm install --verify` command, which performs verification and installation in a single command, assuming that the `.tgz` and `.tgz.prov` files are both downloadable from a chart repository.

The following command describes how the `helm install --verify` command can be used:

```
$ helm install my-guestbook $CHART_REPO/guestbook --verify
--keyring ~/.gnupg/pubring.gpg
```

By using the methodologies described in this section for signing and verifying Helm charts, both you and your users can ensure that you are installing charts that both belong to you and have been unaltered.

With an understanding of how data provenance and integrity play a role in Helm, let's continue discussing the Helm security considerations by moving on to our next topic—security in relation to Helm charts and Helm chart development.

Developing secure Helm charts

While provenance and integrity play a major role in the security of Helm, they are not the only concerns you need to consider. Chart developers should ensure that, during the development process, they are adhering to best practices regarding security to prevent vulnerabilities from being introduced when a user installs the chart in a Kubernetes cluster. In this section, we will discuss many of the primary concerns around security as it relates to Helm chart development and what you, as a developer, can do to write Helm charts with security as a priority.

We will begin by first discussing the security around any container images that your Helm chart may use.

Using secure images

Since the goal of Helm (and Kubernetes) is to deploy container images, the image itself is a major security concern. To start, chart developers should be aware of the differences between image tags and image digests.

A tag is a human-readable reference to a given image and provides both developers and consumers with an easy method for determining the contents of an image. However, tags can present a security concern as there are no guarantees that the contents of a given tag will always remain the same. The image owner may choose to provide an updated image using the same tag, for example, to address security vulnerabilities, which would result in a different underlying image being executed at runtime, even though the tag is the same. Performing these modifications against the same tag introduces the possibility of regressions, which can cause unexpected adverse effects to users. Instead of referencing an image by tag, images can also be referenced by digest. An image digest is a computed SHA-256 value of an image that not only provides an immutable identifier to an exact image, but also allows for the container runtime to verify that the image retrieved from the remote image registry contains the expected contents. This removes the risk of deploying an image that contains an accidental regression against a given tag, and can also remove the risks of a man-in-the-middle attack, where the tag's contents are modified with malicious intent.

As an example, instead of referencing an image as `quay.io/bitnami/redis:5.0.9` in a chart template, it can instead be referenced by digest as `quay.io/bitnami/redissha256:70b816f2127afb5d4af7ec9d6e8636b2f0f973a3cd8dda7032f9dcffa38ba11f`. Notice that instead of there being a tag after the name of the image, the SHA-256 digest is explicitly specified. This assures you that the image content will not change over time, even if the tag changes, thus strengthening your security posture.

Over time, you can expect a tag or a digest associated with an image to become unsafe to deploy as vulnerabilities are eventually likely to be published against packages or OS versions that this image may contain. There are many different ways to determine the vulnerabilities associated with a given image. One way is to leverage the native capabilities of the registry that the image belongs to. Many different image registries contain capabilities around image vulnerability scanning that can help provide insight as to when an image is vulnerable.

The Quay container registry, for example, can automatically scan images at specified intervals to determine the number of vulnerabilities an image contains. The Nexus and Artifactory container registries are also examples of container registries that have this capability. Outside of native scanning capabilities provided by container registries, other tools can be leveraged, such as Clair (which is also the backing scanning technology of **Quay**), Anchore, Vuls, and OpenSCAP. When your image registry or standalone scanning tool reports that an image is vulnerable, you should immediately update your chart's image to a newer version if available to prevent vulnerabilities from being introduced to your users' Kubernetes clusters.

To help simplify the process around updating the container image, you can develop a regular cadence where image updates are checked. This helps to prevent you from getting to a point where your target image contains vulnerabilities that make it unfit for deployment. Many teams and organizations also specify that images can only be sourced from trusted registries to reduce the potential of running images that do contain vulnerabilities. This setting is configured at the container runtime level and the location and specific configurations vary based on each runtime.

Apart from image vulnerability scanning and content sourcing, you should also avoid deploying images that require elevated permissions or capabilities. Capabilities are used to give a process a subset of root permissions. Some examples of capabilities are NET_ ADMIN, which allows a process to perform network-related operations, and SYS_TIME, which allows a process to modify a system's clock. Running a container as root gives the container access to all the capabilities, which should be limited whenever possible. A list of capabilities can be found in the *CAPABILITIES(7)* page of the Linux manual pages (http://man7.org/linux/man-pages/man7/capabilities.7.html).

Granting a container capability or allowing it to run as root gives malicious processes more leverage to damage the underlying host. Not only does this impact the container that introduced the vulnerability, but also any other container running on that host and, potentially, the entire Kubernetes cluster. If a container does have vulnerabilities but does not have any capabilities granted to it, the attack vector is much smaller and could possibly be prevented altogether. When developing a Helm chart, both an image's vulnerabilities and permission requirements must be taken into account to keep your users, as well as other tenants of the Kubernetes cluster, safe.

In addition to the container image that is deployed, chart developers should also focus on the resources granted to an application. We will dive into this topic in the next section.

Setting resource limits

A pod uses the resources that belong to its underlying node. Without the proper defaults in place, it is possible for a pod to exhaust the node of resources, causing issues such as CPU throttling and pod eviction. Exhausting the underlying node will also prevent other workloads from being scheduled there. Because of the issues that can occur when resource limits are not in check, chart developers should be concerned about setting reasonable defaults either in their Helm chart or in the Kubernetes cluster.

Many charts allow the deployment resources field to be declared as a Helm value. A chart developer can default the resources field in the values.yaml file, setting what is believed by the developer to be the amount of resources that the application should need. The following code shows an example of this:

```
resources:
  limits:
    cpu: 500m
    memory: 2Gi
```

If left at the default, this example value would be used to set the pod's CPU limit to 500m and the memory limit to 2Gi. Setting this default value in the values.yaml file prevents the pod from exhausting the node resources, while also providing a suggested value for the amount of application resources required. Users can then choose to override the resource limits if necessary. Note that the chart developers can also set a default for the resource requests, but this will not prevent the pod from exhausting the node resources.

While you should consider setting default resource limits in the values.yaml file, you can also set limit ranges and resource quotas in the Kubernetes namespace that the chart will be installed on. These are resources that are typically not included in a Helm chart but are instead created by a cluster administrator before application deployment. Limit ranges are used to determine the number of resources a container is allowed to use within a namespace. Limit ranges are also used to set the default resource limits for each container deployed to the namespace that does not already have resource limits defined. The following is an example limit range defined by a LimitRange object:

```
apiVersion: v1
kind: LimitRange
metadata:
  name: limits-per-container
spec:
  limits:
    - max:
        cpu: 1
        memory: 4Gi
      default:
        cpu: 500m
        memory: 2Gi
      type: Container
```

LimitRange enforces the specified restrictions in the namespace where the LimitRange object was created. It sets the maximum amount of allowed container resources to 1 core of cpu and 4Gi of memory. If a resource limit is not defined, it automatically sets the resource limit to 500m of cpu and 2Gi of memory. Limit ranges can also be applied at the pod level by setting the type field to Pod. This would ensure that the sum of resource utilization of all containers in the pod are under the specified limits. In addition to setting limits against CPU and memory utilization, you can also set a LimitRange object to default the storage claimed by a PersistentVolumeClaim object by setting the type field to PersistentVolumeClaim.

This would allow you to create the following resource to set a storage limit for a single PVC:

```
apiVersion: v1
kind: LimitRange
metadata:
  name: limits-per-pvc
spec:
  - max:
      storage: 4Gi
    type: PersistentVolumeClaim
```

Of course, you could also set a default storage amount in your Helm chart's `values.yaml` file. The default set in the `values.yaml` file reflects the amount of storage you think is required for a default installation, with the `LimitRange` object enforcing an absolute maximum that the user can override to.

In addition to limit ranges, you can also set resource quotas to add additional restrictions against a namespace's resource usage. While limit ranges enforce resources at a per-container, -pod, or -PVC level, resource quotas enforce resource usage at a per-namespace level. They are used to define the maximum number of resources a namespace can utilize. The following is an example resource quota:

```
apiVersion: v1
kind: ResourceQuota
metadata:
  name: pod-and-pvc-quota
spec:
  hard:
    limits.cpu: '4'
    limits.memory: 8Gi
    requests.storage: 20Gi
```

The preceding `ResourceQuota` object, when applied to a Kubernetes namespace, sets the maximum CPU utilization to 4 cores, the maximum memory utilization to 8Gi, and the maximum storage request to 20Gi for the sum of all workloads in the namespace. Resource quotas can also be used to set a maximum amount of `secrets`, `ConfigMaps`, and other Kubernetes resources per namespace. By using `resource quotas`, you can prevent a single namespace from over-utilizing cluster resources.

By setting reasonable default resource limits in your Helm chart, along with the existence of `LimitRange` and `ResourceQuota`, you can ensure that users of your Helm chart do not exhaust cluster resources and cause disruptions or outages. With an understanding of how you can enforce resource limits, let's move on to the next topic around Helm chart security—handling secrets in Helm charts.

Handling secrets in Helm charts

Handling secrets is a common concern when working with Helm charts. Consider the WordPress application from *Chapter 3*, *Installing Your First Helm Chart*, where you were required to provide a password to configure an admin user. This password was not provided by default in the `values.yaml` file because this would have left the application vulnerable if you forgot to override the `password` value. Chart developers should be in the habit of not providing defaults for secret values such as passwords and should instead require users to provide an explicit value. This can easily be done by leveraging the `required` function. Helm also has the ability to generate random strings using the `randAlphaNum` function.

Note, however, that this function generates a new random string each time the chart is upgraded. For that reason, developers should design charts with the expectation that users will provide their own password or other secret key, with the `required` function serving as a gate to ensure that a value is provided.

When a user provides a secret during chart installation, that value should be saved in `secret`, not `ConfigMap`. ConfigMaps display values in plain text and are not designed to contain credentials or other secret values. Secrets, on the other hand, provide obfuscation by Base64-encoding its contents. Secrets also allow you to mount its contents to a pod as a `tmpfs` mount, meaning the contents are mounted to the pod in volatile memory instead of on a disk. As a chart developer, you should ensure that all credentials and secret configuration managed by your Helm charts are created using Kubernetes Secrets.

While chart developers should ensure that secrets are handled appropriately using Kubernetes Secrets and the `required` function, chart users should ensure that secrets such as credentials are provided to a Helm chart securely. Values are most commonly provided to a Helm chart with the `--values` flag, where additional or overridden values are declared in a separate `values` file and are passed to the Helm CLI during installation. This is an appropriate method when working with regular values, but caution should be taken when using this approach with secret values. Users should be sure that the `values` files that contain secrets are not checked into a `git` repository or an otherwise public location where those secrets could be exposed.

One way that users can avoid exposing secrets is by leveraging the `--set` flag to pass secrets inline from their local command line. This reduces the risk of credentials being exposed, but users should be aware that this would reveal the credentials in the bash history.

Another way that users can avoid exposing secrets is by leveraging an encryption tool to encrypt `values` files that contain secrets. This would continue to allow users to apply the `--values` flag and push the `values` file to a remote location, such as a git repository. The `values` file could then only be decrypted by users who have the appropriate key and would remain encrypted for all other users, only allowing trusted members access to the data. Users can simply leverage GPG to encrypt the `values` files, or they can leverage a special tool such as **Sops**. **Sops** (`https://github.com/mozilla/sops`) is a tool designed to encrypt the values of YAML or JSON files but leave the keys unencrypted. The following code shows a secret key/value pair from a Sops-encrypted file:

```
password:ENC[AES256GCM,data:xhdUx7DVUG8bitGnqjGvPMygpw==,
iv:3LR9KcttchCvZNpRKqE5LcXRyWD1I00v2kEAIl1ttco=,
tag:9HEwxhT9s1pxo9lg19wyNg==,type:str]
```

Notice how the `password` key is unencrypted but the value is encrypted. This allows you to easily see what kind of values are contained in the file without exposing their secrets.

There are other tools capable of encrypting the `values` files that contain secrets. Some examples include `git-crypt` (`https://github.com/AGWA/git-crypt`) and `blackbox` (`https://github.com/StackExchange/blackbox`). Additionally, tools such as HashiCorp's `Vault` or CyberArk Conjur can be used to encrypt secrets in the form of key/value stores. Secrets can then be retrieved by authenticating with a secret management system and then by utilizing them within Helm by passing them with `--set`.

With an understanding of how security plays a role in Helm chart development, let's now discuss how **Role-Based Access Control** (**RBAC**) can be applied in Kubernetes to provide greater security to your users.

Configuring RBAC rules

The ability of an authenticated user in Kubernetes to perform actions is governed through a set of RBAC policies. As introduced in *Chapter 2, Preparing a Kubernetes and Helm Environment*, policies, known as roles, can be associated with users or service accounts, and Kubernetes contains several default roles that can be associated. RBAC has been enabled by default in Kubernetes since version 1.6. When thinking about Kubernetes RBAC in the context of Helm usage, you need to consider two factors:

- The user installing a Helm chart
- The service account associated with the pod running the workload

In most cases, the individual responsible for installing a Helm chart is associated with a Kubernetes user. However, Helm charts can be installed through other means, such as by a Kubernetes operator with an associated service account.

By default, users and service accounts have minimal permissions in a Kubernetes cluster. Additional permissions are granted through the use of roles that are scoped to an individual namespace, or cluster roles that grant access at a cluster level. These are then associated with a user or service account using either a role binding or a cluster role binding, depending on the type of policy being targeted. While Kubernetes has a number of included roles that can be applied, the concept of **least-privileged access** should be used wherever possible. Least-privileged access refers to a user or application that is granted only the minimum set of permissions that is needed to properly function. For example, take the guestbook chart that we developed earlier. Imagine we wanted to add new functionality that can query the metadata of pods in the guestbook application's namespace.

While Kubernetes contains a built-in role called **view** that provides the necessary permissions to read pod manifests in a given namespace, it also gives access to other resources, such as ConfigMaps and deployments. To minimize the level of access that is granted to an application, a custom policy in the form of a role or cluster role can be created that provides only the necessary permissions that the application needs. Since most typical users of a Kubernetes cluster do not have access to create resources at a cluster level, let's create a role that is applied to the namespace that the Helm chart is deployed in.

To create a new role, the `kubectl create role` command can be used. A basic role contains two key elements:

- The type of action (verb) made against the Kubernetes API
- The list of Kubernetes resources to target

As an example, to demonstrate how RBAC can be configured in Kubernetes, let's configure a set of RBAC rules to allow an authenticated user to view pods within a namespace.

> **Important note**
>
> If you want to run through this example on your local workstation, make sure that Minikube is started first by running `minikube start`.

You can then create a new namespace called `chapter9` by running `kubectl create ns chapter9`:

1. Use the `kubectl` CLI to create a new role called `guestbook-pod-viewer`:

```
$ kubectl create role guestbook-pod-viewer
--resource=pods --verb=get,list -n chapter9
```

With this new role created, it needs to be associated with a user or service account. Since we want to associate it with an application running in Kubernetes, we will apply the role to a service account. When a pod is created, it makes use of a service account called `default`. When attempting to abide by the least-privileged access principle, it is recommended that a separate service account is used. This is to ensure that no other workloads are deployed in the same namespace as the `guestbook` application as it would also inherit the same permissions.

2. Create a new service account called `guestbook` by executing the following command:

```
$ kubectl create sa guestbook -n chapter9
```

3. Next, create a role binding called `guestbook-pod-viewers` to associate `guestbook-pod-viewer` with `guestbook ServiceAccount`:

```
$ kubectl create rolebinding guestbook-
pod-viewers --role=guestbook-pod-viewer
--serviceaccount=chapter9:guestbook -n chapter9
```

Finally, to run the `guestbook` application itself using the newly created `guestbook` `ServiceAccount`, the name of the service account would need to be applied to the deployment.

The following shows how the `serviceAccount` configuration appears in the deployment YAML:

```
serviceAccountName: guestbook
```

You can easily install the `guestbook` application by using the chart you created in *Chapter 5, Building Your First Helm Chart,* or by using the chart located in the Packt repository at `https://github.com/PacktPublishing/-Learn-Helm/tree/master/helm-charts/charts/guestbook`. This chart exposes a set of values for configuring the deployment's service account.

4. Install the `guestbook` Helm chart by running the following command:

```
$ helm install my-guestbook Learn-Helm/helm-charts/
charts/guestbook \
--set serviceAccount.name=guestbook \
--set serviceAccount.create=false \
-n chapter9
```

Notice that in *step 4*, the `serviceAccount.create` value is set to `false`. When you scaffolded your Helm chart in *Chapter 5, Building Your first Helm Chart,* using the `helm create` command, the ability to create a service account upon chart installation was provided. Since you already created a service account using `kubectl` previously, this was not needed. However, the ability to create additional resources related to RBAC during chart installation does not need to end at creating service accounts. In fact, you could perform steps 1, 2, and 3 in a single chart installation if your Helm chart contained the YAML resources necessary to create roles and role bindings as well.

5. At this point, the `guestbook` application has the permissions necessary to list and get pods. To verify this assumption, `kubectl` has a command that queries whether a user or service account has the authority to perform an action. Execute the following command to verify that the `ServiceAccount` guestbook has access to query all the pods in the `guestbook` namespace:

```
$ kubectl auth can-i list pods
--as=system:serviceaccount:chapter9:guestbook -n chapter9
```

The --as flag makes use of the user impersonation feature in Kubernetes to allow the debugging of authorization policies.

6. The result of the command should print yes as output. To confirm that the service account cannot access a resource that it should not be able to, such as listing deployments, execute the following command:

```
$ kubectl can-i list deployments
--as=system:serviceaccount:guestbook:guestbook -n
chapter9
```

7. Feel free to delete your release with the helm uninstall command:

```
$ helm uninstall my-guestbook -n chapter9
```

You can also stop your Minikube instance, which is not needed for the remainder of this chapter:

```
$ minikube stop
```

As you can see from the output of no, the expected policies are in place.

When used effectively, Kubernetes RBAC aids in providing Helm chart developers with the tools needed to enforce least-privilege access, protecting users and applications from potential errant or malicious actions.

Next, we will discuss how chart repositories can be secured and accessed in a way that enhances the overall security of Helm.

Accessing secure chart repositories

Chart repositories provide the ability to discover Helm charts and install them on your Kubernetes cluster. Repositories were introduced in *Chapter 1, Understanding Kubernetes and Helm*, as an HTTP server that includes an index.yaml file containing metadata related to charts present in the repository. In previous chapters, we made use of charts that were sourced from various upstream repositories and also implemented our own repository using GitHub Pages. Each of these repositories is freely available for use for whoever may be interested. However, Helm does support incorporating additional security measures to protect the content stored within the repository, including the following:

*   Authentication
*   **Secure Sockets Layer/Transport Layer Security (SSL/TLS)** encryption

While the majority of public Helm repositories do not require any form of authentication, Helm does allow users to perform basic and certificate-based authentication against a secured chart repository. For basic authentication, a username and password can be provided when adding a repository using the `helm repo add` command through the use of the `--username` and `--password` flags. For example, if you want to access a repository that is protected using basic authentication, adding the repository would take the following form:

```
$ helm repo add $REPO_URL --username=<username>
--password=<password>
```

Then, the repository can be interacted with without needing to repeatedly provide the credentials.

For certificate-based authentication, the `helm repo add` command provides the `--ca-file`, `--cert-file`, and `--key-file` flags. The `--ca-file` flag is used to verify the chart repository's certificate authority, while the `--cert-file` and `--key-file` flags are used to specify your client certificate and key, respectively.

Enabling basic authentication and certificate authentication on the chart repository itself depends on the repository implementation that is used. For example, ChartMuseum, the popular chart repository, provides the `--basic-auth-user` and `--basic-auth-pass` flags that can be used at startup to configure the username and password for basic authentication. It also provides the `--tls-ca-cert` flag to configure the **Certificate Authority (CA)** certificate for certificate authentication. Other chart repository implementations may provide other flags or require you to provide a configuration file.

Even with authentication in place, it is important that the transmission between the HTTP server and your Helm client is facilitated securely. This can be performed using Secure Sockets Layer (SSL) / Transport Layer Security (TLS) based encryption to secure communication between your Helm client and your Helm chart repository. While a requirement for certificate authentication, repositories requiring basic authentication (and unauthenticated repositories) can still benefit from encrypting network traffic as this will protect authentication attempts as well as the contents of the repository. As with authentication, configuring TLS on the chart repository depends on the repository implementation that is used. ChartMuseum provides the `--tls-cert` and `--tls-key` flags to provide the certificate chain and key files. More general web servers, such as NGINX, typically require a configuration file that provides the location of the certificate and key files on the server. Offerings such as GitHub Pages already have TLS configured.

Each of the Helm repositories that we have used so far have used certificates signed by publicly available CAs that are stored in both your web browser as well as your underlying operating system. Many large organizations have their own CAs that can be used to produce the certificates configured in the chart repository. Since this certificate is likely not from a publicly available CA, the Helm CLI may not trust the certificate, and adding the repository results in the following error:

```
Error: looks like '$REPO_URL' is not a valid chart repository
or cannot be reached: Get $REPO_URL/index.yaml: x509:
certificate signed by unknown authority
```

To allow the Helm CLI to trust the chart repository's certificate, the CA certificate, or CA bundle containing multiple certificates, can either be added to the trust store of the operating system or explicitly specified using the `--ca-file` flag of the `helm repo add` command. This allows the command to be executed without error.

Finally, depending on how the chart repository is configured, additional metrics can also be obtained to perform request-level auditing and logging to determine who has attempted to access the repository.

Through the use of authentication and managing certificates governing the transport layer, additional capabilities are realized for enhancing the security footprint of Helm repositories.

Summary

In this chapter, you learned about some of the different topics around security that need to be considered when working with Helm. First, you learned how data provenance and the integrity of Helm releases and Helm charts can be proven. Next, you learned about Helm chart security and how a chart developer can employ best practices around security to write a stable and secure Helm chart. Finally, you learned how RBAC can be used to create an environment based on the concept of least privilege access and how chart repositories can be secured to provide HTTPS encryption and to require authentication. Now, with these concepts, you are better equipped to create a secure Helm architecture and working environment.

Further reading

- To learn more about data provenance and integrity in the context of Helm charts, go to `https://helm.sh/docs/topics/provenance/`.

- To learn more about Kubernetes RBAC, check out the *Using RBAC Authorization* page from the Kubernetes documentation at `https://kubernetes.io/docs/reference/access-authn-authz/rbac/`.

- Check out the chart repository guide from the Helm documentation to learn more about chart repositories at `https://helm.sh/docs/topics/chart_repository/`.

Questions

1. What is data provenance and integrity? How are data provenance and data integrity different?

2. Imagine you want to prove the data provenance and integrity of a Helm download. Besides the release archive, what file does a user need to download from Helm's GitHub release page to accomplish this?

3. What commands can a user run to verify the data provenance and integrity of a Helm chart?

4. As a Helm chart developer, what can you do to ensure that you are deploying a stable container image?

5. Why is it important to set resource limits on your Helm chart? What other Kubernetes resources can be used to configure a pod and namespace's resource limits?

6. What is the concept of least privilege access? Which Kubernetes resources allow you to configure authorization and help achieve least privilege access?

7. What command and set of flags can be used to authenticate against a chart repository?

ASSESSMENTS

Chapter 1: Understanding Kubernetes and Helm

Here are some answers to the questions presented in this chapter:

1. An application is `monolithic` if it contains all necessary logic and features in a single application. Monolithic applications can be broken up into multiple different applications, referred to as **microservices**.

2. Kubernetes is a container orchestration tool. To give a few examples, it solves problems around workload scheduling, availability, and scalability.

3. `create`, `describe`, `edit`, `delete`, and `apply`

4. There are many different types of resources a user must understand in order to deploy an application. It is also challenging to maintain synchronized local and live states, manage application life cycle, and maintain boilerplate YAML resource files.

5. Helm includes four life cycle commands that provide users with the ability to easily manage Kubernetes applications. Users apply these commands to interact with Helm charts, which is a packaging of the Kubernetes resources required to deploy an application. Helm abstracts the complexity of Kubernetes resources and provides a history of revisions for a given application, allowing applications to be rolled back to a previous snapshot. It also allows YAML resources to be dynamically generated and simplifies the synchronization between local and live state. Finally, Helm applies Kubernetes resources in a predeterministic order and allows automated life cycle hooks, which can be used to perform various automated tasks.

6. You can use the `helm rollback` command. Helm assigns a revision to each application snapshot. A new revision is assigned when one or more areas of an application are modified from their previously applied state.

7. `Install`, `Upgrade`, `Rollback`, and `Uninstall`.

Chapter 2: Preparing a Kubernetes and Helm Environment

Here are some answers to the questions presented in this chapter:

1. Windows and Mac users can install Helm using the Chocolatey or Homebrew package managers, respectively. All users (Windows, Mac, and Linux) can also install Helm from its GitHub releases page at `https://github.com/helm/helm/releases`.

2. Helm authenticates using the local `kubeconfig` file.

3. Kubernetes roles provide authorization. An administrator can manage these privileges by creating a `RoleBinding`, which binds a role to a user or group.

4. The `helm repo add` command is used to locally configure a Helm chart repository. It is a requirement to install the charts contained within that repository.

5. The three `XDG` environment variables used by Helm are `XDG_CACHE_HOME`, `XDG_CONFIG_HOME`, and `XDG_DATA_HOME`. `XDG_CACHE_HOME` is used to assign the location for cached files (which includes downloaded charts from upstream chart repositories). `XDG_CONFIG_HOME` is used to set the location for Helm configuration (which includes repository information saved by `helm repo add`). `XDG_DATA_HOME` is used to save plugin information, added using the `helm plugin install` command.

6. `Minikube` allows users to easily create a single-node Kubernetes cluster on their local machine. `Minikube` automatically configures the `Kubeconfig` for authentication and assigns users with `cluster-admin` to perform any desired action.

Chapter 3: Installing Your First Helm Chart

Here are some answers to the questions presented in this chapter:

1. The Helm Hub is a centralized location for upstream chart repositories. Users can interact with it by using the `helm search hub` command, or by visiting the Helm Hub website at `https://hub.helm.sh/`.

2. The `helm get` commands are used to get details of an installed Helm release such as the applied values and generated Kubernetes resources. The `helm show` commands are used to show general information of a Helm chart such as the list of supported values and the chart `README`.

3. The `--set` flag is used to provide inline values and is useful for providing simple values or values that contain secrets that should not be saved to a file. The `--values` flag is used to provide values by using a values file and is useful for providing large amounts of values at a time and saving applied values to a source control repository.

4. The `helm history` command can be used to list the revisions for a release.

5. If you upgrade a release without providing any values, the `--reuse-values` flag is applied by default, which will reuse each of the values applied in the previous release. If at least one value is provided, the `--reset-values` flag is applied instead, which resets each value to their defaults and then merges the provided values.

6. The `helm history` command would reveal six releases, with the sixth release indicating that the application was rolled back to revision 3.

7. The `helm list` command can be used to view all of the releases deployed to a namespace.

8. The `helm search repo` command can be used to list each of the repository's charts.

Chapter 4: Understanding Helm Charts

Here are some answers to the questions presented in this chapter:

1. YAML is the format most commonly used, though JSON can be used alternatively.

2. The three required fields are `apiVersion`, `name`, and `version`.

3. Values from a chart dependency can be referenced or overridden by placing desired dependency values in a map whose name is equal to the name of the dependency chart. Values can also be imported using the `import-values` setting, which can be used to allow dependency values to be referenced using a different name.

4. You can create an upgrade hook to ensure that a data snapshot is taken before running the `helm upgrade` command.

5. You can provide the `README.md` file to provide documentation for your chart. You can also create the `templates/NOTES.txt` file, which can dynamically generate release notes upon installation. Finally, the `LICENSE` file can be used to provide legal information.

6. The `range` action allows chart developers to generate repeating YAML portions.

7.   The `Chart.yaml` file is used to define metadata about a Helm chart. This file is also called the Chart Definition. The `Chart.lock` file is used to save chart dependency state, providing metadata about the exact dependency versions used so the `charts/` folder can be recreated.

8.   The `helm.sh/hook` annotation is used to define a hook resource.

9.   Functions and pipelines allow chart developers to perform complex processing and formatting of data within a template. Common functions include `date`, `include`, `indent`, `quote`, and `toYaml`.

Chapter 5: Building Your First Helm Chart

Here are some answers to the questions presented in this chapter:

1.   The `helm create` command can be used to scaffold a new Helm chart.

2.   Declaring the Redis dependency prevented you from needing to create Redis templates in your Helm chart. It allowed you to deploy Redis without needing to know the proper Kubernetes resource configuration required.

3.   The `helm.sh/hook-weight` annotation can be used to set the execution order. Hooks are executed in ascending order by weight.

4.   The `fail` function is used to immediately fail rendering and can be used to restrict user input against a set of valid settings. The `required` function is used to declare a required value, in which chart templating will fail if that value is not provided.

5.   To publish a Helm chart to a GitHub Pages chart repository, you must first use the `helm package` command to package your Helm chart in TGZ format. Next, you should generate the repository's `index.yaml` file with the `helm repo index` command. Finally, the repository contents should be pushed to GitHub.

6.   The `index.yaml` file contains metadata about each of the charts included in a chart repository.

Chapter 6: Testing Helm Charts

Here are some answers to the questions presented in this chapter:

1.   The `helm template` command is used to generate your Helm templates locally. The `helm lint` command is used to lint for errors in your chart's structure and chart definition file. It also attempts to find errors that will result in a failed installation.

2. To validate your chart templates prior to installation, you can run the `helm template` command to generate your YAML resources locally to ensure they were generated properly. You can also use the `--verify` flag to check with the API server that your YAML schemas are correct without installing the resources. The `helm install --dry-run` command can also perform this check with the API server prior to installation.

3. One tool that can be used to lint the style of your YAML resources is the `yamllint` tool. It can be used alongside `helm template` to lint your generated resources (for example, `helm template my-test test-chart | yamllint -`.

4. A chart test is created by creating a chart template with the `helm.sh/hook: test` annotation added. Chart tests are typically Pods that execute a script or short command. They can be executed by running the `helm test` command.

5. The Chart Testing (**ct**) tool allows Helm chart maintainers to more easily test Helm charts in a git monorepo. It performs thorough testing and ensures that charts that are modified have had their versions incremented.

6. The `ci/` folder is used to test multiple different combinations of Helm values.

7. Adding the `--upgrade` flag will help ensure regressions have not occurred for charts that have not had their major version incremented. It will first install the older version of the chart and then upgrade to the newer version. Then, it will delete the release, install the new version, and attempt an upgrade against itself. Testing will take place between each installation/upgrade.

Chapter 7: Automating Helm Processes Using CI/CD and GitOps

Here are some answers to the questions presented in this chapter:

1. CI is an automated software development process that can be repeated when a software change occurs. CD is a set of defined steps written to progress software through a release process (commonly referred to as a pipeline).

2. While CI/CD describes the software development and release process, GitOps describes the act of storing configuration in Git. An example of this is storing a values file in Git, which can be applied to deploy an application to Kubernetes.

3. A CI pipeline for creating and releasing Helm charts can lint, install, and test the Helm charts. The Chart testing tool can help perform these steps more easily, especially when maintaining a chart monorepo. The pipeline should also package each Helm chart and deploy the charts to the chart repository. For GitHub Pages chart repositories, the `index.yaml` file must be generated, and the contents must be pushed to the repository.

4. CI allows charts to be easily and quickly tested and released. It can also help prevent regressions as new features are added.

5. A CD pipeline would deploy Helm charts to each desired environment, with each environment being a different pipeline stage. Smoke testing can be performed by using the `helm test` command after each deployment.

6. A CD pipeline allows users to easily deploy their applications without needing to manually invoke the Helm CLI commands. This can help prevent the possibility of human error when deploying applications with Helm.

7. To maintain configuration for multiple environments, separate folders can be used to separate the values files by environment. To reduce boilerplate, a file containing the common values used across each environment can be saved and applied to each Helm deployment.

Chapter 8: Using Helm with the Operator Framework

Here are some answers to the questions presented in this chapter:

1. An operator works by leveraging a custom controller and custom resources. When a new custom resource is created, the operator will perform the logic implemented by the custom controller. Changes to the custom resource also trigger the controller logic. Operators are typically implemented to install and manage the life cycle of an application.

2. When using the Helm CLI, you must execute the `install`, `upgrade`, `rollback`, and `uninstall` commands from the command line. However, when using a Helm-based operator, these commands are performed automatically when you `create`, `modify`, or `delete` a custom resource. When using a Helm-based operator, you don't have to run any Helm CLI commands locally.

With regard to the application life cycle, the Helm CLI allows users to roll back to a previous revision, while the Helm operator does not allow this because it does not keep a history of revisions.

3. You could first use the `operator-sdk new` command to scaffold a new Helm operator, pointing the command to an existing Helm chart with the `--helm-chart` flag. Next, you could build the operator using the `operator-sdk build` command. Finally, you could push the operator image to a container registry.

4. Installation is performed by creating a new custom resource. Upgrading is performed by modifying the custom resource. Rolling back is performed automatically if an upgrade fails, but cannot be explicitly performed. Uninstallation is performed by deleting the custom resource.

5. The `crds/` folder allows **Custom Resource Definitions (CRDs)** to be created before the contents in `templates/` are created. It provides an easy way to deploy operators that are dependent on CRDs.

6. Answers will vary, but an example of these charts has been provided at `https://github.com/PacktPublishing/-Learn-Helm/tree/master/ch8-q6-answer`. The example creates one chart called **guestbook-operator**, which is used to deploy the operator resources (including the CRD), while the other chart is called **guestbook-cr** and is used to deploy the custom resource.

Chapter 9: Helm Security Considerations

Here are some sample answers to the questions presented in this chapter:

1. Data provenance is about determining the origin of data. Data integrity determines whether the data you received is the data that you expected.

2. A user needs to download the accompanying `.asc` file, which contains the digital signature.

3. The `helm verify` command can be used to verify locally downloaded charts, while the `helm install --verify` command can be used against charts stored in an upstream chart repository.

4. You can incorporate regular vulnerability scanning. You can also try to avoid deploying images that need to be run as root or a subset of root capabilities. Finally, you can reference images using a `sha256` value instead of a tag to ensure that you are always deploying the expected image.

5. Resource limits help prevent an application from being able to exhaust the underlying node resources. You can also leverage `LimitRanges` to set the maximum amount of resources per Pod or PVC, and you can leverage `ResourceQuotas` to set the maximum amount of resources per namespace.

6. Least privilege refers to a user or application being granted only the minimum set of permissions that is needed to properly function. To achieve least privilege access, you can use Kubernetes `Roles` and `RoleBindings` to create least privilege roles and bind those roles to users or groups.

7. The `helm repo add` command provides the `--username` and `--password` flags, which are used for basic authentication and the `--ca-file`, `--cert-file`, and `--key-file` flags, which are used for certificate-based authentication. The `--ca-file` flag is also used to verify a chart repository's certificate authority.

Other Books You May Enjoy

If you enjoyed this book, you may be interested in these other books by Packt:

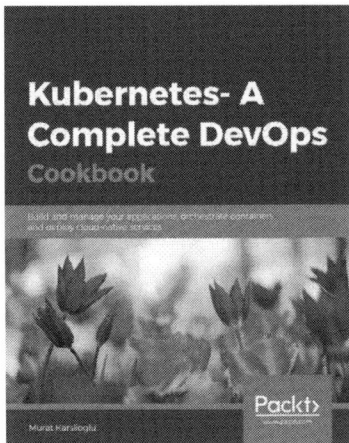

Kubernetes - A Complete DevOps Cookbook

Murat Karslioglu

ISBN: 978-1-8388-280-42

- Deploy cloud-native applications on Kubernetes
- Automate testing in the DevOps workflow
- Discover and troubleshoot common storage issues
- Dynamically scale containerized services to manage fluctuating traffic needs
- Understand how to monitor your containerized DevOps environment
- Build DevSecOps into CI/CD pipelines

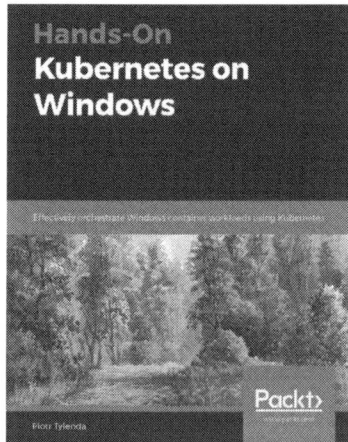

Hands-On Kubernetes on Windows

Piotr Tylenda

ISBN: 978-1-83882-156-2

- Understand containerization as a packaging format for applications
- Create a development environment for Kubernetes on Windows
- Grasp the key architectural concepts in Kubernetes
- Discover the current limitations of Kubernetes on the Windows platform
- Provision and interact with a Kubernetes cluster from a Windows machine
- Create hybrid Windows Kubernetes clusters in on-premises and cloud environments

Leave a review - let other readers know what you think

Please share your thoughts on this book with others by leaving a review on the site that you bought it from. If you purchased the book from Amazon, please leave us an honest review on this book's Amazon page. This is vital so that other potential readers can see and use your unbiased opinion to make purchasing decisions, we can understand what our customers think about our products, and our authors can see your feedback on the title that they have worked with Packt to create. It will only take a few minutes of your time, but is valuable to other potential customers, our authors, and Packt. Thank you!

Index

Printed in Great Britain
by Amazon